TO DWELL WITHIN THEM

Neo-Hasidic Reflections on the Weekly Torah Reading

ARTHUR GREEN

BOOK PUBLISHING COMPANY
RHINEBECK, NEW YORK

Paperback ISBN 9781966608219
eBook ISBN 9781966608226

Library of Congress Control Number 2026000586

Book and cover design by Colin Rolfe
Cover art: "Mizrah," papercut by Israel Dov Rosenbaum, 1877

Monkfish Book Publishing Company
22 East Market Street, Suite 304
Rhinebeck, New York 12572
(845) 876-4861
monkfishpublishing.com

CONTENTS

SEFER VA-YIKRA (LEVITICUS)

SEFER BE-MIDBAR (NUMBERS)

SEFER DEVARIM (DEUTERONOMY)

INTRODUCTION

אין לך פרשה שאין בה תחיית המתים אלא שאין בנו כח לדרוש
ספרי האזינו ש"ו

"There is no portion in the Torah *that cannot be brought back to life*, if only we had the strength to interpret!"

The "strength to interpret" is mostly a matter of courage. The early masters of *aggadah* (narrative/interpretation) combined a relationship of utter faithfulness to the biblical text with almost unlimited daring in reinterpretation and reapplication of its words. They understood that the true intent of the *darshan* (preacher) was to address issues that were central—or that they thought should be central—to the lives of their hearers, and that the biblical text was a powerful vehicle with which to do that. While deriving normative praxis (*halakhah*) from biblical verses was restricted by carefully drawn hermeneutical principles, the much looser rules for *aggadah* were themselves widely ignored. Only rarely, according to an old tale, did others say to Rabbi Akiva, father of the school that led the path toward wide-ranging expansion of scripture's meaning: "Akiva! What are you doing here in *aggadah*? Go back to the rules of infection and impurity!" There he would have to play within the interpretive norms.

If we Jews are really "the people of the book" (it was Muslims who first called us that), it really means that we are a society of re-interpreters. "Seventy faces has the Torah," a medieval *midrash* called out, which was really a way of saying that every verse, word, and letter could be interpreted in multiple ways, ultimately offering the teaching that you, the preacher, sought to find in it. Of course, every re-interpreter of a great text at some point discovers that the process is quite mutual. As you engage in the re-shaping of the text to deliver or underscore your message, the text, through your deep engagement with it, is busy re-shaping you. The wise re-interpreter learns to be grateful for that gift.

The courage for all this creative re-interpretation faded over the course of history. The early medieval rediscovery of the *peshat*, the "simple" and presumably intended meaning of the text, engendered a revolution in Jewish thought. *Aggadah* had gone too far, often seemingly to ridiculous lengths, as the Karaite critics of rabbinic Judaism had been quick to point out. It was no longer in fashion to support a point by creative reinterpretation of scripture's words, taking them completely out of context. Even a commentator like RaSHI, one of our great conduits to the early aggadic tradition, sometimes had to say, "I intended only the *peshat* understanding of scripture."

The boldest in defying this trend in medieval Jewish thinking were the early Kabbalists, culminating in the incredible world of *Sefer ha-Zohar*. Their greatest achievement was the introduction of a new symbolic language into Judaism, constructed around the scaffolding of the ten *sefirot.* This lent a new profundity to the interpretive process, leading to what has been termed a renaissance of the midrashic art. In claiming that the Zohar was itself an ancient text, dating back to Rabbi Shim'on ben Yoḥai of the second century, they were donning the mantle of the early aggadists, seeking to recover that radical freedom to interpret, and they used it with great creativity and bravado.

This renaissance of bold reinterpretation took place once more in the early years of Hasidism, in mid-eighteenth-century Poland. The movement was inspired by the figure of R. Israel Ba'al Shem Tov, whose teachings are often transmitted in the form of startling rereadings of well-known biblical verses and single lines from the rabbinic tradition. It is likely (history and legend are thoroughly intermingled here) that he was originally a relatively unlettered healer and miracle worker from the Carpathian Mountains, who was accepted, after some difficulty, into a community of much more learned Jews. They would share verses or teachings with him and he would interpret them in simple but utterly new and powerful ways. These readings served as something like "shock therapy" (or think of the Zen master's slap), awakening them to a new level of consciousness and inspiring something of a religious revolution.

This ability to use bits of scripture and tradition as tools of spiritual awakening survived well through two more generations, and is often seen in the writings of the school of Mezritch, those who truly founded the Hasidic movement. It achieved new heights in the wildly associative thinking of R. Nahman of Bratslav, and survived, or was again resurrected, in the writings of some nineteenth century masters, most notably those of central Poland. But its degeneration could already be seen in the early years of that century, as new generations of rebbes, mostly holding that position by inheritance, began to rely excessively on such tools as numerology (*gematria*) and abbreviation (*notarikon*) in order to derive new—and often uninspired—meanings.

For Jews seeking to live more fully in the Western world, a new rediscovery of *peshat* was the order of the day. The spirit of Moses Mendelsohn's German translation and *Bi'ur* ("explanation") was one of sober and straightforward consideration of the text itself. One might say that it was the precise opposite of the *midrash* and folklore-filled reading found in the Yiddish *Tsenah u-Re'enah* (or, for Sephardic Jews, the Ladino *Me-'Am Lo'ez*). It was followed by the mid-nineteenth-century emergence of critical and contextual Bible scholarship, originated by Christians but widely accepted in "enlightened" Jewish circles. The emergence of "the science of Judaism" and critical-historical scholarship as the apogee of non-Orthodox *talmud torah* had a choking effect on Jewish spiritual creativity insofar as it was based on ancient sources. "Mere *drash*," the ability to make the text say *anything*, was mocked and derided by professors in universities and seminaries alike.

As modern Hebrew and Yiddish literature began to emerge in the late nineteenth and twentieth centuries, creative reinterpretation of biblical tales and characters often became the playing field of literary authors, especially poets. Those most deeply rooted in tradition had the greatest access to the treasures of Jewish imagination and often produced remarkable readings. In Yiddish, one thinks of such figures as Itzik Manger and Aaron Zeitlin. In Hebrew, Yehuda Amichai and Zelda Schneurson first come to mind. Their works, however, were considered part of the new genre of creativity called Modern Jewish Literature, certainly not seen as part of "Torah" in the broad sense of ongoing creative re-reading of the sources. Amid more western (i.e. German and English speakers) Jewry, these works were hardly known.

This consensus that critical history and philology were the be-all and end-all of understanding the canonical sources of Judaism began to break down among American Jews as well by the late 1960's. In circles of early Jewish feminists, *ḥavurot*, and later the Jewish Renewal movement, personal and often psychological readings of the *parashah* were welcomed in the "Torah discussions" that had come to replace rabbis' sermons. These strove to place hearers and readers *inside* the narrative, rather than standing apart from it as a historical artifact. One was allowed to ask "Why did Jacob do that?" or Why did Moses react that way?" rather than "Why did the Elohist choose to tell it that way?"

This was not a new fundamentalism, returning to pre-modern literal belief in the text. Not at all. But it was a sense that the text is *torah, teaching*, and we are here to learn from it. We do so best by permitting ourselves to enter the text and its reality. The prior example of Hasidism was rediscovered in those circles, and the frequent refrain of the early Hasidic sources ("Torah is eternal, speaking to each generation. What does this text have to teach us today?") echoed loudly in the ears of a very different generation of listeners, one determined to set its own course. While the vocabulary of postmodernism had not yet emerged, there was a growing sense of the readers' right to take an active role in allowing the text to speak. Twin understandings of this process, *one seeing a new generation of seekers wanting to enter the text, and the other seeing the ancient sources in quest of new and creative readers and interpreters,* have continued to emerge in tandem over the course of the past half-century. This way of reading Torah in quest of ever new levels of meaning has entered many a mainstream synagogue as well.

That is the spirit in which the present collection of *divrey torah* is offered. I do not need to call here for a new renaissance of the midrashic art or the Hasidic boldness in reading scripture. This rebirth is already present in our midst; it only needs to be noticed and nurtured, primarily by example.

The inspirations that stand behind this volume are many. They include Torah discussions held in our little Havurat Shalom community some sixty years ago. But it is a lifetime of engagement with the early Hasidic sources that is hopefully most to be felt in these pages. Those works repeatedly say something like: "This book is called *torah*, which means 'teaching,'" followed by the call for a new reading, the voice of the current generation.

I have tried to ask that same question for Jews living in a very different era. What is it that we might learn, both for our spiritual journeys and the growth of our moral conscience (I find these two to be inseparable), from the verses that stand before us? I believe that the most essential task of religion is what I call *the cultivation of inwardness*, and I have tried to follow the Hasidic example of reading the entire Torah as a guide to that process.

In that spirit, I very much welcome Christian readers as well. We share this sacred scripture. Hear these readings as an invitation to join us in a deep and personal reading of the Sacred Word. The ongoing process of *midrash* is one that I hope you are learning to make your own. It has kept our tradition creative and vital over a couple thousand years, and it can offer that blessing to yours as well.

To understand these teachings, read them slowly and thoughtfully. Have the Torah text open alongside these comments. Look at the full verse. Always ask (as I train my students to do): "How is the verse being read here? What is the insight that I hadn't seen previously, and where does it lead?"

The relatively brief insights I have chosen to share are intended to stimulate discussion. Ideally, I would like to see them read and discussed at a *shabbat* table, in a *ḥavurah*, in a rabbi's study group, or perhaps that of a minister as well. Some will undoubtedly use them as kernels around which to construct longer sermons. That too is welcome, although the give-and-take of *ḥevruta*, pairs or small groups of readers, thinkers, and conversation partners, is more of what I have in mind.

I hope, in fact, to remain a *ḥevruta* partner of yours in this conversation long into the future. The Mishnah teaches that one who claims that there is no reference to resurrection of the dead in the Torah has no place in the World to Come. The World to Come, as I understand it, is the future, right here on earth, beyond the lifetime of the individual, the life of the coming generations. This book is my way of saying, as in the motto I have chosen above, that I do indeed have faith in the ongoing *resurrection of the Torah*. I hope that also means that through these words something of me will remain present in the world that keeps on coming.

SEFER BERESHIT

THE BOOK OF GENESIS

בראשית
BERESHIT
(Genesis 1:1-6:8)

1 בראשית ברא אלהים

Torah begins with the secrets of Creation. Its opening verse is filled with puzzles. *Bereshit* seems like a *semikhut* or construct form, to be linked to a noun following it. But the next word is a verb, *bara*, "created." That is followed by *Elohim*, which looks like a plural noun, but is paired with a singular verb. Why the definite articles? ***Et ha-****shamayim* ve ***-et ha-****arets*, rather than *shamayim va-arets*, meaning "***the*** heaven and ***the*** earth?" Might there be others?

RaSHI reads the first two words as *bereshit bero'*, "As God ***began*** to create." But of course! Creation is an ongoing process, one that is still taking place. Even now, in this very moment, Y-H-W-H is breathing existence into all that is. Our greatest teaching is that with which Torah opens: ***We live in a created – and ever re-created – world***. That is not primarily a statement about planetary origins, billions of years ago. It is a faith that the entire world and every process that sustains it, that which we usually see as "nature," is fraught with divine mystery. ***Evolution is a sacred narrative, telling us of a never-ending process of Creation. Torah, which means "teaching," is a guidebook to discovering that truth and living in response to it.*** That is why it begins with this tale of Creation. We need to hear this message today more than ever.

The Targum renders the opening word of Torah as *be-ḥokhmata*, "through wisdom." Wisdom comes before all. This Teaching/Wisdom is unknown to us. It is "Torah before it became garbed in material clothing," say the Kabbalists. The holy Zohar then reverses the subject-object order of the verse. "Through wisdom did the Hidden Source – unknown, mysterious, beyond language – create *Elohim*." That One brought forth a single God in plural form, the One now appearing with many faces. ***Elohim*: *As soon as there was a world, there were multiple***

pathways to Truth. This multi-faced God was the first creation, emerging out of mystery. Your God, my God, God as I need to imagine Him/Her/It today, the God I will need to encounter tomorrow – they are all One. This also means that the Talmudic teaching "Both these and those are the words of ***living Elohim***" is an underlying principle of Torah. There is more than one way to attain truth.

Et, says the Talmud, always comes to add something. ***Et*** the heaven and ***et*** the earth includes everything that is ever to exist within them. The word is written with two letters, *aleph* and *tav*, the first and the last. If everything was created by divine speech, says an old Midrash, all was formed by the letters of the alphabet. It is all part of the One.

והארץ היתה תהו

"The earth" – as long as existence is only earthly, material, it is *tohu*, "chaotic" – without meaning. But then you discover *bo hu*, that the hidden One is in fact hidden ***right there within it***, or ***within you***, that the spirit of God is hovering over your own inner Torah, the "waters" that rise up from within you.

ויאמר אלהים יהי אור

The next step is finding a spiritual language. As the *Me'or 'Eynayim* reads it: "When you say *Elohim*, you create light." The person who finds the words to articulate sacred truth brings light into the world.

But then you come to realize that this light was there already, long before there were words. "A light that already was." You are not creating, but ***discovering*** a light that was there all along.

Welcome to Torah. ***Torah or.*** The teaching ***is*** light.

2 יהי מאורות ברקיע השמים והיו לאותות ולמועדים ולימים ושנים

"Let there be luminaries in the firmament of heaven, that they be signs and occasions, marking days and years." Torah is light, and the plural refers to our two Torahs, the written and the oral. Yes, they exist in the highest heavens – or in the deepest depths – of the human soul. Out of them come forth *otot*, "signs," symbolic forms, rituals, and *mo'adim*, "occasions," special events and moments that transform *yamim*, the days of the year, and *shanim*, the years of a person's life.

The story of Creation is also the story of Revelation. **Cosmos and Torah, *existence and meaning,*** are parallel outward manifestations of the same secret One. This is a core teaching of Judaism as a devotional path. The light of Creation – our sense of wonder at the magnificence of the natural world – and the light of revelation – the inner enlightenment that fills us as we open ourselves to the words of Torah – is the same light.

3 וירא אלוהים כי טוב...וירא אלוהים את כל אשר עשה והנה טוב מאד

"God saw that it was good...And God saw all that He had made, and it was very good" (1:25, 31). The "It was good" for the sixth day is spoken after the land animals are created. ***Then*** God created humans. The Torah knows humans too well to say "It was good" after we were created. There is just a general view of Creation after it was completed, saying "It was altogether good," regarding the project as a whole. No judgment is offered concerning this particular creation called humanity.

Humans are created in the image of God, the One who "creates light and forms darkness, makes peace and creates evil" (Is. 45:7). A true monotheist must believe that evil, too, has its root in God. As God's image, we must contain it as well. Therefore, the Torah holds back in notable silence.

True evil, needless and malicious harm to others, brutality as a form of sport or entertainment, indifference to suffering, unwillingness to share even when we have more than plenty – these are human inventions, not found in the world of "lower" creatures. As we struggle against them within ourselves as well as with others, we struggle also to understand why we were given them by the One who creates and is all.

4 וכל שיח השדה טרם יהיה בארץ...כי אדם אין לעבוד את האדמה

In the spirit of R. Nahman of Braslav: **"There was not yet conversation in the fields...for there was no human to work the ground"**

(2:5). The precious conversations people have with God – and perhaps with themselves as well – so often happen out in the open fields. The sight of the sky, the freshness of the air, the feel of real soil beneath our feet – these can always inspire us to open our hearts. But we know how to do so because we have "***worked*** the ground," toiled at a life of service, **from the ground up**. Opening the heart in *siaḥ ha-sadeh*, "conversation in the field," which may appear to be so spontaneous, requires lots of work in preparation.

5 ועץ החיים בתוך הגן ועץ הדעת טוב ורע

"The Tree of Life was within the Garden, and the Tree of Knowing Good and Evil" (2:9).

The Tree of Life had a natural connection to "the Breath of Life" that God had just (2:7) breathed into Adam's nostrils. That was the tree of which we were ***supposed*** to eat (before we ate of the other), linking the life-force within us to the life all around us in the Garden. The serpent understood that eating this tree would make humans immortal, meaning that we would be aware in each moment of the eternal life-force breathing through us. He therefore tried to distract us from it, showing Eve how beautiful and tasty the Tree of Knowledge – lifeless knowledge, even life-destroying knowledge – could be. She and Adam fell for it, and we are still paying the price.

If you are not convinced that the two trees have been rent asunder, try studying at a nearby university. Unless you're unusually lucky, you will quickly see how divorced our "higher education" has become from the affirmation of life, how obsession with "critical distance" and "objectivity" have led us toward a fear of affirming values. The creative juices that flow from the Tree of Life are too easily stifled by the dryness of learning as accumulating information, by the choice of cleverness over wisdom.

We get a second chance at Eden by means of Torah, she who is called a ***"Tree of Life"*** (Prov. 3:18). True Torah learning (not easily found) offers an opportunity to engage with text and tradition in a way that heals the ancient breach, linking us back to life, reuniting the two trees. This is the meaning of *torah li-shemah*, for the sake of the letter *heh, shekhinah*, the force of Y-H-W-H within us.

The "union of The Blessed Holy One and *shekhinah*," say the Kabbalists, is also the reunification of the two trees of Eden.

6 ויבא קין...והבל הביא גם הוא

"Cain brought...and his brother Abel also brought." Here you are, the first human being born outside the Garden. You are grateful for your life, so you get the idea of expressing that gratitude by bringing an offering. As a farmer, you bring your best veggies. Then your smart brother decides to one-up you. He's a shepherd, so he offers barbeque. And it turns out that God is no vegetarian and seems to prefer the aroma of burning meat.

It is in no way fair that God pays attention to his offering and not to yours. Unable to strike God in your fury, you raise a hand against your brother and kill him, not quite understanding what you were doing. Immediately God calls out "Where is Abel, your brother?"

Here we are, out of Eden. We are all Cain, the world's first absurd hero. We are adults now, outside the protected Garden of childhood. Our deeds make a difference and they cannot easily be undone. ***Life is totally unfair, yet you are totally responsible.*** No wonder there is a voice in the tradition that says: "Better if we had never been created!" But here we are. We'd better get used to it.

נח
NOAḤ
(Genesis 6:9-11:32)

1 נח איש צדיק תמים היה בדורותיו את האלוהים התהלך נח

"Noah was a righteous man, perfect in his generations; Noah walked with God" (6:9). The tradition's judgment of Noah, based on this verse, is well-known. The Midrash holds him up to the standard of Abraham, to whom God said "Walk ***before*** Me" (Gen. 17:1), indicating greater trust than He had in Noah. Especially telling is Noah's indifference to the fate of the rest of humanity, beyond his own family. Noah neither preached to them to repent of their ways nor did he argue with God in an attempt to save them. Compared to both Abraham and Moses, he was a failed leader.

I think about what it would mean to be a Noah in our day. I'm sure that he has solar panels on his roof and that he uses only recycled toilet paper. He is probably a well-trained survivalist, with lots of bottled water in his basement. He might even own a cabin in the country, somewhere on high ground, where he and his family can flee in time of need.

He's given up on the political system, judging it just impossible to change. He used to give a little money to environmental organizations, but he's given up on them as ineffective. Our contemporary Noah does nothing wrong, but nothing right, either. What's the point?

I guess he's just waiting for the word to come. Meanwhile, he's keeping an eye out for a stockpile of gopher wood.

2 בוא אתה וכל ביתך אל התיבה

"Come, you and all your household into the ark" (Gen. 7:1). The Ba'al Shem Tov loved the fact that the biblical term for "ark," *teyvah*, also means "word" in rabbinic Hebrew. Several teachings are attributed to him around this link. This verse becomes "Bring your whole self with you into every word of prayer or teaching." "Make a window for the ark" (Gen. 6:16) turns into "Let the light shine through as you speak the word." The light within you seeks a way to shine forth. Words spoken in wholeness and holiness can become a pathway for that light. "Words that come from the heart will enter the heart." Learn to use your words as a way for your inner light to shine.

Yes, this begins with what we know to be holy words, those of prayer and Torah. You need to bring your whole self into them. But the message of *ḥasidut* is that these are paradigmatic. They are meant to teach us about ***all*** words, all language. Learning to make and keep your language holy is not only about avoiding gossip, malice, and "dirty words" (though this too is important). It is also about being thoughtful about words, using them to let the light shine through. This is a spiritual practice that we could spend our whole lifetime learning.

3 ותנח התיבה בחודש השביעי

"The ark rested in the seventh month" (8:4). A later Hasidic master, the rabbi of Radomsk, added to the Ba'al Shem Tov's quip about *teyvah* as "word" a comment on "The ark rested in the seventh month" (8:4). The seventh month in the biblical calendar is *Tishrey*, the month of the Days of Awe, which has just concluded when we read this *parashah*. It is there, in that time when integrity is most demanded, that the *teyvah*, the word, finds rest. *Ḥat'anu*, "we have sinned," is a word that is spoken with the whole self. So too is God's *salaḥti,* "I have forgiven."

The largest and most challenging frame into which the tale of Noah forces us is the ultimate question of whether we, or our human society, ***deserve*** to exist. God is here our voice of self-judgment, thunderously asking, in the language of Gen. 6:13, "Are we too so filled with *ḥamas* – violence or malice – that we ought to be destroyed?" Would a Creator God, looking down upon our world, also conclude that "great is the evil in humans…just evil, all day long" (6:5), and that we are therefore irredeemable? But then comes the seventh month, and those two words – *ḥat'anu* and *salaḥti* – are spoken.

True repentance – for societies as well as for individuals – is never too late. But it needs to begin in that same verse, where this *parashah* begins: "The ***land*** was destroyed in the presence of God" (6:5). We, too, have destroyed the land. *Teshuvah* and "clean-up" – reforestation, soil conservation, and the parallels for air and water – go hand in hand. Once we get those in hand there will be time to deal with the rest of human evil.

4 לא אוסיף לקלל עוד את האדמה בעבור האדם כי יצר לב האדם רע מנעוריו

"I will no longer curse the land because of humans, since the evil of the human heart is due to childishness" (8:21). This verse, as I render it here, would record a change in God's attitude toward human evil from the moment before the flood (6:5). This reading of the verse would mean that He has learned, while still taking it seriously, to treat it with more patience and compassion.

How much of human evil and aggression is really a matter of immaturity? Childhood fears and childish needs that we never get over? Defenses created in childhood, needs to protect our very real vulnerability, often turn into limits in our ability to perceive reality when we become adults. We then lash out with aggression to "defend" territory that is threatened only in our outdated imagination.

Rabbinic tradition says that the *yetser ha-ra'*, the "evil urge," is there within us from birth. Its opposite, the *yetser ha-tov*, "good urge," enters us only at puberty. This really means that we are needy beings from birth on, always seeking assurance, from parents and others, that our needs and desires will be fulfilled. Maturity (both physical and emotional) means realizing that we have something to ***give*** to others, not just an endless need to receive. That process of maturation needs to be cultivated. "Wicked" adults are often those who never made it across that bridge.

5 ומוראכם וחתכם יהיה על כל חית הארץ

"Your fear and your life-concern must be for all that lives on earth, every bird in heaven, every thing that creeps across the ground, every fish in the sea. They have been placed in your hands" (9:2). We used to think this meant that ***they*** would be afraid of ***us***. But life in our century calls forth a new reading here. We live in the first era – or maybe the first time since Noah - when the fate of all creatures on this planet has indeed been "placed in our hands." Now we indeed need to fear ***for them***.

The following verses tell us that creeping things may be eaten, just like vegetation. But a careful look might make us wonder whether the text really meant to permit consumption of warm-blooded animals. The wording surely opens the doorway for a biblically-based vegetarianism.

The Noahide covenant, the text goes on to say very emphatically (9:10, 15, 17), is not just with humans, but with all living creatures, all those that had been with Noah in the ark. We humans have forgotten that, or have intentionally distorted it. In our treatment of our non-human fellow-members of that covenant, we have filled the whole earth with *ḥamas*, violence, once again.

Beware. We've only been promised that it won't be a flood next time.

6 ויהי כל הארץ שפה אחת ודברים אחדים

"The whole earth spoke a single language and single words" (11:1). That was the sin of the generation of Babel: they were all saying the same thing! Everybody thought and spoke alike. New ideas, unconventional ways of thinking and speaking, were not permitted. Babel before its destruction was a sort of proto-fascist state, everyone obliged to think and speak alike.

People were so confident in their universally-held opinions that they decided to turn them into bricks and mortar, a tower, like a spired cathedral or a modern "skyscraper," reaching up to heaven to proclaim their single truth.

But "heaven" is not to be reached in that way. In order for human ***creativity*** to carry forward God's open-ended and evolving ***creation***, multiple voices need to be heard. "Both these and those are words of the living God" is a cornerstone of Judaism.

Our Torah is constructed as a portable tent religion, the opposite of Babel's brick tower.

לך לך
LEKH LEKHA
(Genesis 12:1-17:27)

1 לך לך מארצך וממולדתך ומבית אביך אל הארץ אשר אראך

"Y-H-W-H said to Abraham: 'Go toward yourself, from your land, your birthplace, and your father's house to the land that I will show you'" (12:1). This verse marks the beginning of the Jewish journey. ***All*** of our journeys, through all generations, are a continuation of the one begun in this moment. The Hasidic readings of the verse do not tie it to a particular place. The call to Abraham is about more than that. *Erets,* "land," in the verse refers to the entire physical world, to corporeality itself. You have a certain habitual way of seeing the physical world, taking things around you, including your own physical self, for granted. That is the worldview you were born into and the way you were raised in your father's house.

Now you are being called to leave all that behind. "Go forth from your land," from ***the attitude toward the world that you had been given***. "Go to yourself," turn inward to a deeper truth that you will find within. That is "the land that I will show you," a new way of seeing all that is around you. I will show you a physical universe that serves as an outer garb to the spiritual treasure that lies within it, just as your own body houses a divine soul. I will show you a world filled with shining sparks of holiness, waiting to be discovered and uplifted.

The journey has begun.

2 והיה ברכה, ואברכה מברכיך ומקללך אאור, ונברכו בך כל משפחות
האדמה.

"Become a blessing. I will bless those who make you into a blessing, but will curse those who make you into a curse. May all the families of the land become blessings through you" (12:2-3). Here, it's all in the translation. The phrase *ve-heyeh berakhah* is striking. Abraham is told not just that he is blessed, but that he is to be a blessing to others. But then the next verse needs to be read in the same spirit. *Mevarakhekha* is not "those who bless you," but those who use you, their spiritual descent from you, to become blessings as well. May those who pass on that blessing also be blessed! The opposite should be the fate of those who turn your heritage into curses and hatred. *Ve-nivrekhu vekha* means that all families ***should become blessings*** through the legacy of Abraham.

Abraham is the father of the three great religions of the West. Each of them has brought great blessing into the world, but also more than a few curses. Teach us, Father Abraham, to remember you in a way that makes us, too, into fonts of blessing. Let us never make your legacy into a curse, or an excuse for cursing others.

3 ויסע אברם הלוך ונסוע הנגבה

"Abram travelled back and forth to the Negev" (12:9). Abraham is the original seeker of our tradition. He rejected religion as he had inherited it and struck out to find Y-H-W-H on his own. This is a long and lonely quest. Everyone who undertakes it goes "back and forth to the Negev." Sometimes we find deep wellsprings within ourselves and are nurtured by the path we have chosen. But yes, there are dry times as well. Every seeker goes through days – sometimes even years – in the barren wastelands, sometimes leading us to question whether the whole journey was worthwhile. We need to acknowledge these and accept them as part of the journey, trusting that we will get back to the fertile plain and its deep wellsprings soon again – or at least before it's over.

ו

4 אברהם כבד מאד במקנה כסף וזהב

"Abram was very loaded down with ownership, [including] silver and gold" (13:2). *Mikneh* can refer to anything you acquire. Too much of it makes you *kaved*, "heavy" or loaded down. This chapter is a brief but sad tale about how possessions can drive a family apart. "There's no room for both of us" in this burgeoning business, says the uncle to his nephew, who has been his closest family until this time. "Separate from me"; it is time to strike out on your own. He does, but it comes to a bad end. Lot goes to Sodom. Perhaps Abraham should have foreseen this.

This is the first of our patriarch's family decisions, and it is not necessarily a good one. Couldn't they have worked out their shepherds' quarrel and found a way to stay together? As this family narrative goes on, we will be learning of many decisions made and roads taken, not always for the good. We are meant to learn from all of them.

5 ובן משק ביתי הוא דמשק אליעזר

"What are You giving me? I am barren; my household is managed by Eliezer of Damascus" (15:2). He will be the only one left to inherit me! RaSHI quotes an *aggadah* that Damesek is an abbreviation for *doleh u-mashkeh*: "he dips into my teaching and serves it up to others." On this the *Ma'or va-Shemesh* suggests that Eliezer was incapable of innovating, just passing the teaching along unchanged. Only a true son of Abraham would dare to seek out his own path in the service of Y-H-W-H.

Might our situation today be reversed? Could it be that the direct heirs of the Hasidic masters have taken the path of Eliezer, and that it will take newcomers like ourselves to bring the teachings back to life?

6 באר לחי ראי

(16:14) How are we to translate this enigmatic phrase? "The Well of Seeing Life?" "The Well where I had a living vision?" "The Well where the Living One sees me?" Any of these meanings could fit this elusive name. When we add to it the fact that *be'er* ("well") can also mean "explain," as in *be'ur* or "commentary," the possibilities get ***really*** interesting. Try some.

וירא
VA-YERA
(Genesis 18:1-22:24)

1 והוא עומד עליהם תחת העץ

"He was standing over them beneath the tree" (18:8). Literally, it could also be translated "He stood upon them." Here the *Degel* brings the Ba'al Shem Tov's parable of a beautiful bird sitting on the highest branch of a tree. No one can reach the bird up there, unless they stand on top of one another and make a human ladder. So too, we cannot reach the beautiful bird called *shekhinah* who hovers over us unless we stand on the backs of one another. Here he quotes the Talmudic teaching "from my students I learned most of all."

Each of us ***stands over them***, on the backs of both our teachers and our students as we reach upward (or ***inward!***). Today we also stand on the backs of the rich legacy left us by those early Hasidic generations.

2 היפלא מה' דבר

"Is anything too wondrous for Y-H-W-H?" (18:14) This response to Sarah calls to mind two verses in the Book of Proverbs (1:8; 6:20) that refer to *torat imekha*, "your mother's teaching." There is something in the transmission of Torah that requires mothering, both giving birth and nursing. One of the earliest Kabbalists suggested that the true teachings can only be absorbed "by way of nursing," rather than by intellect alone.

But is our mother too old? Are the breasts of Torah too dried up to nourish anymore? That challenge is not a trivial one in an era like ours. The answer is found in these words. Sarah stands as witness that this aged mother of ours can still nurse new generations of seekers.

Why can Sarah still do that? ***Because she doubted and laughed***;

there was still some sparkle in those elderly eyes. And that was accepted as part of her journey.

3 המכסה אני מאברהם

"Shall I hide from Abraham what I am about to do?... All the nations of earth shall be blessed through him...by keeping the way of Y-H-W-H, acting in righteousness and justice" (18:17-19). God foresees Abraham's challenge and wants to bring it on. This is Y-H-W-H the Teacher's great educational moment. The plan is that Abraham is to bless all nations by bringing them a sense of *mishpat* and *tzedakah*, judgment and righteousness.

Looking back from a distance, we may say that this was a great success, through the birth of three great religions descending from Abraham, and the moral conscience they have aroused in humanity (in their better moments). But this is the moment when God first has to educate Abraham to that role. The divine mind must be saying: "How will I help this person grow into being a source of blessing, bringing justice to the world? The words sound great, but how do I make it a reality? He will only learn about justice if he has stood up for it and fought for it! I need to give him this opportunity to challenge Me, to cry out for justice, to ***demand*** it of Me! That's how he – and all his descendants – will learn!"

It is in the context of this educational moment that Abraham cried out "***Will the Judge of the whole earth not do justice?***"

4 ואברהם שב למקומו

"And Abraham went back to his place" (18:33). This means that in arguing with God he had indeed stepped beyond his own place! In verse 22, we saw him "still standing before Y-H-W-H." In the boldness of his approach, he had entered into the place of God, *ha-Makom*. God seems to permit that to those who stand up to Him in order to save human lives. It was when Moses was arguing at Sinai to save the lives of Israel that God said to him *hineh makom iti*, "Here is a place, with Me."

Ordinarily, the *makom* of God is beyond us. Even the angels call out *Ayeh mekom kevodo*, "Where is the place of His glory?" But there are moments when the One who loves all of God's creatures makes room for those who seek to defend them.

These moments of "holy audacity" indeed have their place. But it is also important to be able to step back from them with one's faith unbroken. As the author of Job teaches us, even after the greatest of protests we must be able to submit.

An early Hasidic author, R. Mendel of Premyshlan, interprets these words in precisely the opposite way. Abraham was one of those people who was always attached to the One. He knew that his real place was that of *devekut,* intimacy with Y-H-W-H. Out of concern for the fate of these people he stepped out of that place for a moment, standing back to confront God with questions as an "other." But once it was over, "Abraham went back to ***His*** place," the place of which we say "Blessed is the glory of Y-H-W-H from His place." That was the place where Abraham belonged.

5 הוציאם אלינו ונדעה אותם

"Bring them out to us, that we may know them" (19:5). The reading that interprets this "knowing" sexually, giving rise to the whole language of "sodomy," is not completely clear from the text and is possibly a later interpretation.

Suppose we read it this way. Strangers have come to town, and the townspeople (to whom Lot is also a relative newcomer) are suspicious, and want to find out who they are. "We want to question them." This is similar to the people of Jericho seeking out possible spies in the house of Rahab, many years later. Lot is being an excessively protective host (something he learned from his Uncle Abe), and his offering up of his daughters is indeed horrifying. But of what, exactly, are these Sodomites really guilty? Curiosity? Excessive caution?

Pirkey Avot tells us what it means to be a Sodomite. "A person who says 'What's mine is mine and what's yours is yours' has the quality of Sodom." The Sodomites had built a society that existed completely without generosity. "What's mine is mine! Don't ever ask me for anything! Don't give anything away! Charity? Generosity? *Pfui!* "Don't offer hospitality to strangers! We don't do that here!"

Such a society is indeed doomed to be destroyed.

6 מי מלל לאברהם הניקה בנים שרה

"Who said to Abraham that Sarah would be nursing children" (21:7). Why the plural? Sarah had only one child. RaSHI says that after Isaac was weaned, noble women from among the nations brought their babies to Sarah to be nursed. A rumor had spread that she had not really given birth to Isaac, but that he was a foundling. Her ability to nurse quelled those rumors.

The Kotzker Rebbe suggested that these babes formed the root of the souls of future converts. We often encounter Jews by choice, having no known Jewish ancestors, who say; "I always knew" or "I always felt that I had a Jewish soul." Herein lies an explanation – or at least a hint that this experience is not a new one in our times, but an insight that was shared from within the tradition as well.

This may open a door for Jews by choice to consider themselves as descended from Sarah's nurslings. Not a bad start in life!

7 ויהי אחר הדברים האלה והאלוהים נסה את אברהם

"It was after these things that God tested Abraham" (22:1). We need to understand the *'akedah* as a ***mutual*** test: God tests Abraham and Abraham tests God. Although the text does not permit it easily, we can bend it to mean "***God was tested along with Abraham.***"

Functionally, the tale of the binding of Isaac sets a boundary in the evolution of Israelite religion. It is an announcement that God does not command or desire human sacrifice. Abraham was willing, but God did not want it to happen. But God is also tested in this process.

Abraham, the truly faithful servant says: "Is this what you ***really*** want, Master of the Universe? If it is, I will do it for You. But are You sure that You want it? Have You thought about how I will feel about You afterwards? Yes, I will continue serving You, but with bitterness, rather than devotion, filling my heart. Is that what You want?"

Abraham is challenging God again, drawing a line in the sand. ***"Is this what You will demand of a faithful servant? Then here it is."***

Abraham binds Isaac to the altar and takes the knife into his hand. And God backs down.

What gave Abraham the unbelievable courage to do this? Perhaps it is hinted at in "On the third day Abraham lifted his eyes" – *va-yar' et ha-makom me-raḥok* (22:4) – "he saw that God, *ha-makom*, was far away." He understood that it could not really be that this would be demanded of him, ***that the God he knew*** couldn't really be present in this command. And he was right.

Never again were humans supposed to be forced to play this Russian Roulette with the lives of their children.

Listen, generals!

חיי שרה

ḤAYYEY SARAH

(Genesis 23:1-25:18)

1 ואברהם זקן בא בימים וה׳ ברך את אברהם בכל

"Abraham was old, come into days, and Y-H-W-H blessed Abraham with All." The Midrash adds: "Abraham had a daughter whose name was *ba-kol*, "In All" or "With All."

The Midrash points toward an esoteric meaning. The Abraham of this verse is not our earthly ancestor, but his counterpart within the divine realm. Abraham is called by the prophet (Is. 41:8) *Avraham ohavi*, Abraham who loves Me. He is the human representation of *ḥesed*, the divine quality of compassion, the force that constantly flows into and renews all that is. Abraham is thus the Elder among the seven qualities (*middot* or *sefirot*) that manifest both in humans and in their divine Source, which are also referred to as the seven primal Days (although existing in a realm prior to time!). But His love courses through all of those "Days," flowing finally into Shabbat, the manifestation in time of *shekhinah*, the divine presence that fills the world. She is also the "Daughter" who is both the fulfillment of divine compassion and the "Mother of All Life," the Source of love that animates this world. Any Judaism that calls itself Hasidic must be one built on *ḥesed,* the sense that compassion comes first in the list of divine qualities with which we humans are blessed. All the rest follows from it, as we all follow from Abraham, both through his son (who will add *gevurah*, strength of character, to the mix) and through this daughter.

2 וכל טוב אדוניו בידו

"All the good of his master in his hands" (24:10). What "good" of Abraham's did Eliezer take with him when he went to seek out a bride for Isaac? The use of the vague term *tuv* here lets us think that it was more than just evidence of wealth. He brought with him something of the ***goodness*** with which Abraham had conducted himself in the Land. This included welcoming strangers, making treaties with local chieftains, treating the locals fairly in buying land, and caring enough for the people of Sodom to risk all in order to defend them. This came as part of the effort to discern God's teaching from within himself and trying to live by it. All this is part of the "good" that Eliezer bore with him on his journey. He cared about his neighbors.

When he came upon Rebekah and saw her kindness toward both him and his camels (24:18-20), he knew that she was the one. This was behavior than was familiar to him from the ***goodness*** he had seen in the house of Abraham. "She'll fit in well," he thought, "with this family and its values."

3 הנה אנוכי ניצב על עין המים

"There I was standing over the well" (24:43). But the Hasidic *Degel* takes this verse totally out of context and reads it: "Behold! The ***anokhi*** or "***I am***" of God stands upon the flowing spring of Torah!" Awareness of Y-H-W-H comes about through the process of fruitful learning. It is the renewing and refreshing power of ever-new learning and understanding that brings you to such awareness.

Does it not work that way for you? The Ba'al Shem Tov (the Degel's grandfather) would say that it's because you're not yet really learning Torah. Maybe the wrong books, maybe the wrong teacher, maybe the wrong mindset. Try again.

4 ויצא יצחק לשוח בשדה

"Isaac went out *la-suaḥ* in the field, toward evening." The verb is left untranslated because its meaning is unknown. Some biblical scholars have sought to emend it. Yet so much of Jewish spiritual life is woven around it! This is a good place to meditate on how much of Judaism is created by such obvious later re-reading of the biblical legacy. The rabbis read *la-suaḥ* as "to speak softly" or "converse," based on other biblical occurrences. They then added (Berakhot 26b) that such "conversation" must refer to prayer. From here they derived that Isaac established the *minḥah* prayer, recited daily at sundown. But they also concluded from it that *la-suaḥ* indicated the proper tone for prayer, to be recited quietly, like one would speak in conversing with oneself.

In a still later development, R. Nahman of Bratslav used the verse to suggest that the field itself was an active participant in this "conversation" between Isaac and his God, that all the grasses of the field entered into his words as he prayed. He is reading the *bet* of *ba-sadeh* as indicating more than place; he was praying ***along with*** the field.

All this from the single incomprehensible word!

5 ויתן אברהם את כל אשר לו ליצחק

"Abraham gave the 'all' that he had to Isaac" (25:6). This is the same "all" that we met above, when "Y-H-W-H blessed Abraham with all." For the Kabbalist, ***kol***, "all," refers to the fullness of blessing, the wholeness of existence, the total flow of divine energy into the world. Abraham's gift was an opening of the inner eye to see this "all." He passed it on to Isaac, and Isaac to Jacob. This what Jacob means when he says ***yesh li kol*, "I have all"** to Esau (Gen. 33:11). Accept my gifts, for I have the only true inheritance that I need.

6 ויקברו אותו יצחק וישמעאל

"Isaac and Ishmael buried their father" (25:9). This is a very touching and somewhat startling moment. We have heard nothing of the relationship between these brothers since Hagar and her child were sent away. Did they know each other throughout their lives? Had there been some contact between them over the years? What did they both think about their family history?

What happened when Abraham died? Did Isaac, in an act of reconciliation, seek out Ishmael in the desert to join him in the burial? Or had Abraham remained in contact with his elder son all along? We are given some hint about this in the rabbinic tradition to the effect that Keturah, Abraham's "new" wife, whom he married after Sarah's death, was none other than Hagar. What does this say about the entire family dynamic?

We have heard the story only as told among the descendants of Isaac. But there must be another version, the family story as told from Hagar and Ishmael's side. Are we open to hearing it?

תולדות
TOLEDOT
(Genesis 25:19-28:9)

1 ויתרוצצו הבנים בקרבה ותאמר אם כן למה זה אנכי ותלך לדרוש את ה׳

"The children bounced about (or 'smashed one another') within her. She said: 'If this is so, why am I?' And she went in search of Y-H-W-H" (25:22).

Rebekah is the first God-seeker in the Torah. It is God who calls to Adam, to Noah, and to Abraham. It is notable that the first one to be called a God-seeker in this very patriarchal narrative is a woman. Her words also offer a strong three-word expression of existential crisis: *lamah zeh anokhi*? ***"Why am I?"*** It is in being confronted with that question that we become *dorshey Y-H-W-H*, seekers of God. All of us seekers, in every generation, are Rebekah's children, asking her question.

2 ויאהב יצחק את עשו כי ציד בפיו

"Isaac loved Esau because of the hunt in his mouth, but Rebekah loved Jacob" (25:28). As every parent knows, this stark choice by each parent of one child – especially a twin – over the other is not going to end well.

Isaac's preference for Esau looks something like because he's a real "man's man." He's always out there hunting, and his father takes pride in that. Rebekah's choice of Jacob is unexplained; it was just pure maternal love, and Jacob was nourished by it. Let us recall that the story we usually call "Jacob and Esau" is also the story of a powerful mother, and the ways she, acting behind the scenes, exercises crucial control over her family's future. Both she and Sarah are original *yiddishe mamas*; they seem to make the most important decisions about who will rule the roost.

3 מכרה כיום את בכורתך לי

"Sell me your birthright as of this day" (25:31). How young are the brothers here? We are not told, but they seem to be adolescents. Why does Jacob make this demand of Esau? Something in their upbringing must have prepared him to do it.

Jacob must always have known the origin of his name, the fact that he was born grasping onto his brother's heel. That might have been part of his identity from early childhood. Perhaps his mother also shared the prophecy with him, especially the line "the elder will serve the younger." He suffered from the denial of his father's love, who gave it all to the firstborn. Here was a chance, he thought, to change all that in an instant.

4 ויחפור את הבארות

"He dug out the wells that had been dug in the days of Abraham... Isaac's servants dug in the valley, and they found there a well of living waters" (26:18-19). The Hasidic authors see these as internal wellsprings that have to be dug anew by each generation. Based on an old midrashic linking of Torah and water, they speak of a deep reservoir of inner Torah that lies within each human soul. It awaits our "digging," meaning the effort of discovery. Yes, the wells were already dug by earlier generations; we learn from the accumulated wisdom of the past. But the effort has to be undertaken anew by each generation. The language in which the teachings can best be heard and absorbed keeps changing, due to the unique experiences that each generation undergoes. How especially true this is in our day, as the pace of change has so much quickened!

But how do we undertake this vital task of renewal? Yes, we believe that wellsprings of Oral Torah exist within each of us, waiting to pour forth in creativity. But this can only happen as we become connected to Torah, both to the text and to the long tradition of re-reading it. We need an education, for adults as well and children, that combines these efforts, teaching the tradition in a way that remains open and welcoming to its renewal for a new era. A contemporary Hasidism has to stand both for a deep learning and for a re-opening of the interpretive canon, just as did the disciples of the Ba'al Shem Tov.

5 וישב יצחק ויחפור את בארות המים אשר חפרו בימי אברהם אביו

"Isaac settled and dug the wells of water that they had dug in the days of Abraham his father. The Philistines had sealed them up after Abraham's death...They dug in the wadi and found there a well of living waters...The shepherds of Gerar quarreled with Isaac's shepherds, saying 'The water is ours!'" (26:18-20).

Water represents both Torah and *ḥesed* in the Jewish symbolic imagination. Abraham embodied both, having discovered the flowing wisdom of compassionate and loving Torah from within his own self. But then he died, and with his death the era of Isaac began. Isaac represents judgment, the restraining of compassion. Immediately all the "Philistines" saw their chance. "This is a time of severity!" they proclaimed. "No more forgiveness, no more overlooking of the slightest sin! The water of Torah is ***ours*** now!"

This is the battle that Isaac had to fight, both against those forces of judgment that so quickly reveal themselves to be demonic, but also against that same inclination within himself. **One of the most important truths of Jewish mystical teaching is that judgment untempered by compassion will quickly turn wicked and demonic.** His first two attempts at achieving this balance were failures, resulting in wells called "Conflict" and "Devilry." Only on the third try did he feel that Y-H-W-H opened him up wide enough to regain some of his father's compassion. He named that well *Reḥovot,* "broad places" or "wide open spaces." It is the antithesis of *Mitsrayim*, "the narrow straits."

The waters of Torah flow only in a mind wide open, not in the tight and narrow spaces.

6 ויהי כאשר זקן יצחק

"When Isaac grew old and his eyes dimmed from seeing, he called Esau, his older son, saying to him "My son. And he said to him: Here I am" (27:1). Notice how closely the language here tracks to the dialogue of Abraham and Isaac on Mount Moriah. The Torah wants to tell us how close Isaac and Esau really were. This is clear at the end of the story as well (27:33-38), with the account of Isaac's trembling and Esau's loud cry.

It is too easy just to attribute this to Isaac's failing eyesight, a stand-in for moral blindness. We know the story from Jacob's side of the family and have always defended his narrative and the deeds of his mother. But Esau, as the ultimately rejected son, also calls out for our sympathy. The Torah wants to teach us something here, and we ignore it at our peril.

"Do you have only a single blessing, my Father? Bless me too, my Father!" We cannot but hear in this cry an echo of the promise to Abraham: "Through you will **all the nations of the earth** be blessed." How much are we missing when we read the patriarchal tales only as the story of our own people?

7 למה אשכל גם שניכם יום אחד

"Why should I lose both of you on the same day?" (27:45) In sending Jacob away, Rebekah seems to understand that she has already lost Esau, but she cannot bear the loss of both. Hear in the text a mother's terrible pathos in this moment, that of a parent who had to choose. She gambled heavily for what she believed was right. Our version of the story affirms her deed; the spiritual legacy of Abraham and Isaac went where it needed to go. But she paid a heavy price. And not only she. We are still paying it.

ויצא
VA-YETSE
(Genesis 28:10-32:2)

1 ויחלום והנה סולם

"He dreamed: Behold a ladder...divine messengers going up and down on it" (28:12). Our dreams reflect a lot of who we are and what we need to see. The text cannot ignore the moral ambiguity of Jacob's character. As he sets forth on this life-journey, one forced upon him by his own actions, he encounters this presentiment of the possibilities that lie before him. Life itself is the ladder, on which the most earthbound of deeds and people can rise to heaven, and the most heavenly intentions can be ground into the dust. Just as the Torah tells us that we can never be quite sure who is human and who is an angel (see Gen. 18:2 and 32:4), so we can never know in which direction on the ladder they (or we!) are moving, until we see the results of their actions.

The ideal of *ha'ala'ah*, "uplifting," is a key teaching of Hasidism. Everything can be raised up, revealed to be part of the divine order, taken "back to its Root." That is the essential task of the devotee, raising everything up to its Source, finding the One within it. ***All of religious life is a training course for this way of living in the world.*** Sometimes, indeed, we need to "descend for the sake of ascent," reaching down into darker places – in the world and within ourselves – in order to raise things up and restore them to the light.

But everything heavenly can be dragged down, as well. The Hasidic sources teach that all our basest desires are distortions of divine qualities implanted within us. It is our task to discover them as such and to turn them around. This is the work called *tikkun ha-middot*, an essential part of Hasidism. "Working on yourself," we might call it, paying attention to your moral and emotional life and how it's working out. The angels going up and down on the ladder reminds us that a fall is always possible. We are God's messengers (*mal'akhim*) on the rungs of the ladder, and we are always moving, whether up or down. The ladder's rungs seem to be made of glass. If you try to stand still on any of them, you are in danger of falling. Then you have to begin the long climb back up all over again.

2 והיה זרעך כעפר הארץ ונברכו בזרעך כל משפחות האדמה

"Your seed will be like the dust of the earth, and. All the families of the earth will be blessed by them" (28:14). Could there be an understood conditionality in this sentence? "***If*** you and your seed are as humble as the dust of the earth…" This promise of becoming a source of blessing for all the earth's families had already been made to Abraham, the first to worship Y-H-W-H by saying "I am dust and ashes" (18:27). Perhaps Jacob and his seed need to be told that these two aspects of Abraham's legacy – the humility and the blessing – are inseparably linked together. Otherwise, the promise of the land might lead him to become haughty, to lord over others, as he did to his brother. There was a danger that lay buried in the blessing he had just received and the way he attained it.

We need to pay special attention to this today. Control over territory and haughtiness toward others often seem to go together.

3 וייקץ יעקב משנתו ויאמר אכן יש יהו"ה במקום הזה ואנוכי לא ידעתי

"Jacob awoke from his sleep and said 'Wow! There is Y-H-W-H in this place, the 'I am' that I had not known!" (28:16) This is the first great revelation to Jacob, the first step in his transformation. *Anokhi,* God's "I am" that is the essence of the Teaching, is revealed to him here. Jacob thus becomes the outer form of *da'at* or awareness, of which Moses, to whom Torah is fully revealed, is the inner.

This awareness of Y-H-W-H is, however, only the first step. The "Wow!" moment is crucial, but it is the first step, not the last. He still has to undergo the great confrontation with the angel who is both his own shadow self and the brother he has wronged. That will happen next week. But this great discovery of the ladder and the "Wow!" has set him on his way.

4 וישק את הצאן...וישק יעקב לרחל

"He watered the sheep...and Jacob kissed Rachel" (29-10-11). The words *va-yashk*, "watered" and *va-yishak*, "kissed" appear identical in the unvocalized Torah text. The name "Rachel" can also mean "lamb." What are we to make of all this?

5 ויאמר לו לבן אך עצמי ובשרי אתה

"Laban said to him: 'But (*akh*) you are my bone and flesh" (29:14). The idiom seems to mean what we would call "my own flesh and blood." Does Laban perceive that Jacob is somehow like him, that he has met a fellow trickster? From this very first encounter, the parallel between the two of them leaps off the page.

But our sages say that the words *akh* and *rak* in the Torah text always come to hint at an exception, pointing at something missing. Yes, Laban immediately sees that clever and devious side of Jacob, someone with whom he could be quite comfortable doing business. But he is missing something. He does not see the Jacob who is capable of becoming Israel, of being transformed by inner struggle. That part of Jacob remains beyond him, inconceivable to him. The power of insight, in that branch of the family, seems to have gone to his sister.

6 ויהי כאשר ילדה רחל את יוסף

***Va-yehi ka-asher yaldah Raḥel et Yosef.* "When Rachel had given birth to Joseph, Jacob said to Laban: Send me forth..."** (30:25).

Sometimes you develop ways of living that last for a long time, even though you know deep within you they are not really the best you have to offer. You just fall into a pattern, one that is hard to leave behind. Then something happens, a life milestone – perhaps the birth of a child, the sadness of a loss, a significant birthday – and you say, "I just can't live this way anymore."

Jacob had lived in Laban's house for a long time. He had seen ten sons and a daughter grow up in the setting of Laban's extended family. He, too, felt a certain kinship with Laban. They both knew how to be tricksters when they needed. But Jacob knew he was also someone else, that he was destined for more than this. He somehow understood that he was the one who had to inherit Abraham's mantle. Now, as his beloved wife gave birth to Joseph, the next chosen son, it was completely clear. "I've got to get out of this place – and this life," he said to himself.

This makes for a different reading of the famous RaSHI comment in the next chapter. "I dwelt (GaRTI) with Laban," Jacob says to Esau (32:5). RaSHI switches around the letters and GaRTI becomes TaRYaG, 613. "I lived with Laban and kept all 613 commandments." But *shamarti* can also mean "I waited" or "held back" (see Gen. 37:11). All those years he was with Laban, Jacob is saying, he knew that there was a spiritual path he would eventually need to follow. But he was waiting, abiding his time, not able to do it while living in Laban's house. Thus the verse continues: "I delayed until now."

וישלח
VA-YISHLAḤ
(Genesis 32:3-36:43)

1 קטנתי מכל החסדים

Katonti mi-kol ha-ḥasadim. Usually, this verse is taken as a statement of Jacob's humility, and it is often quoted in that spirit. **"I am too small to have deserved all this good."** But suppose we try: "I have ***been made small*** by all the kindnesses and faithfulness You have shown to Your servant" (32:11). You have treated me too well. It has not been good for my moral development. I've never paid the price for what I've done because I never had to. Now, standing in the moment when I need to reclaim my legacy, I recognize that.

Many of us have experiences like that in the context of interpersonal relationships – with parents, a spouse, or others. "You've been too good, too forgiving, too generous, for my own growth." Here the Torah suggests that we can have such a feeling in relationship with God as well. "Life has gone so well for me that I haven't had to pay the price for my moral failings." But recognizing and admitting it requires courage.

We have really met two Jacobs in the Torah text: the man in relation with God and the man in relation to family. We might call them the Jacob of night visions and of daytime deeds. The trickster who outsmarts both Esau and Laban hardly seems to be the same person (about to be called "Israel") who dreams of angels on the ladder and wrestles with a holy being. When will the nighttime Jacob succeed in converting his daytime twin?

By next week's Torah reading, we are going to see a very different Jacob/Israel: loving and knowing parent, tribal elder, eventually the bestower of blessing. Perhaps this *katonti* is the first sign of growing up, a statement that "I know I have to change."

2 ויאבק איש עמו

"A man struggled with him" (32:25). Man or God? Angel, brother, or brother's angel? Where does the notion of alter ego fit into this story? Remember that *ish* can sometimes refer to an angel in this Genesis narrative (18:2), just as *mal'akhim* can sometimes be human (32:3). *Ish* can also be God, as in *Y-H-W-H ish milḥamah* (Ex. 15:3), "God is a ***man*** of war."

The word for "struggled" in this verse (*va-ye'avek*), says the medieval commentator Rabbenu Baḥya, is related *ḥabbek*, "to embrace." In an all-night wrestling match, isn't there a moment when you look up and say: "Just what is it that we are doing here? Are we wrestling or embracing? Battling or making love? And that is precisely where we are in our relationship with God.

3 וישאל יעקב ויאמר הגידה נא שמך ויאמר למה זה תשאל לשמי

"Jacob asked, saying: 'Tell me your name.' He said: 'Why do you ask my name?'" (32:30) This being, who is surely all of the above and more, now calls Jacob's bluff. "Why do you ask My name?" You know very well who I am.

So, too, for all of us who engage in that struggle, sometimes more than once in the same day or night. ***Nafshi yoda'at me'od*****, "My soul knows very well,"** as the poet says (Ps.139:14) – even if my mind cannot admit it. Yes, we are wrestling with God, struggling to say: "I love You, I need You, I want to do Your will!" while also crying out: "I need to be free!" "Let me find my own path!" "Do not smother me with love!" Above all, "Do not abandon me!"

4 ויאמר לא יעקב יאמר עוד שמך כי אם ישראל כי שרית עם אלוהים ועם
אנשים ותוכל...ויקרא יעקב את שם המקום פניאל

"He said: 'Your name will no longer be said to be Jacob, but Israel, for you have wrestled with God and men, and succeeded'.... He called the name of the place Peniel, because 'I saw God face to face and my life was saved'" (32:2-30). The struggle needed to be with both God and humans; Jacob's transformation into Israel is spiritual and moral at once, with no separation between them. This leads to a moment of bliss, one in which he sees the Face of Y-H-W-H.

Seeing the divine Face is a matter much discussed in the Torah text. The elders at Sinai "saw the God of Israel" (Ex. 24:10). Moses asked to see God's glory, but was shown only His back. Still his own face shown so brightly after Sinai that he needed to wear a mask to hide it. In retrospect, at his death, he is called one whom Y-H-W-H knew "face to face" (Deut. 34:10).

Jacob is the first human said to have this experience. His transformation opens the doorway to what will become the revelation at Sinai. That is why he is called the "outer" awareness (*da'at mi-le-var*), the first stage in the process, while Moses is "awareness from within." But Jacob has now become Yisra'el. The Torah takes it to mean "struggler with God. But later readers also saw in it *shur el*, "one who has seen God." Both are true, perhaps not even separate.

5 על כן ראיתי פניך כראות פני אלוהים

"I see your face, like seeing the face of God" (33:10). The cruelest thing Esau can do to Jacob is to refuse his offering. Now that Jacob has come home to reclaim his mission, he finds himself obsessed with guilt. He feels Esau's embrace and does not know how to handle it. Surely it recalls his brother's tears, shed so many years ago. Jacob has just been through a heart-wrenching and transformative experience. He knows that this angel with whom he wrestled has something to do with his struggle with Esau and the events in their past. ***He sees that angel again in the face of his brother.*** Now he cannot move forward without his brother's acceptance.

The psalmist's *bakkeshu fanav tamid,* "Seek His face always" (105:4), makes a tough demand. Seek out the face of Y-H-W-H in every human face you encounter. There are situations where that is made easy for us, either because of beauty or responding to the natural impulses of love. But sometimes it is extraordinarily difficult, especially when we encounter the faces of those to whom we know we have caused great pain. Jacob – or Israel – has taken the first step here, recognizing this task in his encounter with his brother.

6 ותצא דינה בת לאה לראות את בנות הארץ

"Dinah, daughter of Leah, went out to see the daughters of the land" (34:1). The terrible story of Dinah's rape and its aftermath begins with an innocence that prior generations did not seem to understand. There was nothing wrong with this "going out." Here she was, an only daughter (at least the only one mentioned!) in a family of so many men. They had just moved to a new country. She must have been asking herself: "What is it like to be a woman in this place?" My mother can't teach me, since she too is a foreigner. I will have to go explore for myself, meet other girls like me, and find out how they live.

Think of daughters of immigrants we have seen in our time. They still come from societies where women are locked away, supposedly for their own protection. But then they come to a new country, a place where their parents' ways are not shared by the society around them. They need to "go out," to see for themselves, perhaps to get an education that would not have been possible in the land from where they came.

And, indeed, there are dangers out there; not a few of them become victims. But they should not be blamed. The Torah text does not blame Dinah, as it might have chosen to do, but condemns her rapist, as well as her brothers, for their awful revenge.

7 ויאמר יעקב אל שמעון ואל לוי עכרתם אותי להבאישני ביושב הארץ בכנעני ובפריזי".

"Jacob said to Simeon and to Levi: 'You have made me ugly, disgracing me before those who dwell in the Land, the Canaanites and the Perizites'" (34:30). Jacob fully understands that in returning to the Land he will have to learn to live together with those who already dwell there. The Torah does not tell us that Jacob himself wanted to reject the offer of the Shechemites to mingle and intermarry with them. He was silent (34:5) and left it to his hot-headed sons. Now he curses them for having disgraced his name.

Might there be something to learn here, both for those of Israel who have chosen to live near to Shechem, and for the rest of us who have remained silent?

וישב
VA-YESHEV
(Genesis 37:1-40:23)

1 אלה תולדות יעקב יוסף

"These are the generations of Jacob: Joseph" (37:2). The whole preceding chapter has been a list of Esau's descendants and the kings of Edom. The Kabbalists viewed these as princes of primordial chaos, prior attempts at Creation that did not succeed. Over against them stands one figure, the key to their redemption. "These are the generations of Jacob: Joseph." He is the only biblical figure regularly designated by the early rabbis as ***ha-tsaddik***, the righteous one. He is the one Jacob has brought forth. One righteous or upright human being can redeem the world, even hidden worlds that cry out to be uplifted.

2 את אחי אני מבקש

"It is my brothers that I seek!" (37:16) This verse echoes loudly, indeed shouts itself out, throughout Jewish history, indeed through human history as a whole.

Jealousy and hatred, as in the preceding verses, have separated us brothers and sisters, made us "unable to speak in peace" (37:4) with one another. Maybe it was the unequal treatment we received from a parent, or at least our perception that things were that way. Maybe it was someone's dreams, or a sibling's need to say things aloud that might best have been kept quiet. Joseph and his brothers were troubled by all of the above and so are many other siblings throughout the world, in literature as well as in life. Whatever it is that has driven us apart, we long for that *shalom*, peace or wholeness, that only comes about through *shevet aḥim gam yaḥad*, "brothers dwelling together" (Ps. 121).

This is the place to pass on a teaching I heard from my teacher Rabbi Abraham Joshua Heschel, of blessed memory. He asked, "What is the central topic of the Book of Genesis?" His answer: ***"How do I live with my brother***?" From Cain and Abel through Joseph and the tribes, that is the theme that holds the book together.

The rest of the Torah, he taught, is an attempt to respond to that question.

3 וידע אונן כי לא לו יהיה הזרע

"And Onan knew that this offspring would not be considered his own" (38:9). Here the theme of brothers continues. Onan's real sin was not being willing to give this gift of a child to his deceased brother. This was an act of generosity that would have cost him nothing. Why should he refuse it? Perhaps he had seen, in the long and painful history of his family, that brothers too easily become rivals, and feared that this offspring might be a rival to his own child who would come later. This might be a hint at the dangers of family patterns that become hard to break, even in ways that should seem easy. Overplanning and strategizing can sometimes be enemies of doing the right and simple thing in the moment when it is needed.

Levirite marriage is very far from the sort of family structure familiar to us. In fact, it was abandoned as a Jewish practice already in antiquity. But in its context, it must have felt like "the right thing to do," an act of generosity toward the poor widow.

Think of the generosity of today's birth mother who gives a child to an adoptive family and what a great gift that is. I know.

4 וימאן ויאמר אל אשת אדוניו

"Joseph refused, saying to his master's wife…" (39:8). His refusal, emphasized by the *shalshelet* that lengthens the word as chanted, is a key moment in the story. The sages said that "the image of his father appeared before him," giving him the strength to resist. But what was that image? Was it just parental superego, making him ashamed of sexually going astray? Or was it the memory of real love, that of his father for him, perhaps even of Jacob's for his mother Rachel, that allowed him to reject this travesty of the act of love? Reading the text closely, we also see that this *va-yema'en*, "refused," is the same word used about Jacob in the previous chapter (37:38), when he ***refused*** to accept consolation over Joseph's alleged death.

The "image of his father" that Joseph now saw was the truth that his father had not given up on him. He did not accept that his son was dead and continued to pray for him and send love to him. The radiance of that continuing parental love reached him, all the way off in distant Egypt. That is what gave him the strength to resist and remain faithful.

5 ויעזוב בגדו בידה

"He left his garment in her hand" (39:12). Think about Joseph and clothing. His troubles began with the special striped cloak his father made for him, the one his brothers soaked in blood to prove to Jacob that he had died (37:31). When he is brought before Pharaoh, in next week's reading, we will be told that he first made sure to change his clothing (41:14). When he sends the brothers up to fetch Jacob, he sends for his brother Benjamin five new suits (45:22)! Everything in the story is expressed through garments.

We are told that Joseph was a good-looking guy, and the Midrash adds that he cultivated his fine appearance. But here, like in that pit back in Canaan, he is stripped of his fancy garments. The Hebrew word *beged*, "garment," is related to a root that can also mean "betrayal." Often, we hide who we are behind prettied-up garments – or make-up, or titles, or poses. Only when they are stripped away and we are forced to stop hiding is our true self revealed.

6 ואשר הוא עושה ה׳ מצליח

"Whatever he did, Y-H-W-H made it succeed" (39:23). The chapters of the Joseph narrative are a remarkably "secular"-seeming tale. Things happen mostly without divine interference. But here we have a hint that the hidden divine hand remains active, that Joseph's success, in prison as well as in Potiphar's house, is not only a matter of his own skills.

The narratives of Joseph and Esther are remarkably parallel, though said to take place in very different eras. They are both tales of the "Hebrew youth" – or the Jewish young woman – off in the king's palace in a foreign land. Courtiers and the glory of royalty become their surroundings. Most significantly, they both seem to live in a world where the hand of God in history is not readily apparent.

How is a Jew supposed to behave in a world where God does not intervene? How do you act when you feel yourself a stranger ***inside*** the king's palace? Here the kings are not Jewish, but their careful protocols of behavior all need to be followed. This is a situation familiar to not a few Jews in our time.

The most important thing in both of these stories seems to be not forgetting who you are and from where you come. Joseph remains a Hebrew in the eyes of the Egyptians; Esther is a Jew in the Persian court. Neither of them hides or flees from their origins. When the moment of real need comes, they are able to save the day for their tribe or people.

Think about members of minorities we know when have attained positions of power in various societies. We should stand with them and bless them for reaching out to help members of the tribe from which they came – whether that tribe is ours or another.

מקץ
MI-KETZ
(Genesis 41:1-44:17)

1

שבע פרות בריאות בשר ותרעינה באחו

"Seven healthy-fleshed cows who pastured in the reeds (*va-tir'enah ba-aḥu*)" (41:18). The Zohar (1:194a) reads *ba-aḥu* to mean "in brotherhood" or "fellowship." They are parallel to the seven maidens and the seven royal servants of the Book of Esther (Es. 1:10; 2:9), all of them representing the harmony among the seven lower *sefirot*, representing both aspects of divinity and qualities of human personality that need to be kept in balance. In good times, they are all together, eating of the same grass. But their shadow side, seven rungs of discord, trails closely behind them. Watch out.

The message is that brotherhood is relatively easy in times of plenty. It is in times of want, all of us competing for the same bit of food or living space, that we are tested. But we, even living as we do amid unimaginable plenty, are not very good at brother-and-sisterhood. How will we do when the seven years of plenty are over and things start getting rougher?

2

וקמו שבע שני רעב אחריהן

"Seven years of famine will arise after them, and all the satiety will be forgotten in the Land of Egypt" (41:30). Periods of starvation happen in our spiritual lives as well. The prophet speaks of "a hunger not for food, and a thirst not for water, but for hearing the words of Y-H-W-H" (Am. 8:11). It would do us well to anticipate such periods in our lives, and to store up spiritual "grain" to help sustain us through them.

The text goes on to speak of this storing up as a *pikadon* (41:36). The word *pikadon* comes to be much used in later *halakhic* sources. It is a pledge, an object placed in trust with another, assuring that a debt will be repaid or an obligation fulfilled. For a sign of this in nature, think of the beauty of fall foliage (I write these words in New England!) as a spiritual *pikadon,* something we can store up and keep close, that will help to sustain us through the bleakness of winter.

In the many moments of blessing that fill our inner lives, can we learn to store away some of their radiance as a trust, assuring us in times of darkness that such illumination will come again?

3 והנה פרעה חולם...ויישן ויחלום שנית.

"Pharaoh dreamed...He slept and dreamt again" (41:1-5).

Pharaoh's pair of dreams are parallel to Joseph's pair of dreams that we read about last week. Joseph remains a believer in dreams and their meaning. Even in his worst moments in those two pits, one in the field and the other in Egypt, he never thought his life would end there. He knew that he was destined for greatness. All that happens as this chapter unfolds appears to be the fulfillment of Pharaoh's dreams, but it really fulfills Joseph's as well. He is ready for his role. Without knowing the details, he has been preparing for it throughout his life.

4 אתה תהיה על ביתי ועל פיך יישק כל עמי

"You will be over my house, and by your mouth will all my people be sustained" (41:40). Once again, now for the fourth time, Joseph is set "over the house." Although the next to youngest brother, he is set over the household of Jacob, causing the resentment that sets up the whole story. He is then set over Potiphar's "house" (39:4), and then over the "house of detention" (39:22), and now the "house" of Pharaoh, which means all of Egypt.

Here we turn to a Kabbalistic reading of the verse. ***Bayit*** or house is a symbol-term for *malkhut*, the receptive element within divinity. The house is empty, needing to be filled. Joseph (his name means "the one who adds") is the fulfiller, the one who constantly adds more of divine blessing, filling the empty house.

Can we imagine these as psychic states, aspects of our inner lives? Need and fulfillment (*malkhut* and *yesod*, for the Kabbalists) exist in constant dialogue with one another. Male and female, giver and receiver, yin and yang, each needing and calling out to the other, reversing roles from one moment to the next.

This metaphor is greatly enriched by the verb used here. *Yishak*, "sustained," is subject to the same play that we saw above with Jacob and Rachel at the well. One could also read this verse to mean "by your mouth will all my people be kissed." The fulfillment of need comes as a divine kiss.

5 ויקרא יוסף את שם הבכור מנשה

"Jacob called his first-born son Manassah..." The names that Joseph gives his two sons (41:51-52) have a poignancy that is often ignored. Menasheh looks like a form of *n-sh-h*, "to forget'" and that is how the verse understands it. God has forgotten me, or forsaken me, in this strange land where I have come to dwell. Ephraim is read as derived from *p-r-h*, "to be fruiful." But at the same time God has blessed me, made me fruitful, in this land where I started off so poor.

What a strange, anomalous situation this seems to be! How can one with so much success, starting from nowhere, now blessed with a family as well, feel forsaken by God? Is this consecutive, accounting for the course of Joseph's life? "First I was forsaken, but now I am fruitful?" Perhaps. But how could a person so successful that he ruled all of Egypt name his son "God forgot me?" Who knew that there would be a second son?

But there is something within us that can understand him. All the outward blessings and achievements one can imagine do not in themselves give us the fulfillment we could have from feeling the presence of Y-H-W-H in our lives. The world is full of successful people who still feel a great emptiness in their lives. This is even more likely if their success, like Joseph's, leaves them cut off from their roots. An inner longing remains, not quieted by "success" or any of its rewards. Joseph, who "succeeded in everything he did" (39:33) in Egypt, knows that inner longing.

Awareness of that need can be the beginning of a great journey.

6 ויּרא יעקב כי יש שבר במצרים

"Jacob saw that there was produce (*shever*) in Egypt" (42:1). The identical word, *shever*, can also mean breakage or brokenness. This play on words may be seen as the beginning point in the Torah narrative of the Hasidic explanations of Israel's bondage in Egypt and the (ongoing) redemption from it. Jacob sent his sons down to Egypt not only to bring back food, but because he suspected there was something broken there that the presence of Israel, carrying the faith of his forefathers, could help to mend.

The culture and religion of ancient Egypt were focused on death, preparing the soul for the afterlife. The surviving tombs of the Pharaohs are testament to the great value the Egyptians placed the next life, including all the worldly goods that were to accompany the dead. The culture of Israel was one of life; Jacob embodies that affirmation.

When the tribes, in next week's reading, tell Jacob that Joseph is alive, we are told that "Jacob's spirit **came to life"** (45:27)! The following portion, telling of Jacob's death, will begin with "Jacob **lived** in the Land of Egypt" (47:28). With the spirit of ***Israel,*** say the Hasidic masters, wrestling with the angel and surviving that struggle, one can really ***live,*** even in the Land of Egypt.

ויגש
VA-YIGGASH
(Genesis 44:18-47:27)

1 ויגש אליו יהודה ויאמר בי אדוני. ואל יחר אפך בעבדך כי כמוך כפרעה.
"Yehudah approached him saying: "Please, my lord (or: "*My lord is within me*"). Do not be angry at your servant, for you are like Pharaoh" (44:18). The meeting of Yehudah and Yosef is seen to be of great significance throughout the Hasidic readings, taken in various directions.

Here's mine: The two brothers represent two sorts of leaders, but also two personality types. Yosef is "ruler over all the land" (42:6). His very name refers to "adding;" he is always accumulating more and more successes, greater and greater confidence. In this sense he is an incarnation of *netsaḥ*, the ever-victorious, or seeking to be victorious, side within us. Now he is addressed by Yehudah, whose name contains *hod*, referring to *hoda'ah*, which means both "gratitude" and "acceptance." This is the part of us that is grateful for who we are, accepting our limits, realizing that we cannot achieve everything, and that we are not always right. Yehudah was able to say of Tamar *tsadkah mimeni*, "she is more right than I am" (38:26). Yosef represents grandeur of vision. Being a visionary requires a certain self-confidence, an ability to believe in your dreams. Yehudah is humility and generosity of spirit. He is a ***good*** person, but not necessarily a high achiever. He leads by example more than by vision.

Yehudah opens his speech to Yosef, trying to arouse within him a compassion that he has not shown (Yosef has been turning away and hiding, so that his brothers have been unable to see his tears). He begins with ***bi adoni,*** "My lord is within me." "I recognize that I have some of you within me. I am not all pure humility and gratitude. I too think that my life has value, that there is something I have to offer, and that I have accomplished something along the way. Now I challenge you to ask the same question: Do you have any of ***me*** within ***you***?"

"No," Yehudah continues, before Yosef has a chance to reply. "Do not go immediately to that place of anger. You have something within you that can act just like Pharaoh. But there is something more to you as well. ***I know, because I am your brother.*** You have not fooled me by that hiding."

There are souls in whom this dialogue takes place every day. We say in our prayers that God is *mashpil ge'im*, "lowers the haughty," and *magbiah shefalim*, "raises up the humble." Sometimes both of these take place in the same person, on the same day.

2 ויצא האחד מאתי ואומר אך טרוף טרף ולא ראיתיו עד הנה

"One went away from me, and I said: '*Akh* he has been torn apart, and I have not seen him until now'" (44:28). This is Judah's version of what Jacob would say about Joseph. But the untranslatable *akh*, the rabbis tell us, always comes to lessen something, to teach about an exception to what the verse says. Here it indicates that the father has never quite given up on his missing son, has not quite believed the tale as he himself has told it. This is the Jacob of Gen. 37:38, who has refused consolation, never coming to terms with Joseph's alleged death. Thus, he can say: "I have not seen him ***until now.***" There is still hope in his voice. Judah, too, ever concerned for his father, has kept this in his heart. Remember that he was the one who convinced the brothers not to kill Joseph in the first place.

Perhaps this is why Jacob's blessing, coming in the next *parashah,* will give primacy to Judah (49:8-10). His father recognizes these qualities of kindness and hope. This is the right son to carry on the future of Israel.

3 איך אעלה אל אבי והנער איננו עמי

"How will I go up to my father, if the lad is not with me?" (44:34) This is the line that is meant to break Joseph's heart – as well as that of the reader – and it does. "What you and I have in common," Judah tells his brother, "is that we still love and care about the same father." No wonder the Zohar read the verse about the soul's return to its Father in heaven.

We have all come down into this "Land of Egypt." We saw there was food here, and we were hungry. "I have to make a living, after all." How many compromises have we made in order to get along? Take immigrant Jews saying: "But in America you ***have to*** work on Shabbos!" as a symbol of all the compromises we make as we go through life. How much has our original vision of who we are been squeezed into the ever-narrowing straits that constitute our particular *mitsrayim*? The worst part of it is that we have "the lad" still within us. It is none other than the self of our youthful dreams whom we have taken captive along the way. Is he – or she – still alive? Or have we squelched them completely?

Then we discover the spiritual journey, seeking our way out of Egypt. We need to be sure that our inner "lad" is still with us as we begin to climb the ladder. We cannot show up without him.

4 "ואל ירע בעיניכם כי מכרתם אותי, כי למחיה שלחני אלוהים לפניכם...
ועתה לא אתם שלחתם אותי הנה כי האלוהים (מ"ה:ה-ח)."

"Let it not be bad in your eyes that you sold me into Egypt, for God was sending me ahead of you in order to sustain life…. Now it was not you who sent me here, but God" (45:5-8). Joseph surely sees in these moments the fulfillment of his early dreams. Here he is sitting on the ruler's throne and his brothers are shamed and desolate, bowing before him. Note the word ***"now"*** in the verse, meaning that this is how things are to be seen as of now. He understands immediately how a *netsah̲*-person, one who is indeed victorious, is supposed to act with regard to his defeated rivals. He treats them generously and with forgiveness, offering a hand to help them in their need. He does so by invoking the presence of God in the story, seeing it as all part of a divine plan.

What might there be to learn from a story like this, one to which our Torah has devoted three long *parshiyyot*? Might it have something to do with how we treat those we have defeated? Will we ever learn?

5 ויסע ישראל וכל אשר לו ויבואו בארה שבע. ויזבח זבחים לאלוהי אביו יצחק. ויאמר אלוהים לישראל במראות הלילה...אל תירא מרדה מצרימה (מ"ו:א-ג)".

"Israel journeyed, he and all that was his, until they arrived at Beersheva. He offered sacrifices to the God of his father Isaac… God said to him in a night vision… "Do not be afraid to go down to Egypt; I will make you a great nation there" (46:1-3).

It is interesting that Israel makes an offering specifically to the God of Isaac, and not to that of both his predecessors, as we might expect. This is a moment of great fear in his life and it is to the "left side" that he feels a need to turn. His father's God – the one who helped him to survive the *'akedah* without turning bitter – assures him that he does not have to fear going down into that narrowing place, the land of enslavement. "By turning to Me as God of Isaac, you have shown that you still have the Great Fear, the awe of heaven. If you keep that with you as you go down there, all the lesser fears will be manageable. Out of all the pain that is about to come, something great will happen. Keep that faith with you as you go down into Egypt."

All of us who go into Egypt need to take with us the sense that Y-H-W-H is a powerful and fearsome force, one that has the power (along with the love) to redeem us.

6 כי תועבת מצרים כל רועי צאן

"For all shepherds are repulsive to the Egyptians" (46:34). Once the Egyptians realized that they were shepherds, they would be given a separate place to live, outside the city, because the Egyptians would not want them as closer neighbors. It is hard not to hear in this verse an echo of Jewish life in much later times, when various European cities permitted Jews to live only on the "other side" of the river or outside the city limits.

But why did the Egyptians so disdain shepherds? Rabbi Abraham Ibn Ezra, a rather worldly fellow among twelfth-century Jews, suggests the following: "In those days, the Egyptians did not eat meat and would not tolerate anyone who slaughtered sheep, just like the people of India today. Whoever is a shepherd is considered repulsive, because they drink the milk. To this day, the people of India do not eat or drink anything that comes from a living and sensate creature."

Insofar as I know, Ibn Ezra was wrong about India. Perhaps this was a monastic practice that he confused with the Indian diet altogether. It is only the slaughter of cattle that is forbidden to Hindus, and milk is considered a privileged rather than a forbidden beverage. But Ibn Ezra may be considered a founder of the vegan diet! Had he sent his readers to California of our day rather than to the India of his, he would have had a great explanation.

ויחי
VA-YEḤI
(Genesis 47:28-50:26)

1 ויתחזק ישראל וישב על המיטה

"Israel strengthened himself and sat up on his bed" (48:2).

ויכל ישראל לצוות את בניו ויאסף רגליו אל המיטה ויגווע ויאסף על עמיו

"Israel finished commanding his sons; he gathered his feet into the bed and died and was gathered with his people" (48:33).

Jacob's deathbed scene, painted so beautifully in this chapter, is depicted in the midrash to be the original setting of the *Shema'*. Of course, the verse "Hear O Israel, Y-H-W-H our God, Y-H-W-H is one" is first found in Deuteronomy 6:4, amid Moses' final speeches. But the tale is that this was originally the reassurance the twelve sons (Where was Dinah? Where were the other daughters?!!) gave to their father as he lay dying. Addressing him by the name he had acquired while wrestling with the angel, they called out: "Listen, Israel!" to him, promising that they would remain loyal to his faith, even as they raised their children in Egypt.

Egypt prior to the enslavement stands in our mind as representing the threat of assimilation. Immigrants, especially the poor and needy among them, look up toward what seems like the higher culture of their new homeland and long to be accepted into it. This was surely the case here. We are told that the Egyptians would not even break bread with shepherds from Canaan. Jacob, or Israel, was right to be worried. Think of Eastern European immigrants, Jews and others, who came westward to Germany and France in the nineteenth and early twentieth centuries. When his children called out this proclamation of faith, he responded, "Blessed be God's glorious name forever," and breathed his last.

Loyalty to ancestral tradition has a significant place in our persistence as Jews. We seek to pass on what we have received from our parents and grandparents. At the same time, we want that tradition to be open to change. Otherwise, it would really become a "dead letter." How much faithfulness and how much change? The call for change is inevitably influenced by the surrounding culture and its values. Where do we draw the lines? The pressures of assimilation are indeed constant as we try to maintain the best of our own identity. These are constant questions for us as we live and raise our families in this comfortable Land of Goshen called America.

2 וישם את אפרים לפני מנשה

"He placed Ephraim before Menasheh" (48:20). This very carefully told narrative of Jacob switching his hands in blessing of course repeats that which his mother Rebekah had arranged for him. Like her, he is quite sure that the blessing belongs with the younger son, and he violates the norm of primogeniture in order to make that happen.

But we know nothing of the character of these two boys. Why is Jacob doing this? Is it just a family pattern? All we are told are their names. (See also the comment on the names above in *parashat mi-kets*.) Joseph had named his first son Menasheh, "Forgotten," reflecting the despair that must have accompanied him through his early years in Egypt. Only later does his life turn "fruitful," which is the meaning of Ephraim.

The Hasidic master R. Zvi Elimelech of Dinov asks why we still bless our sons with "May God make you like Ephraim and Menasheh." He explains that Menasheh, the real firstborn, did not protest when Jacob switched his hands. Nor did Ephraim, receiving the blessing, lord it over his brother. Both accepted that this was God's will, bringing a proper conclusion to all the rivalry between brothers that has so filled this first book of the Torah.

Special thanks to my friend Reb Levi, a descendent of the Dinover, who brought this to my attention.

3 ויקרא יעקב אל בניו ויאמר האספו ואגידה לכם את אשר יקרא אתכם
באחרית הימים

"Jacob said to his sons: "Assemble and I will tell you what will become of you at the end of days" (49:1). A famous RaSHI comment here, quoted from the Midrash, says that "Jacob sought to reveal the end, but the *shekhinah* vanished from him, and he began to speak of other things." This certainly accounts for the curses that he heaps upon his three eldest sons. Does *shekhinah* return and begin speaking through him when he gets to Judah? We are not quite sure.

What does this disappearance of the divine voice mean? One can imagine deathbed scenes where the dying parent is going to reveal too much, letting go of secrets that have been held inside for many years. This may include predictions of how each his/her children "is going to turn out." That is usually not a good idea. Such thoughts are better taken to the grave. The new generation needs to live its own life in the best ways it can, without the burden of a fate dictated by those who have departed.

The *shekhinah* seems to know this and keeps Jacob from saying it all. But how much of the truth does come through in the words of this blessing? Does *shekhinah* speak through him again when he gets to Judah? We are left unsure.

4 הקבצו ושמעו בני יעקב ושמעו אל ישראל אביכם

"Gather and listen, O sons of Ya'akov, and listen to Yisra'el your father" (49:2). He calls them to him using both of his names, wanting them to *listen* and learn the lessons of both.

"You are the sons of Ya'akov," he is telling them. "The story of my life, with all its moral ambiguity and resulting suffering, is part of your inheritance. Do not forget the trickster who bore you. Learn from my mistakes, but also know that you are clever enough to turn to that power, if you truly need to.

But remember also that Yisra'el is truly your father, the one who came away transformed from that long night of wrestling – with God, with an angel, and with his own demons. It is this figure, *yisra'el sabba*, Israel the Elder, that the tradition calls upon you to emulate and to pass on. The tribe that is to emerge from the loins of Jacob, described as a people for the first time in the coming narrative of *Shemot,* is to be called Israel, not Jacob, throughout its history. It is the legacy of that inner struggle with all those powers that will define us for all time.

5 שמעון ולוי אחים...בסודם אל תבוא נפשי

"Simeon and Levi are brothers…" (49:5-6). RaSHI interprets the verse as speaking in the second person, Jacob addressing his soul. "Do not be linked, O my soul, to these two sons, for they are ill-tempered killers."

It is interesting to see that Levi has no separate blessing. There is no hint that his offspring are to serve Y-H-W-H in the tabernacle or the Temple. The two brothers are known here only for the atrocity they committed against the people of Shechem, with whom Jacob was initially prepared to live in peace. Even as he lies on his deathbed in distant Egypt, he wants nothing to do with them. Instead, he recalls how they desecrated the name of Israel. This is something not to be forgotten.

We should pay attention. These brothers are not the last ones to have desecrated the good name of Israel.

6 יהודה אתה יודוך אחיך

"You are Judah; your brothers will acknowledge you" (49:8). Or "will *thank* you." The word can have either meaning or both. Surely, they will thank him for not having let them kill Joseph, an act that ultimately allowed them all to survive the famine. But it is interesting to see Judah here inheriting something of Joseph's place, all the brothers gathered around him and (48:10) seemingly acknowledging his rule.

Ultimately, it was Judah, the grateful and humble one, rather than Joseph the victorious, who for so long defined and carried on the legacy of the people Israel. But today we are in a time when our inner Joseph has taken the leading role. Can we keep the two of them in balance?

7 גור אריה יהודה...

"Judah is a lion's whelp…" (49:9-11). The description of Judah here is that of a conquering military hero, his clothes dripping with bloodlike wine. This seems to reflect the continuing power of the Kingdom of Judah, following the destruction of northern Israel, which the prophets considered a wicked, idolatrous kingdom, by the Assyrians.

There is no stronger example of the complete transformation of biblical imagery effected by the rabbis than their reading of this verse. Listen to it as rendered in the Aramaic Targum: "Rule will never depart from Judah, nor **the book of law** from among his children. The kingdom is his and nations shall submit to him. **Israel will surround his city and build his Temple. The righteous will be about him, fulfilling the Torah that they study with him.** He shall be garbed in purple, fine silk of red and other colors."

Now that Israel is also the name of a state, so well-known as a military power, has the time for this transformation of Jacob's vision simply passed away? Is there any way for these two readings of the verse to survive side by side?

SEFER SHEMOT

THE BOOK OF EXODUS

שמות
SHEMOT
(Exodus 1:1-6:1)

1 ואלה שמות בני ישראל הבאים מצרימה את יעקב איש וביתו באו...שבעים נפש

"And these are the names of the Children of Israel as they came into Egypt. Together with Jacob, they came along with their households...seventy souls" (1:1-5). But *ha-ba'im mitsraymah* can also be read as a continuous present tense: "As they ***come*** into Egypt." We are ***always*** coming into Egypt, all seventy of us. We bring our full "*household*," our whole selves, with us, as we come into Egypt.

The psalmist (118:5) says "Out of the strait (*meytsar*)," the narrow, constricting place, "I call to YaH; YaH answers me with a broadening," liberating me from that strait. *Mitsrayim*, "Egypt," is a pair of straits, as though I am being squeezed from both sides. (The word likely originally meant "Delta," which is precisely that.) Our attempt to liberate ourselves from our own varied forms of *mitsrayim* goes on forever, because we are always "coming into Egypt," letting ourselves fall back into those narrow places and getting squeezed in them.

The seventy who enter Egypt, in the kabbalistic imagination, represent a full ten-fold measure of each of the seven *middot*, the moral/emotional qualities through which we conduct our lives. These are the seven lower of the ten *sefirot*, viewed as the essential human qualities. Our love-energies (*ḥesed*), our power-energies (*gevurah*), our pride (*tif'eret*), our triumph or sense of accomplishment (*netsaḥ*), our gratitude and submission (*hod*), our fundamental sense of self (*yesod*), and our turning outward (*malkhut*) – all of them can become distorted and lead us into those narrow and constricted places. Then those *middot* themselves need to be liberated. But how do we go about that? The liberation of our *middot* can be a lifelong process!

The verse ***min ha-meytsar kara'ti YaH*** offers a hint. **YaH**, comprising the first two letters of the great name, refers to the uppermost (or deepest!) *sefirot*. This represents a deeper part of us, one that has never been enslaved. YaH is the mysterious innermost self (for the kabbalists, the *hokhmah/binah* within the hidden chambers of the mind), but also the place where our individual self is ever connected to the single cosmic Self that dwells within us, the place where the soul is ever rooted in the One (the tip of the *yod* pointing upward). It is there that we turn for liberation.

Again the psalmist: "***Mi-ma'amakim*, From the depths I call unto You, Y-H-W-H"** (130:1). I call You forth ***from within my own inner depths*** to redeem me from *mitsrayim*.

2 ויעצמו במאד מאד

"And they became very, very strong" (1:7). *'Atsum*, "strong," seems related to a root that also comes to mean "self," perhaps deriving from *'etsem*, "bone." As Israel's numbers increased in Egypt, their distinct identity continued to develop. They came ***more fully into themselves***. That was their strength, and Pharaoh (1:9) noticed it. "A greater and more '*atsum* nation than we are" might mean "more self-defined," closer to their own root. That was enough to frighten even mighty Pharaoh.

The thought that *'otsem*, "strength," appears to derive from the same root as *'etsem*, the "self" or the bone, meaning the innermost self, is an interesting insight built into the Hebrew language. The unusual double *me'od* may also be taken as "they became more and more themselves." From that first step, their liberation became almost inevitable.

3 ויקוצו מפני בני ישראל

"The more they afflicted them, the more they increased and spread forth. They [the Egyptians] became exasperated by the Children of Israel" (1:12). *Va-yakutsu* is formed from *kets*, "end." The Egyptians were "at their wits' end" with regard to Israel. It may also be understood as "Israel became a thorn in their collective body." Reading this in our generation, we cannot fail to see that the genocidal decision to kill all the male infants came about slowly, as the end product of this feeling of exasperation. They just ***couldn't stand*** those Israelites any more – and they had the power to do something about it. Sound familiar?

As descendants of the Israelites, we naturally read the tale as one of the terrible oppressions that our ancestors suffered. But this word makes it sound like the Egyptians felt like they were victims as well, that they were ***threatened*** by the Israelites.

People in power who nevertheless feel and act like victims can do some pretty terrible things. The misguided sense that "***I am the real victim here***" is a very dangerous weapon. What might the Torah be trying to teach us? Can we listen?

4 וידע אלוהים

"And God knew" (2:25). This precipitously hanging phrase, with no object, becomes a statement of great power. God knew it all, the bitter suffering of Israel in Egyptian bondage. But God also knew that the Israelites remembered who they were, that they had the wherewithal to leave Egypt if the right leader and moment were to come forward. Thus, the verse leads right into that which comes next: "Moses was a shepherd." The *vav* of *u-Mosheh* indicates continuity with what comes before it. Moses was getting ready to lead, practicing on the sheep.

But suppose we take *Elohim* as the ***object*** rather than the subject of the sentence. "They (collectively, meaning Israel) knew God." Their suffering itself opened them up to a certain profundity within themselves, a place from which God could be known. This "knowledge of God" has nothing to do with either the RaMBaM's *da'at Elohim* (based on reason and conceptual purity) or that of the Kabbalists (esoteric knowledge and tradition). It is born of pain and a refusal to surrender to it. Some Jews came to know it in the Holocaust, alongside many who lost their faith during those awful years. Some American Jews have re-discovered this way of knowing God in the deep faith of African-American neighbors, the legacy of slavery and oppression. It has nothing to do with philosophy. This may be the sort of faith with which our ancestors began the journey into freedom. Maybe we need some of it for our journeys as well.

Remember that the word "Amen!" is a form of the word *emunah*, "faith." To call out "Amen!" is an affirmation of that faith. The tradition places great value on that calling out, especially in responding to the *kaddish*. Think about the sayers of those *amenim*, or maybe even of some anglicized "Amens!" you have heard when you want to "know God."

5 ומשה היה רועה את צאן יתרו חותנו כהן מדין וינהג את הצאן אחר המדבר

"And Moses was herding the sheep of Jethro, his father-in-law, priest of Midian, leading the sheep toward the wilderness" (3:1). The phrase *aḥar ha-midbar* is surprising enough that the Midrash sees him as "pursuing" the wilderness; it kept retreating before him, and he kept chasing after it.

The wilderness is the place where Moses is going to make his mark and where he will also be tested. It is wilderness in the sense that it is owned by no one; all are free and equal within it, struggling to survive. Only there, in that place where all prior civilizational rules were suspended, could the Teaching be revealed. *Midbar,* wilderness or wasteland, is also *midbar*, the locus of true speech, the divine Word. Moses the shepherd, also the one who is "hard of speech," is drawn toward that place, taking his flock along with him, as though presaging what he will do with that other flock he will soon lead out into the wilderness.

This chapter, along with several in the prophets, constitutes the original account of "being called" in the Jewish tradition. As one who has given much of his life to training future religious leaders of the Jewish people, I have been privileged to hear many personal tales of such callings. Some have known nearly since childhood that this is what they are supposed to do. They echo the call to the young Samuel. Others are somewhere in mid-career doing something quite different, but surprisingly find themselves being drawn, like Moses, ever closer to the Wilderness of Sinai, the place of the Word.

The voice in which such calls are heard is almost never in spoken words, and the "heaven" from which it comes is located deep within the human heart. Nevertheless, it is a divine call, and its message is clear.

There is no reason to believe that this original call, that of Moses, was any different.

6 ואמרו לי מה שמו מה אומר
אליהם...אהיה אשר אהיה. כה תאמר אל בני ישראל אהיה שלחני אליכם
"If they say to me: 'What is His name?' What shall I say to them?...' I will be whatever I will be.' He said: 'Thus shall you say to them: EHYEH has sent me to you'" (3:13-14).

EHYEH asher EHYEH is a statement of the utter elusiveness of the divine. You cannot grasp hold of it, because it can take on any form, while at the same time transcending them all. Then, in the very same verse, EHYEH is presented as an answer to the questions "What is His name?" and "Who sent you?" There is something of a riddle or a great joke in this reply. Think of the laughing buddha or the smiling sphynx, perhaps even of the Mona Lisa. "The endlessly and utterly elusive, is the One who sent me here."

EHYEH represents the verb *hayah*, "to be" preceded by an *aleph*. *Aleph* also represents the number one, so that another possible rendition is "the oneness of being" or "all being as One." But that same *aleph* also represents the future tense; "I will be." ***The oneness of being, yet to be revealed***.

This is the most potent of all truths, not to be revealed until the end. It is the realization of oneness that ever stands before us, drawing us closer to it. That which liberates us from all our Egypts is always beyond our grasp. But we, like Moses, are given a hint of it at the beginning of our journey, to help set us on our way. It is the One to whom we call "***Draw me after You, let us run***" (Cant. 1:4).

7 ויפגשהו בהר האלוהים וישק לו
"He met him at the divine mountain and kissed him" (4:27). The second book of the Torah opens with love between brothers. The first thing that Moses does, after receiving his call, is to share it with his brother.

This simple act stands as a response to the entire Book of Genesis.

The central question of that book, my teacher A. J. Heschel taught, was the question: "***How do I live with my brother***?" From Cain and Abel through Ephraim and Manasseh, it is a tale of rivalry, distrust, and competition between brothers, one set over the other. Here the Torah is saying that a new chapter is beginning, and it can only come about through brothers working together.

The redemption of Israel from Egypt and their formation as a religious community is to become Moses and Aaron's shared life's work. None of it could have happened without Moses' boldness and clarity of vision. He was the one who "turned here and there and saw there was no man" – and took decisive action. It was that slaying of the Egyptian, a Midrash tells us, that convinced God that Moses was the one who could bring Israel out of Egypt.

But they never could have made it through the wilderness without Aaron's unifying project of making Israel's ragged camp of former slaves into a *mishkan*, an earthly dwelling-place for Y-H-W-H. Perhaps the same God who saw Moses' strength in the sinful act of killing the Egyptian also saw Aaron's power when he made the Golden Calf. He understood and responded to the human need for a sacred center, for something to dance around. The beginning of ritual.

But Moses was hot-tempered, while Aaron is always known as a pursuer of peace. More than once, it was his pursuit of peace that kept the people together. The blessing that radiates through the rest of Torah has much to do with this *shevet aḥim gam yaḥad*, the closeness of these two brothers dwelling together.

Their meeting here is epitomized in a verse from the Psalms (85:11, as interpreted in the Midrash): "***Compassion and truth met; justice and peace kissed.***" Moses is the man of truth and justice, demanding them of God as well as of humans. Aaron is the pursuer of peace, the embodiment of compassion. Redemption is brought about by the brotherly embrace of these two.

The point is underscored in the following *parashah* (6:26-27): "That was Aaron and Moses to whom Y-H-W-H said to take the Children of Israel out of Egypt, with all their hosts. It was they who spoke to Pharaoh, king of Egypt, to bring out the Children of Israel. It was Moses and Aaron."

The chiasm (beginning with "Aaron and Moses" and concluding with "Moses and Aaron") is there to emphasize how equal and balanced they need to be.

It takes both of their qualities to liberate ourselves from the straits of all our mental and social *Egypts*. Learning to treat ourselves, as well as others, with this balance is the work of a lifetime.

וארא
VA-ERA
(Exodus 6:2-9:35)

1 וארא אל אברהם אל יצחק ואל יעקב באל שדי ושמי יהו"ה לא נודעתי להם
"I appeared to Abraham, to Isaac, and to Jacob as El Shaddai, but I did not become known to them as My name Y-H-W-H" (6:3).

The first Hasidic book published, *Toledot Ya'akov Yosef* says briefly that "this rung (he really means "process") is found in every person." We begin our spiritual journeys with an immature religious mind, able to grasp only the form of divinity known as *Ze'ir Anpin*, "the lesser face," which is also God as Shaddai. He is suggesting that this is parallel to the religion of the patriarchs, as compared to that now revealed to Moses. This is the divine as an authoritarian male personality, the God of our childhood. As the mind matures, we are able to attain *da'at*, best translated as "**awareness**." This is a higher rung of consciousness, that which opens us to **Y-H-W-H**, the name that bears within it the fulness of Being, all that was-is-will be, the One who both surrounds and fills all the worlds.

"The purpose of human existence," the *Toledot* goes on to say, "is that we subjugate matter to holiness." This is what is meant by "redemption from Egypt," which leads to receiving the Torah. "Each person is born as a wild creature; the 'evil urge' is the eldest part of us." Our desire for worldly things, including worldly love and power, are with us from the beginning. From infancy, we are grasping onto that which will fulfill our needs, both physically and emotionally. Only with maturity does the 'good urge' begin to engage us as well, bringing forth *hesed* or compassion for others. The God we need in childhood, he means to say, is that of *Ze'ir*, the One who rewards and punishes, who keeps our selfish and needy instincts in line. As we mature, our awareness takes us to a higher (I would say "deeper") place.

The language of the verse points as well to a different aspect of this maturation of religious faith. We begin with the worship of *El* ("Powerful One") and *Shaddai*, the God who exists to fulfill our needs, the One who always gives us "enough." This may also be (though I doubt that the *Toledot* intended this) God as Mother, the One who nurses us at the breast (*shad*).

It is this inner process of maturation that names us as **Israel,** strugglers or wrestlers with God. We are seeking to reach Y-H-W-H, the divine reality beyond the "God" embodied in *Ze'ir* or in *El Shaddai*. Each of us has to engage in that struggle in a unique way. For some, the God of childhood grows naturally and matures with us, helping to lead us toward that awareness, *da'at Y-H-W-H. Ze'ir* serves as a bridge that takes us to that deeper place. For others, the hold of childhood fantasies is too powerful, blocking our ability to grow beyond it. Sometimes that "God" can even become the "Pharaoh" of our inner "Egypt." Then we need to escape His rule, to flee into the wilderness, where we will be free to discover in our own way that "the whole earth is filled with the glory of Y-H-W-H."

2 וגם אני שמעתי את נאקת בני ישראל אשר מצרים מעבידים אותם

"I too have heard the cry of the Children of Israel, whom Egypt is making into slaves" (6:5). *Ve-gam ani,* "I too," sounds like: I have heard the same cry that you heard, Moses, when you rose up and slew the Egyptian."

The word *ma'avidim* has two meanings. One is the actual enslavement, the forced labor and oppression. But the other refers to the effect upon the Israelites: they are becoming a slave people. The commentators say that there are fifty measures of degradation in the world. Israel had been dragged down to the forty-ninth. This "degradation" may have to do with the course that runs between hope and despair. Had they remained in Egypt any longer, or sunk any deeper into it, they would have given up all hope and would have been beyond redemption.

3 ולקחתי אתכם לי לעם והייתי לכם לאלוהים

"And I will take you unto Me as a people, and I will become your

God" (6:7). This climax of the proclamation that God will redeem Israel has such a strong echo of marriage running through it! I will take you as Mine, and I will become yours! "My beloved is mine and I am His" (Cant. 2:16). We do not yet have the Song of Songs in the canon here (King Solomon has not yet written it!), but we can feel its implied presence. When I take you out of here, the verse goes on to say, and take you home with Me, "you will know that I am Y-H-W-H your God, who takes you forth (notice the present tense, suggesting constant motion) from beneath the sufferings of Egypt." We might hear this liberated slave-girl respond with "…until I have brought him into my mother's house, the chamber of the one who bore me" (Cant. 3:4).

Exodus as a fairy tale. God as Prince Charming, sweeping up the beautiful maiden imprisoned by the evil king, taking her on his mighty steed, or flying on eagles' wings, and bringing her home to become his bride. Something of that universal archetype is present in this story. In what ways does it shape our spiritual lives? Are we waiting to be "swept off our feet?" Are we disappointed on those days (quite a few, by my last count) when we are not?

Our love of Y-H-W-H also needs to mature. God and Israel are in fact an old married couple who have been through a long life together, with a love that never ends. They have been through lots of hard times together, when that love was mightily tested. Perhaps the greatest miracle of this relationship is that the magic of those first moments of love has never been forgotten. Reading these verses each year, celebrating the Exodus from Egypt at our seder table, reciting phrases such as *yedidim he'evarta*, "You brought Your lovers across the sea" in our prayers, serve to reinforce that memory.

Does this romance demand a sense of ***exclusive*** relationship between Israel and her God? It is certainly ***unique***; there is none other quite like it. But can we admit that the same One may be the Prince Charming of other maidens' dreams as well?

4 וידבר ה׳ אל משה ואל אהרן ויצוום אל בני ישראל

"Y-H-W-H spoke to Moses and to Aaron, fastening them to the Children of Israel and to Pharaoh, king of Egypt" (6:13). Here, the well-known Hasidic derivation of *mitsvah* from the Aramaic *tzavta*, "attachment" or "togetherness," seems to work best. God's word fastens the unbreakable link of the brothers with both the people and their oppressor. Neither side will be able to let go. Both Israel and Pharaoh understand that their fate is tied up with these two brothers and their God. This bond will survive all the ups and downs, the betrayals and disappointments, that will take place in the coming chapters, until the liberation of Israel and the downfall of Pharaoh both become inevitable.

Suppose we take Moses, as we did above on Ex. 4:27, as **the striving for justice**, for doing good in the world, and Aaron for **the pursuit of inner peace**. Our journey out of our own inner Egypt requires that we be linked to both of them.

That might be true of our collective Egypts – social and even political – as well.

5 ויחזק לב פרעה ולא שמע אליהם...כבד לב פרעה

"Pharaoh's heart was strengthened; he did not listen to them, as Y-H-W-H had said. Y-H-W-H said to Moses: Pharaoh's heart is heavy" (7:13-14). What is the problem with Pharaoh's heart? Is it too strong (*ḥazaq*) or too heavy (*kaved*)? A few verses earlier (7:3), yet another verb is used. God says "I will harden (*aqsheh*) Pharaoh's heart." This multiplication of terms in the text wants to tell us something.

Why does the oppressor hold so tightly to the reins of power? Is he truly strong, or does he need to reassure himself that he is? Might he in fact be heavy-hearted, depressed or insecure, only making him more anxious to show himself the tough guy? Or could he be *qasheh*, just hardened or "stuck" in his role, unable to make changes even when he knows he should?

How about our inner Pharaoh, the part of us that keeps us from being free? What combination of these describes the hold "he" has on us? What "signs and wonders" can we call upon that might weaken that hold? How about the turning of the life-giving waters of the Nile to blood? Is that a sign that this "heart condition" can only lead to death?

And how about those same Pharaohs on today's political stage? Strong, insecure, or just stuck and unable to change?

6 והיה דם בכל ארץ מצרים ובעצים ובאבנים

"There will be blood throughout the Land of Egypt, on the trees and on the rocks" (7:19). We understand that the water of the Nile was to turn into blood, and even "their rivers, deltas, and lakes," as the verse says earlier. But trees and rocks?

The phrase is identical to an old midrashic reading of Genesis 4:10-11. "Where is Abel your brother?" God calls to Cain. "The voice of your brother's blood screams out to me from the soil." The Midrash comments, in language clearly influenced by this verse: "His blood was cast upon the trees and the rocks." Everything appeared blood-red to Cain in that moment, even the rocks and the trees.

Think about how the soil of Europe appeared to most Holocaust survivors in 1945. Or how Rwanda might have looked to both Tutsi and Hutu victims after the year of genocide there. The Israelites in Egypt, having watched their male children slaughtered by Pharaoh's soldiers, saw an Egypt soaked in blood. Even the landscape of that place was colored in blood. They had to get out.

No wonder they had so little sympathy for the Egyptians, even during the terrible final plague, or at the shore of the Reed Sea.

But what are we supposed to do with that piece of our legacy? And what do we do with it when we understand that we are sometimes experienced by others as the "Pharaoh" rather than the "Israel" in another struggle for liberation in which we are involved? Can this help us to find a little more room for compassion?

בא
BO
(Exodus 10:1-13:16)

1 בא אל פרעה

"Come to Pharaoh" (10:1). All the commentators ask why the text says "Come" rather than "Go." A brief Hasidic comment from the *Me'or 'Eynayim*: *Bo* is spelled *bet aleph*. Only when you see the One (*aleph*) hidden behind the mask of "twoness," duality (*bet*) will you have the courage to deal with Pharaoh.

This implies, at least, that Y-H-W-H, Source of all, is present in Pharaoh as well. Approaching him, as is true of every other situation in life, is a coming close to Y-H-W-H. The choice of the reflexive verb *hit'alalti*, "I wrought," in the following verse may be taken to hint at this as well. "I have written Myself into the plot" of what is happening here. I am there, waiting to be discovered, even – or maybe "especially" – in this difficult moment of confronting Pharaoh.

Remember the Ba'al Shem Tov's teaching on Pharaoh's words quoted in the Song at the Sea: **אמר אויב ארדוף אשיג אחלק שלל** – "The enemy said: I shall pursue, catch up, divide the spoils." These five words in a row beginning with *aleph* – found only here in the Torah – teach us that Y-H-W-H, the Cosmic Aleph, is to be found everywhere, even behind the most grotesque masks of evil.

This is not an easy teaching when we try to apply it to the expressions of evil we have encountered in our time. But it is an essential part of the Hasidic message.

2 לא ראו איש את אחיו ולא קם איש מתחתיו שלושת ימים

"They did not see one another; no person rose above his lowest self for three days" (10:23). Read the second half of this verse in a very earthy way. "No one got up off his *tokhes* to help anyone else! The ninth plague may be taken to be one of moral blindness. Until then, we might say, the Egyptians still cared for one another, even if they had little regard for their Hebrew slaves. But after the hail and the locusts, when there was no green thing left to eat (10:15), they became so desperate that there was no longer any caring for one another; they did not ***see*** one another's suffering.

We live in a land of plenty and we like to think of ourselves as generous, concerned with the fate of the less fortunate around us, indeed all over the world. "For just pennies a day," those impassioned television ads tell us, "you can help those poor starving children in Africa." When we have so much more than we need, it is easy to think of ourselves as caring about others, and to pat ourselves on the back for it. But the account of the plagues, like some narratives we read of other disasters, including the Holocaust, stands to challenge us. How deep is our commitment to one another? When there is nothing left to eat, will we still "see" the other? Is that the sort of "darkness" that enveloped the Egyptians? How can we prepare ourselves for such a coming "plague of darkness?"

3 ואנחנו לא נדע מה נעבוד את ה׳ עד בואנו שמה

"We will not know with what we will serve Y-H-W-H until we come there" (10:26). Do we ***ever*** know with what we will serve Y-H-W-H, until we "come there" – until we arrive at that moment?

Moses' absolute demand ("with our elders and our youth we will go; with our sons and our daughters, our sheep and our cattle" [10:9]) and Pharaoh's attempts at bargaining (Just the men! No children! Leave the flocks behind!) all sound too familiar to students of Jewish history. So too do they echo with the history of American slavery and that of other struggles for liberation as well. "Can I go to freedom and leave my children – or my parents – behind?"

Moses is calling for a liberation where no one and nothing is left behind. We are leaving Egypt not only to escape bondage, but because (that same verse says) "We have a festival of Y-H-W-H." We want to ***celebrate*** our freedom, and that means being out of there completely, everyone coming along.

How does this work when we are seeking liberation from a Pharaoh who lives within us? What compromises are we secretly negotiating? What parts of us are we trying to leave behind, perhaps because we are afraid to take them with us?

Here we turn to a later verse in our *parashah*. As Israel were leaving, the text (12:39) tells us, "they had also made no provisions for themselves." In the end, we just ran and trusted. The *Haggadah* of Rabbi Nahman of Bratslav comments on this verse that once you stop to ask ***"But how will I make a living out there?"*** you will never leave Egypt. Sometimes you just have to get up and run.

4 ואם ימעט הבית מהיות משה ולקח הוא ושכנו...במכסת נפשות

"If the household is too small [to consume] a lamb, he and a neighbor close to his house, in an overlapping of souls, shall cover the lamb" (12:4). *Mikhsat nefashot* is an unusual phrase; I take it as deriving from *k-s-h*, to "cover."

The choice of a close neighbor is interesting here. In a society still so tribally defined, one might have expected a brother's family, or some larger kinship unit, to share the paschal lamb. *Shakhen*, "neighbor," is not a term widely found within the Torah. If this text, as is widely assumed, is prescribing for *pesaḥ dorot*, future Passovers, and not just that in Egypt, it is saying something interesting about social structure within the Jewish community. All of Israel are together in reliving this experience of liberation. If your household cannot consume a whole lamb, reach out to your very closest neighbors and share it with them. Perhaps your souls were meant to overlap, just like your back yards.

In fact, RaSHI (12:46) quotes a Midrash saying that the paschal lamb should be eaten *be-ḥavurah*, "in community," one of the early occurrences of that word. You have to create *ḥavurah*, community, with your neighbors in order to fulfill the *mitsvah*! To picture this, imagine if American tradition insisted that each of us share our Thanksgiving turkey with the folks right next door. Imagine it in Israel as well: a Pesaḥ seder with your neighbors – *mizraḥim*, Ethiopians, secularists, *ḥaredim* – just the folks next door, whoever they happen to be.

It might start a revolution. **It might even help us get out of Egypt!**

5 למען תהיה תורת ה' בפיך

"So that the teaching of Y-H-W-H be in your mouth" (13:9). This is the first time the word *torah* occurs in this long account of exodus and revelation. It follows the commandments of *haggadah*, passing on the Passover narrative in an entirely personal way, and donning *tefillin*. Note that this first occurrence of Torah refers to *torah shebe-'al peh, torah* as an oral process.

We are taught to think of the Written Torah as the *Urtext* of our tradition, Oral Torah growing out of a series of comments on it. But this passage and others suggest that perhaps it was oral tradition that came first. Historically, that is likely to have been the case as well. In any case, these two means of transmission have been intertwined for millennia.

The word *le-ma'an*, "so that," usually points to reward when used in the Torah ("so that your days be lengthened" (Ex. 20:12; Deut. 22:7, etc.). Here, the reward for doing these *mitsvot* is that your own mouth become a source of living Torah. This is most obviously true of telling the Passover tale, where your mouth is indeed serving in that way as your children listen, receiving *torah* from you. But it is also true of seemingly external rituals, forms of symbolic "speech." The way we perform them daily, being watched by our children and students, makes us into fonts of Oral Torah. Oral Torah is a living and unceasing process.

The *Sefat Emet* reads the blessing that follows an *'aliyah* to the Torah as follows: *asher natan lanu torat emet*, "who ***gave*** us a teaching of truth," refers to the Written Torah, given long ago. *Ve-ḥayyey 'olam nata' be-tokhenu,* "who has implanted eternal life within us," refers to Oral Torah, an ongoing process emerging from within the souls of Israel. Only as the two are joined does the tense of *natan* turn to the present, allowing Y-H-W-H to be seen as *noten ha-torah*, forever "***giving*** the teaching."

It is our oral teaching, bringing forth Torah from within us, that brings the ancient teaching back to life.

בשלח
BE-SHALAḤ
(Exodus 13:17-17:16)

1 ויהי בשלח פרעה את העם ולא נחם אלוהים דרך ארץ פלישתים כי קרוב
הוא

"As Pharaoh sent the people forth, God did not lead them by way of the Philistines' land, for it was close. God said: 'Maybe they will have regrets when they see battle, and will return to Egypt. God caused the people to go by way of the wilderness, the Sea of Reeds'" (13:17-18).

How slow and complex the process of liberation is! We thought it was only Pharaoh keeping us in Egypt, enslaving us to do his bidding. But now he has released us, yet we are still in danger. **When we see that freedom is an ongoing struggle, we might turn back to servitude.** "It's too hard for me out there in freedom! Too many decisions to make! Too many temptations to resist! Let me go back and be a slave, a condition where I know all the rules, and accept that they cannot be violated." **Getting slavery out of the person is a lot harder than getting the person out of slavery!**

But there may be another reading here, as well. God chooses not to send us *derekh erets phlishtim*, "via ***the Philistine way with the land***." It is too close ***to us***; we are too likely to fall into the trap of becoming just like them. The Philistines were a tribe of seafaring merchants and conquerers; they offered a *derekh erets*, a way of living, that God did not want for us. We were still weak and susceptible; we might too easily become enslaved ***to that example***. In order to become ourselves, we needed some time in the wilderness.

There are all sorts of bondage out there, and we need to ***learn*** how to remain free. That happens only in the wilderness. Could it be that history did not give us the forty years of wandering and self-examination we needed between the Holocaust and the Jewish State? Perhaps we needed them in order to absorb the lesson of those terrible events before we were ready *li-heyot 'am ḥofshi be-artseynu*, "to be a free" – ***and responsible*** – "people in our land."

We seem to be paying the price.

2 ויקח משה את עצמות יוסף עמו

"Moses took the bones of Joseph with him" (13:19). *'Atsmot Yosef* (connected to the way we read *'atsum* in *parashat shemot*) can also be translated as "an extra measure of selfhood." Israel are becoming ever more themselves in this journey, just as they did under slavery. Their unique nationhood is evolving in the course of both oppression and wandering, to forms of preparation that were needed for the covenant soon to come.

The two meanings of *'atsmot Yosef* do not contradict one another. We become ever more deeply ourselves when we realize that we are carrying our ancestors' bones within us.

3 ויחנו באתם בקצה המדבר. וה׳ הולך לפניהם...

"And they camped at Ay-Tam, on the edge of the wilderness. Y-H-W-H walks before them, by day in a pillar of cloud, to lead them on the path, and at night in a pillar of cloud, to give them light, so that they walk day and night. The pillar of cloud by day and the pillar of fire at night never disappear before the people" (13:20-22).

These verses virtually cry out to be re-read in terms of ***our*** religion, that of our *midbar*, the place of speech. We too are camped at Ay-Tam, somewhere (based on the Aramaic), anywhere, on the edge of our *midbar.* Two phrases that appear together here, *yomam va-laylah*,"day and night" and *lo yamish*, "will never disappear" echo with the opening admonition of Joshua (1:8) that first defines us as a "People of the Book: לֹא-יָמוּשׁ סֵפֶר הַתּוֹרָה הַזֶּה מִפִּיךָ וְהָגִיתָ בּוֹ יוֹמָם וָלַיְלָה, "May this book of teaching never disappear from your lips; meditate on it by day and by night." '*Amud,* "pillar" here, also comes to mean "page" in the Hebrew of our book-driven tradition. We are led day and night by the living word that constantly re-emerges for us from those pages, which serve as our *midbar*, the place of speech. It never vanishes from our presence. That is how "Y-H-W-H walks before us," in the present tense, day and night.

But what are the "pillars" or "pages" of cloud and fire? The written and oral Torah? The revealed and hidden levels of interpretation, the one traditionally studied during the day and the other at night? Perhaps they say something about the place Torah should have in our lives. By day, when everything seems so terribly clear, Torah appears in the form of a **cloud**. Its message is: "Wait. Look again. Things are not as clear as they appeared to be." Soon (20:18) we will read that "The people stood far off, but Moses entered the cloud, where God was." To be a *ben* or *bat Torah* is to "enter the cloud," to understand the difficulty of finding the proper path. It is all about struggle and negotiation with the unclarity of the message found in the text. But at night, when we are confused, frightened, and on the edge of feeling lost, that same *'amud* has to become an *eshdat lamo*, "a fiery prescription for them (Deut. 332:)," lighting the way for us, kindling a fire in our hearts as well. We need them both, the cloud and the fire, for our day and our night.

4 ופרעה הקריב

"And Pharaoh drew near" (14:10). The Hasidic readings, based on the Midrash, emphasize the *hif'il* form of the verb, meaning "brought near" rather than "came close." The approach of Pharaoh and his army "drew the hearts of Israel close to their Father in Heaven."

Might this mean something more than "There are no atheists in foxholes," as they said during the First World War? How does our confrontation with Pharaoh – or perhaps many pharaohs – shape our religious lives?

Our own inner struggle with faith – the moment of *yisra'el* wrestling within us – is overcome when we see what stands on the other side. Pharaoh represents all that enslaves us, the forces of degradation and dehumanization that exist both within us and around us. Pharaoh is that which seeks to extinguish the divine spark that lives within us. Even as we struggle with questions of God and faith, we know that the inner spark is real. The fact that it is under attack draws us closer to the very resources of faith within our tradition that we find ourselves questioning.

We stand with our backs to Egypt and our faces to the sea. Now come the forces of Pharaoh, riding hard behind us. We need a faith that will give us the courage to be Nahshon, to step into the sea, confident that it will split. Only faith tells us that this sea is *yam ha-ḥokhmah*, the sea of wisdom, and not just a place to drown. The alternative of surrendering to Pharaoh and returning to Egypt, of being squeezed in by the slow death of meaningless existence, is no longer an option. Pharaoh "draws us near," indeed, by pushing us forward with the courage and unity of mind that we need.

Faith requires courage, and the sight of Pharaoh can serve to awaken that courage within us.

5 הנני ממטיר לכם לחם מן השמים

"Behold, I will rain down upon you food from heaven, and they will gather it up each day, in order that I test him. Will he follow My teaching or not?" (16:4) One might have expected the opposite. The ***lack*** of food would be such a test. What will they do when they are really hungry? But the story goes the other way. I will feed them well; they'll have enough to eat every day. ***Then*** let's see how they behave.

An early midrashic teaching says that "Torah was given to be interpreted only by those who eat manna" (Mekhilta to Ex. 16). Only those who are confident about where their next meal is coming from have the luxury of being able to interpret Torah. Our generation has that ability in great abundance. We live with a degree of leisure unimaginable to those who came before us. This is our test. Do we study Torah? Do we live in accord with its teachings, sharing our wealth, including our hearts and time, as well as our food and money, with those in need? That is our "***In order that I test him***." Do we get a passing grade?

Note the abrupt change in the verse from plural to singular. The challenge to what we do with our satiety and wealth falls uniquely on each individual.

6 וימודו בעומר ולא העדיף המרבה והממעיט לא החסיר

"When they measured it by the *'omer*, those who had gathered a lot did not have any extra, and those who had gathered less were not lacking; they had gathered in accord with what they needed to eat" (16:18). The secret is that they shared ***before*** they measured! When we see our sustenance as manna, we neither take too much nor leave too little for the other.

Gratitude is the beginning point of the religious life. As long as we are still thinking that "it was my power and the strength of my hand that achieved all this" (Deut. 8:17), we are pulled toward an ethos of selfishness. This money is mine; I don't want to share it with others, not even in paying taxes. When we realize that it is all manna, the message of sharing is immediately clear. That is the ***real*** miracle that happened out there in the wilderness.

Some of this has to do with age. As I live past my eightieth year, surviving a pandemic in which so many in my age group have died, my life is all about gratitude. The immediate and most natural response is to open both heart and checkbook, and to give. It is all manna.

יתרו
YITRO
(Exodus 18:1-20:23)

1 אל המדבר אשר הוא חונה שם הר האלוהים ...

"to the wilderness where he was camped, the Mountain of God" (18:5). This is the same language used above in the story of the burning bush, the place where Moses first encountered Y-H-W-H. In bringing Israel first to this place, he was fulfilling the words he had heard there: "This will be a sign for you; when you take the people out of Egypt, you will worship God at this mountain" (3:12).

What was it like for Moses to bring this ragged band, already murmuring in discontent, to what had been his own private holy place? Is he hoping that they might come to share in his experience of this place? Perhaps he hoped this might quiet them, inspiring them for the long journey that still lay ahead. If he wants them to see "the sign," to offer a sacrifice and then move on, he is about to get much more than he'd bargained for.

Think about sharing your private holy places – or moments – with others. I am doing that, of course, in these teachings. What do we hope will come out of this intimate sharing? Do we expect our hearers or readers to catch a glimmer of what we have experienced in that "place?" Or do we dare to hope that our ***sneh*** might become the next generation's ***Sinai***?

2 ומשה עלה אל האלוהים ויקרא אליו ה' מן ההר

"Moses went up to Elohim, but Y-H-W-H called to him from the mountain" (19:3). Again, as at the bush, we have a multileveled experience. Moses could ascend to Elohim, the powerful (*gevurah* or *malkhut*) Presence for whom the mountain was named. But then he was called to transcend even that, to go beyond the God of Power. The message he was to deliver would come from Y-H-W-H, from the core of Being itself.

The description of Sinai is certainly one of great power. The thunderbolts and lightning, the loud shofar sound, and all the rest. We cannot but think of them as coming from God's "special effects department." The rabbinic tradition then adds to these the dimension of love. "The Song of Songs was spoken at Sinai," says Rabbi Akiva. From amid the thunderclaps, the Holy One was also whispering the verses of this love poem into His beloved's ear.

That combination of *yir'ah ve-ahavah*, awe and love, is what the Jewish "religious experience" is all about. "Unify our hearts to love and fear Your name" – all at once – as we say before calling out the morning *Shema'.* Sinai is a description of it in graphic terms. Take away all the outer elements of that description, strip it down to its core, and you have the perfect balance of love and awe that constitute the emotion of standing in the presence of Y-H-W-H. "Sinai" is the distillation of that experience, one that exists for all generations.

But there is something beyond them both. Awe and love are the means, not the end. "Right" and "left" come together in *da'at*, best translated as "awareness." *Da'at*, the nominal form of *yada', "to know"* is always linked in the Hasidic sources with its first usage in the Torah: "Adam *knew* his wife Eve." It is an act of intimate union, the fusion of our mind with that of the cosmos. Only from there does it flow into the separate emotional channels of *ahavah ve-yir'ah*.

3 ועתה אם שמוע תשמעו בקולי

"And now, if you truly listen to My voice, keeping My covenant, you will be distinguished to Me from all nations, since the whole earth is Mine. You are to be My priestly kingdom, a holy nation" (19:5-6). Yes, I am the God of all nations, of all the earth. You are to be a priestly kingdom, one dedicated entirely to serving the world by teaching and fulfilling that truth.

A priest exists in order to serve, serving God and serving others. Priesthood is meaningless unless there is a broader community to be served, to be brought near to the One the priest worships. "A priestly ***kingdom***" means that your national purpose, ***the very reason for you to exist as a distinct people***, is your collective career of service to My world. If Israel is to be a "kingdom of priests," the community of nations is the people it serves.

So how are we doing at that? Our *rebbe*, Hillel Zeitlin, wrote in 1939, in the last essay he sent out of Warsaw, that God's experiment with us had been a colossal failure. We did best at it, he said, in Second Temple times, when many people throughout the Hellenistic realm looked to Israel as a source of enlightenment and truth, non-Israelite "fearers of God" filling the Temple courts. But Christianity's success took this away from us, and for the next 1800 years we were an oppressed minority, living under two civilizations who thought they had already inherited the best of what we had to offer. Now that liberation from the ghetto had given us a new chance to speak to and serve the world, he saw us as failing to do so. Western and liberal Jews, he said, were too shallow in their Jewish knowledge and commitment, and Eastern European Jews were abandoning our legacy of Torah and becoming devoted to nationalism and self-assertion, not caring enough to share our spiritual truth with others (He ignored both the Near Eastern and the New World Jewish communities).

Now history (or providence, if you prefer) has given us a new opportunity. We have a Jewish state, one that should embody the best of our values, sharing them with people everywhere. The state contains (and supports!) so many people who have vast Jewish learning, perhaps more than ever before. We diaspora Jews live in great freedom, enjoying an opportunity to share our truth and values with those around us, many of whom are anxious to hear it. We do so while also learning from them as we share our own wisdom, bringing blessing to all.

So how are we doing at our priestly task ***this time***? What is the world learning from us?

4 ויאמר ה׳ הנני בא אליך בעב הענן...ויגד משה את דברי העם אל ה׳

"Y-H-W-H said to Moses: Behold, I come to you in the thickness of cloud, so that the people listen as I speak to you...and Moses told

the people's words to Y-H-W-H" (19:9). The order of the verse makes no sense. Several verses in this chapter seem confusing, not quite clear in reporting the give-and-take. The text seems to be saying: "Here, at Sinai, there is no narrative possible. We have no consecutive verbal 'video' of this event, only a group of 'stills.'" We catch ***glimpses*** of what happened at Sinai, but not more. Time itself has been arrested, eternity entering into the moment. That is all hidden in the "thickness of cloud," amid which the tale is told.

Remember the *aggadah* that reads "My soul went forth as he spoke" (Cant. 5:6) to say that we fainted (or even "died") after each commandment was spoken and needed the dew of resurrection to awaken us. That is why the memory remains so shielded in cloud.

5 משה ידבר והאלוהים יעננו בקול

"Moses spoke; God responded to him in thunder" (19:19). It is this verse that has saved Sinai for me. What are we to do, here at the foot of the mountain, we who do not have a God who uses words, who speaks in human language? In the end, isn't Torah all about a God who speaks? Yes, in God's speaking at Creation we might have taken "God said" as metaphor, meaning something other than speaking in human language. But ***here***?

Yet here we are, we are still Jews, remembering somehow that we were all there at Sinai, and the verse calls out to us to speak its truth. There was indeed a dialogue at Sinai: Moses spoke in words; God spoke in thunder. ***It takes a Moses to translate divine thunder-speech into human language.*** He is indeed the *meturgeman*, translator, as our sages said.

We begin by following what my teacher Heschel calls *shittat ha-tsimtsum,* the narrowing path, in describing the verbal content of this moment. First, we follow the biblical text itself: not the whole Torah, but only the ten commandments were spoken at the Mountain. This is the view of Rabbi Yishma'el. But then note that the Talmud places Ex. 20:17 ("You speak with us, [Moses], but let not God speak with us lest we die") after the first ***two*** commandments. Only these two did we hear *mi-pi ha-gevurah*, from the mighty Mouth; the rest were transmitted – or "translated" – through Moses. These two *dibrot,* "words," come down to "***It is I who make you free. Worship nothing else.***" Do these really have to be spoken in language? Is it not enough that we hear them in our hearts? We are talking about a transformative moment of realization, not words issuing out of the sky.

We then go to the conversation between our masters Franz Rosenzweig and Martin Buber. Is it *anokhi*, "I am," that we really need to hear spoken by Y-H-W-H? Does that suffice, with all the rest of Torah flowing from it? Or is that word itself already "commentary," and only *va-yedabber Elohim*, "God spoke" (20:1) is the primary text?

Then on to the Hasidic master R. Mendel Rymanover, who offered the *alef* of *anokhi* as that which contained it all, the *alef* that in itself is a silent letter. God speaks in silence. Again, it takes a Moses to translate it into words. But the graphic *Alef* itself, as the Rymanover knew well, is a construct. It is made up of a *yod* above, a *yod* below, and an angular *vav* that joins them. The first *yod* is *ḥokhmah,* the inner Mind of God; the second is *shekhinah*, Y-H-W-H as manifest throughout the world and in our own souls, the God within. The *vav*, which means "and" links them together, teaching that the two are one, indeed that there is only One. And that *alef* is itself the number One.

What more does ***torah,*** our "teaching," need to offer? The One is present in all that is. We are called to live our lives in response to that truth.

6 דבר אתה עמנו ונשמעה ואל ידבר עמנו אלוהים פן נמות

"You speak with us and we will hear, but let not Y-H-W-H speak with us, lest we die" (20:15).

Yes, there is a real element of terror in the experience of Sinai. Something in us wants to run away from the divine voice that calls out from within us. We would rather hear it as mediated through Moses, through tradition. That's ***safer*** than really straining to listen to what Y-H-W-H, the eternal presence within the moment, is trying to tell us.

It is quite impressive that the tradition recognizes that. In saying that we heard only those two – "I am" and "Do not make yourself any other gods alongside Me" – from Y-H-W-H, and that these contain the entire teaching, it is admitting that the other 611 commandments are already commentary or expansion. The Zohar refers to them as "counsels" to help us to fulfill these two.

But it remains important to ask ourselves how we really fulfill the two *mitsvot* that contain the entire Torah, without immediately fleeing to the forms of Moses' religion, the "You speak with us." "***I am***" hardly sounds like a *mitsvah* at all, yet it contains all of them within it. It is clearly about intention, awareness, attachment to the ever-liberating One. "Worship nothing else!" requires a being constantly on guard against our own tendency toward idol worship, toward making something else our God.

The Or ha-Hayyim, a Moroccan Kabbalist widely favored by the Hasidic masters, says that the word *la-khem*, "yourself," in the verse is a warning not to turn ***ourselves*** into false gods. This is the most widespread form of idolatry – even more so in our generation.

משפטים
MISHPATIM
(Exodus 21:1-24:18)

1 ואלה המשפטים אשר תשים לפניהם

"And these are the judgments you shall place before them" (21:1). At first glance, this appears to be an abrupt change in the nature of Torah. Until now, it has been a narrative, a book of stories. To learn from it – because Torah means "teaching," after all – has been to learn from those stories, or to seek out wisdom from the words in which they are told. Now, suddenly, Torah seems to turn into a code of laws, and the fear arises in us that perhaps all this long narrative has just been an introduction to that.

A memorable *dvar torah* by Reb Yoel of our *ḥavurah*, more than half a century ago, has helped me to read it differently. The narrative does not stop here. Each *mishpat* or judgment listed here is the result of a story. This is a collection of case laws, not an abstract code. That also accounts for its seemingly haphazard order.

Here's how it must have happened: Sometime, shortly after Sinai, there was an Israelite who owned a slave, because of a debt that could not be paid off. When the time of bondage was over, the man refused to go free, not wanting to leave his wife and kid behind. So they came and asked Moses. Then there was a guy with a daughter…Then there were two guys who had a fight, and one of them died…Then there was this terrible story in the camp of a child who killed his parents…

All of these are readings from **the casebook of Moses' court.** In fact, the *vav* with which it begins, traditionally seen as linking it to what came before, directly ties these chapters back to chapter 18, where Jethro advises Moses to set up courts. Ex. 18:26 reads: "They shall judge the people constantly. The hard things they shall bring to Moses, but small matters they shall judge themselves." Here we have a list of the "hard things" as they came up. They got written down as "laws" for the sake of precedent. But there are real stories, with real people, behind each one.

A Jewish praxis based directly on the Talmud, rather than on the intentionally abstracting codes, would look a lot closer to this. *Halakhah* and *aggadah*, *nomos* and narrative, intertwined at each moment. But think also about your own life and practice this way. Why do you do X or Y? Because of a certain story, a certain memory…

2 כי אם ענה תענה אותו כי אם צעוק יצעק אלי שמוע אשמע צעקתו
"If you harshly afflict him and he cries out to Me, I will surely hear his cry" (22:22); **"If he cries out to Me, I will hear him, for I am compassionate"** (22:26). Note that every verb in the verse is repeated for emphasis. Widows, orphans, and the poor – the helpless within human society – are ***heard*** by Y-H-W-H. This assurance that crime against the helpless does not go unnoticed represents the very beginning of morality within the history of human conscience. The call for righteous behavior toward those who cannot defend themselves begins with this: God hears.

This truth is not lost even on those of us who do not understand "God hears" in a simple way. The human ear that lets itself be transformed when it hears: "I am Y-H-W-H your God who brought you forth from the Land of Egypt, from the house of slaves" (20:2), itself becomes an ear of God. In that hearing, ***we give our ears to God***. This requires us to listen to the outcry of God's creatures, in all their pain. When we do not listen to the cries of others, we diminish the image of God within us.

A statement of faith: Each of us was created – meaning that the miracle of conception was set into motion – in order *le-harbot et ha-demut*, to increase and add a unique dimension to the divine image present in the world. The cultivation of that image is our task in this world. It is made up of equal measures of responsiveness to the cries of others – which are the cry of God, and nurturing of the inner life – the presence of that same God within us. The two are inseparable.

3 ואנשי קדש תהיון לי

"Be persons of holiness for Me" (22:30). The Kotzker Rebbe said on this verse: "Persons" comes first. You have to be a *mensch* before you can try to be holy. His comment shows a good appreciation for the tone of this chapter, which the medieval commentators already referred to as "the Book of the Covenant." For an understanding of Judaism at its core, there is no better example than this thorough mixing of ethical concerns, especially for the helpless and disadvantaged, with an insistence on personal holiness, witnessed especially in our behavior both in the bedroom and at the dining table.

4 הנה אנכי שולח מלאך לפניך לשמרך

"Behold, I send an angel before you to guard you on the path, and to bring you to the place I have prepared. Be careful in his presence. Do not rebel against him. He will not bear your sins, because My name is within him" (23:20-21). This verse, written in the singular, leaps forth to be taken out of context, to be applied to every person and each life's journey.

There is an echo of personal destiny to be heard here. This is different from the usual understanding of particular providence from "above," which is difficult for many of us today. The verse seems more like it is talking about following one's inner star, not rebelling against the course of life that you know to be truly yours. There is an "angel" – sometimes a tough one – who is there to keep you on that path. Pay attention.

5 ויקח משה את הדם ויזרוק על העם

"Moses took the blood and cast it upon the people" (24:8). The most interesting aspect of this very dramatic ceremony of the Sinai covenant is that it does not seem to be commanded by Y-H-W-H. Moses sends the young people in the community to offer sacrifices (this is the only occasion when sacrifice seems to be an activity for the youth!). He then gathers the blood in bowls, dashing half of it upon the altar and half over the people. The message is very clear: God, represented by the altar, and the people of Israel are joined by the sharing of blood. That makes this a link that cannot be broken.

Who is Moses trying to impress by this most powerful gesture? Perhaps it is the people, especially the emerging new generation, one that will not remember the sufferings of Egypt. That would be why he involved the youth in this ritual moment. As the people go forward – whether for a forty-year journey or one of four thousand years – each generation needs to be reminded that the covenant is sealed in blood and can never be broken.

Or might it be God whom Moses is trying to bind permanently to this covenantal moment? "No matter how frustrated or disappointed You become with this people, remember that You are linked to them by a covenant of blood, and You can never leave them."

For us, that blood is no longer just that of an ancient sacrifice, poured upon the altar. It is the blood of martyrs over many generations, including that of a million Jewish children murdered in the Holocaust. The sense that the Jewish people continues to have a divine mission, and that that the covenant is unbreakable from either side, is indeed sealed in blood. For many an Israeli parent, that sealing of the covenant in blood still goes on. But linking it to our sense of holy mission has gotten much harder.

6 ויאמר ה' אל משה עלה אלי ההרה והיה שם

"And Y-H-W-H said to Moses: Come up to Me, to the mountain, and *be there*" (24:12). The phrase *ve-heyeh sham* is very distinctive and surprising. What does it mean for Moses to "be" on the mountain, before Y-H-W-H will give him the tablets and the teaching? Is this a period of adjustment to the "mountain air," to being in the rarified divine presence? Or is there some deeper existential meaning to this word, hinting that Moses needs to make himself fully present in order to hear the Word? Is it an accident that the letters of *ve-heyeh* ("and be") are those of God's own name?

The Kabbalists say that "Moses spreads forth into each generation." We are all Moses. Many of us are blessed with moments on the mountaintop. But do we listen to the command to "***be there***?"

תרומה
TERUMAH
(Exodus 25:1-27:19)

1 ועשו לי מקדש ושכנתי בתוכם

"They shall make for Me a holy place, and I will dwell within them. As all that I show you, the structure of the dwelling and of all its vessels, thus shall you do" (25:8-9).

These seemingly simple verses call forth complex readings. Based on long tradition, extending from Philo through the Hasidic masters, we read *be-tokham* as "within them," within each one of them, rather than "in their midst." The verse then refers to the dwelling-place that we make for *shekhinah* within the human heart. The sanctuary of Israel in the wilderness is a paradigm for the inner *mishkan* each of us spends our lives constructing.

In the following verse, "show" is followed by a direct object (*otekha*), rather than the expected indirect (*lekha*). *Ani mar'eh otekha* means that ***you*** are what I am showing you, a vision coming from within your own self. The commandment to build a *mishkan* serves as an internal mirror, allowing you to look into an inner place that was already there, but of which you were unaware. You build your tabernacle out of materials that are already there within you.

In the next verse, the "you" switches from singular to plural. Only Moses (the "mind" of Israel) has been shown the model, but all – the entire self – are to engage in the construction. Building that holy place is thus set forth as the ongoing work of Israel. (Remember here that "Israel" is also Jacob's *yisra'el* – all those who wrestle with God, in whatever language or religious framework they are do so.) In fact, building the *mishkan* is the task that defines *mel'akhah*, constructive labor. ***That is what we are to do with our lives: build a tabernacle for God's presence.*** "The rest is commentary," as someone once said.

But should you say that that this work within the heart is ***all*** we have to do, and never mind the outside world and how we live in it, the verse comes back and says: "*ve-khen **ta'asu***, and thus shall you ***do***." The end product is not just a heart that contains the divine presence, but an entire life that is built around that truth. The final test of our *mishkan* is the way we live and act in the world.

2 ונתת אל הארון את העדות אשר אתן אליך

"And you will place in the ark the testimony that I will give you" (25:16). The word *'edut,* "testimony," is an abstract term, and its meaning is somewhat vague. It is usually taken here to refer to the two tablets, but that is not clear in the text. *'Edut* is generally an oral process, an act of witnessing, like testimony in a trial. ***What is the testimony or witnessing that we need to place in our inner ark?***

Think of Psalm 19's "The heavens declare the glory of God; the firmament tells of the work of God's hands." That is ***'edut***; it ***witnesses*** to the poet's experience. Our own lives are filled with moments of such testimony. "Place them in the ark" – this is a *mitsvah* for all generations.

"***Atem** 'edai*, "***You*** are My witnesses," says the prophet (Is. 43:12). That too needs to be held in our ark. Our entire lives are meant to serve as testimony to our awareness of Y-H-W-H. Our entire lives are meant to serve as testimony to our awareness of Y-H-W-H.

3 ועשית שניים כרובים זהב מקשה תעשה אותם משני קצות הכפורת

"Make two golden cherubim; of a piece shall you make them, on either side of the covering" (25:18). The two cherubim should not be soldered together, according to RaSHI, but should be fashioned out a single piece of gold.

Hovering over our ark are two angels that are really one. The sages say of the cherubim that seeing (forbidden, of course, except to the high priest) or contemplating them was to remind one of "See how beloved you are before the ever-present One – like the love of man and woman!" This reflects a notion (somewhat out of fashion today) that finding your true love is like discovering the "other half" of your own self. In such a way, two beloveds are like the cherubim, separate angels who come to realize that they were hammered out of a single chunk of gold.

But here we are saying the same thing about the relationship of the soul and the Holy One. It is ***these*** two that are one, Y-H-W-H and the soul. That is the truth that hovers over our ark.

4 חמש היריעות תהיינה חוברות אשה אל אחותה

"The five curtains shall be linked, each woman to her sister, and the five [others], woman to her sister" (29:3). Of course you may say that this female language is just due to the fact that *yeri'ot*, "curtains," happens to be a feminine word in Hebrew. But I rather like the idea that the *ohel mo'ed*, tent of meeting, itself is formed by a *minyan* of sisters, surrounding it by linked embrace. The Torah is hinting that the women who did all that weaving and embroidery came to form a close community as they worked together, and became ***sisters.*** Some aura of their circle was left behind, to be felt by all who would enter its sacred precincts.

5 ולשער החצר מסך עשרים אמה תכלת וארגמן

"The gateway to the courtyard shall have a twenty-cubit curtain, azure and purple..." (27:16). As we come to the conclusion of this description, we realize how incredibly elaborate it has become. Rather than a simple "fold-up and carry" tabernacle for these wandering Israelites, this reminds us of Solomon's Temple in the Book of Kings, and even more of Ezekiel's grand vision of a future Temple. There too we have a gate to the inner courtyard, closed during the week, but kept open every *shabbat* and *rosh ḥodesh* (Ez. 46:1).

We want both of these, the simplicity and the glory, for our inner sanctum. The balance between them will vary. Some days, we are happy just to enter that quiet place. No gold trimmings needed, no azure and purple curtains. At other times, we want to know it as a place of special beauty, fancied up as best we can. The most important part of it is the ***gateway***, something especially decorated so that we can always find it in order to enter.

תצוה
TETZAVVEH
(Exodus 27:20-30:10)

1 ואתה תצוה

"And you! Command..." The *parashah* begins with three uses of this *ve-atah*. **"You! Command"** (27:20); **"You! Draw near"** (28:1); **"You! Speak"** (28:3). This is also famous as the single *parashah* in the latter four books of the Torah in which Moses' name is not mentioned.

There is an echo of a special intimacy in the call to Moses here, and maybe a sharper demand, but one that covers over Moses' pain. All three of these commands – the daily lighting of the lamps, serving as priests, and wearing the priestly garments - concern Aaron *and his sons* or descendants. It is here that Moses realizes that the inherited leadership will belong to his brother, not to him. Moses' own sons are to play no special role in the passing on of his prophecy or teachings.

There must have been some heartbreak in this realization. After all, the revelation at the bush had originally come to him, not his brother. He was the one told to lead his people out of Egypt. He was the one who entered the cloud over mountain alone. Aaron was there to assist, to be his "prophet," in the sense of spokesman, to cover for the fact that Moses was "heavy of mouth and tongue." Why, then, should the inheritance pass through Aaron's children and not his own?

Moses here has to face the difference between prophecy and priesthood, between charismatic and institutionalized religion. Each of the moments he had in God's presence, whether at the bush, in Egypt, or on the mountain, was unique, never to be repeated. To have his sons out there claiming to relive or embody them would have betrayed the unique charism of those moments, the special magic of divine revelation present when each of them took place. Aaron was the great translator of Moses' charism into ritual forms that could be carried on. It was those that could be passed on through the generations. (This was the great failure of Hasidism in its turn to dynastic leadership. Charisma is not carried in the genes.)

But God's voice, as hinted at in the text, understands Moses' pain at this. So it cries out to him three times: "***And you! And you! And you!***" Yes, you too will be present in all that they do, throughout the generations. Each time they light the lamps, approach the altar, or put on the priestly garments, that *ve-atah* will be there within them. The forms exist only to preserve and recall the charismatic moment. Without it they are but empty shells.

2 ונשא אהרן את שמות בני ישראל בחושן המשפט על לבו

"Aaron shall carry the names of Israel, in the breastplate of judgment, on his heart as he enters the holy, as a remembrance before Y-H-W-H, forever" (28:29). Here we see the first of many verses, continuing through the book of *Va-Yikra*, where the priest serves as the prototype of religious leader. The Zohar describes Aaron as the embodiment of *ḥesed*. He always carries the names of all Israel – not just those of the tribes – with him as he enters the holy place, remembering each of them in the presence of Y-H-W-H. Hasidic sources transfer this to the *tsaddik*, whose secret rests in the intimate relationships he has both with Y-H-W-H and with his disciples, allowing him to become a channel of blessing and devotion between the two.

Some part of this priestly function exists in the role of the contemporary rabbi as well. Even though today's rabbis are often less than comfortable with it, we act unwisely when we seek to deny it or flee from it. But we need to be careful and discerning in the way we apply it. The rabbi does not convey the prayers of Israel to God; each Jew must pray on his/her own. Each of us must find our own path in the work of opening our hearts. But we must not run away from the call to "Pray for me, rabbi," that is often heard.

We rabbis carry the names of "all Israel," lots of Jews (and others) we serve and care about, when we "enter the Holy." But we need to remember that we carry those names on the breastplate of *mishpat,* good judgment and proper balance. That means judging ourselves carefully in that role, never using it to promote our own ego needs or to elevate our status. Hopefully, our standing in God's presence fills our hearts with love for all those people we carry with us in our hearts, and makes us a source of blessing in their lives.

3 פעמון זהב ורימון פעמון זהב ורימון על שולי המעיל סביב. והיה על אהרן לשרת

"Golden bell and pomegranate, golden bell and pomegranate, all around the edge of his cloak. It shall be upon Aaron as he serves; its sound will be heard as he enters the holy, and he shall not die" (28:34-35). The little pomegranates served as clappers to the bells. Their sound indicated that it was Aaron who had entered the holy place and not someone else.

But who was it who needed to hear that sound? Does Y-H-W-H not know whether it is Aaron? Perhaps the sound is for Aaron himself. He puts on this cloak as he enters. The sound of the bells reminds him to fix his mind on the sacredness of the place and the moment of transition as he enters it. The garments of the priest are described as *ma'aseh ḥoshev*, deeds that arouse thought.

We do not have bells on our cloaks that ring when we enter our holy space. There are no special garments; our *mishkan* welcomes us on a "come as you are" basis. But the inner place itself and the moment of entry are both *kodesh*. Having them and recognizing their holiness renews our lives and is "upon us as we serve."

4 לשכני בתוכם

"They will know that I am Y-H-W-H their God who brought them forth from the land of Egypt *to dwell within them.* I am Y-H-W-H their God" (29:46). I know of no other verse that so well summarizes the entire Torah narrative. That is why I have named this book for it. God brought us out of Egypt, liberating us from human bondage, so that we would constitute an earthly dwelling-place for divinity. That was the purpose of our liberation. ***We were chosen not because we are better or smarter, not because God likes us better, or because he fell in love with our ancestor and made a promise.*** We were liberated and brought to the foot of Mount Sinai to become an earthly home for the *shekhinah.*

I believe this to be the purpose of Jewish existence throughout the generations. We continue to exist because of it. This is as true of modern Israel as it was of ancient Israel. The two-thirds of us who were not slaughtered in the Holocaust were redeemed for a purpose, to become such a *mishkan,* both in the Holy Land and in our dispersion.

The creation of a Jewish polity in Israel has given us a great opportunity to realize this, but we seem to be wasting it. We seem to be divided between those who think a Jewish State means one that enforces *halakhah* and those who think it means giving greater privileges to Jews over others! It means neither of these, of course! It means a place of peace and justice, one in which nobody does to anyone what was done to us Jews for so long! It means a place where our most essential truths, that knowing the One who is everywhere makes you free, and that every human being is God's living image, are realized in the way we live and govern.

But this immediately takes us back to the theme of brothers. Have we learned from the latter four books of the Torah to solve the problem that Heschel taught us was the key question of Genesis: "How do I live side by side with my brothers?" We are back in the Land of Israel to test whether we can live side by side with brothers from whom we have been away for a long time. How are we doing at that task?

Now there arise Jews in Israel (many of them even called "religious") who say that the problem is too much democracy, a value that is not part of Judaism. Let's get rid of it, for Jews and gentiles alike! But don't they see that ***it is our Torah*** that calls for honest courts, caring for the needy, loving the stranger, and lots more? How can they have missed all those parts?

Those of us in America are also called to be brothers to a great variety of people. But surely there is a special mission to offer brotherhood to another people who are struggling mightily to recover from a slavery that we should understand. How are we all doing in building such a *mishkan* of brother/sisterhood?

This is true of the individual as well. Y-H-W-H delivers you from all your Egypts, all those forces that oppress and constrict you in both body and soul, for a single purpose. Y-H-W-H longs to dwell within you, for you to become a *mishkan*, radiating the light of divine blessing to those all around you, to brothers and sisters near and far away.

5 והקטיר עליו אהרן קטורת סמים בבקר בבקר

"Upon it shall Aaron offer aromatic incense; each morning, as he cleans the lamps he shall offer it. And as he raises up the lamps at dusk he shall offer it, a regular incense offering before Y-H-W-H, throughout your generations" (30:7-8). The conclusion of the verse uses the same language as that of circumcision (Gen. 17:12) or *Pesaḥ* (Ex. 12:14, 17), making it sound like one of those commandments that we are to continue observing forever, even without the Temple. Indeed, in the Sephardic and Hasidic *siddur* these verses are recited each day at those times, before the *shaḥarit* and *minḥah* services, as a sort of verbal fulfillment of the *mitsvah.*

The incense altar stood at the entranceway to the inner sanctuary. Perhaps we need one in the same position, to be there as we enter our inner holy place. The incense we offer is that of *reaḥ ma'asim tovim*, the aroma of good deeds, accompanying us as we enter. We should have to "pass the smell test" before we are ready to pray.

תשא
KI TISA
(Exodus 30:11-34:35)

1 וקדשת אותם והיו קדש קדשים כל הנוגע בהם יקדש

"You shall sanctify them and they will become Holy of Holies; all that touches them will become holy" (30:29). The Tent of Meeting, the ark, the altar, and all the rest were made by humans. As they were being built, the construction crews went freely in and out. Only now, by the act of anointing them with pure olive oil, does Moses make them holy.

We should not be afraid of admitting the human role in creating all the forms of our religious life. Yes, it is Moses – a human being – who makes them holy. Think of the sages in all their generations as the Bezalels, the artisans who fashioned the objects with our *mishkan*, and the "Moses" within them as the one who sanctified them. But that holiness is nevertheless *kodesh kodashim* – Holy of Holies, ultimately real. It is not diminished because of the human role in creating it.

So too with our own inner *mishkan*. The Moses within us is responding to an inner divine voice that says: "Make it holy!" We both construct it and declare it holy. But the "pure oil" with which we anoint it flows from our deepest hearts, and that comes to us from the Unknown that lies within us.

Even though we know that it is our own handiwork, we take that holiness seriously, and then call out: "Let everything that touches it become holy."

"The work of our hands make firm for us; make real the work of our hands" (Ps. 90:17).

2 וביום השביעי שבת וינפש

"On the seventh day God rested and was ensouled" (31:17). RaSHI reads *va-yinafash* as "God took a deep breath." But then he immediately adds that it makes no sense to attribute "rest" to the One who created all simply by speaking it into being. It is only said this way, he suggests, to help us mere mortals understand.

What we need to understand is that pausing in our labors is a precondition for finding holiness. In the Creation story, God rests on the seventh day and then declares it holy. Our prayers speak of Shabbat as *yom menuḥah u-kedushah*, "a day of rest and holiness," with rest coming first. You cannot discover holiness until you let yourself rest.

The notion that ordinary human beings, including slaves, have a right to rest, is a great innovation of the Torah. In the ancient world, rest belonged to the gods and perhaps to their son, the earthly king. Humans were created to work for them, so that they might have leisure. The Torah opens with a proclamation that every human being is created in the divine image. This is immediately followed with the sanctification of a day of rest.

So much of human life is spent on the treadmill of seeking a livelihood, of pursuing our needs, both real and imagined. Parenthood and maintaining a household can also become a treadmill. There can even be a treadmill of serving others that becomes a burden. The Torah gives us a great gift in insisting that *shavat va-yinafash* go together, that you have to ***stop*** in order to truly ***breathe***.

This notion that the right to rest is vital to humanity could only have been created by a nation of recently liberated slaves.

3 ויאמר משה אל ה': ושמעו מצרים...מבלתי יכולת...ועתה יגדל נא כח ה'
לאמר ה' ארך אפים ורב חסד...ויאמר ה' סלחתי כדבריך

"The people opened up all the gold rings that were in their ears and brought them to Aaron. He took them from their hands, fashioned it with a graving tool, and made of it a molten Calf" (32:3-4).

The presence of gold, silver, and other valuables among the Israelites in the wilderness is mentioned in three places. As the slaves left Egypt, they were told (Ex. 11:2) to "borrow" from their neighbors gold and silver vessels. Some of that gold seems to have gone into the making of the Golden Calf. But even after the sinners were forced by Moses to drink that gold in powdered form (32:20), there seems to have been plenty left for them to offer in the construction of the *mishkan* (35:22).

How does all this relate to the simplicity demanded by Y-H-W-H as revealed at Sinai, the voice that seems to shun such display by saying: "Do not fashion and gods of silver with Me; do not make for yourselves gods of gold. Build Me an earthen altar" (20:21-22). Is Aaron going out of his way to do something unmistakably alien to the God his brother is talking to on the mountain above them? Or might the Torah be telling us that there was something inherently polluting about all that gold the Israelites had "borrowed" back in Egypt, that it would inevitably lead them astray?

The school of Rabbi Yishma'el taught that the commandment to build the elaborate tabernacle was given only after the Golden Calf, and hence that the Torah text in these chapters is presented out of order. It was only after Y-H-W-H saw that the people needed a grand manifestation of divine presence on earth, perhaps out of a certain attraction to idolatry, that He commanded gold and silver vessels for His service. Let them use their gold *for this*!

But perhaps the purpose was to empty the pockets of the Israelites, so that all that gold and silver not be a burden to them along their journey and a source of conflict between them.

4 לוחות כתובים משני עבריהם מזה ומזה הם כתובים

"Tablets inscribed on both of their sides, written in both directions" (32:15). We see only our side of the tablets, that which we think of as the front. But they are written on both sides, we are told. What might they look like from the other side?

Sinai is a covenantal moment. In a *brit,* "covenant," commitments are demanded from both parties. Then there must be another set of ten commandments, or a reading of them in the opposite direction, that obligate the other Partner to this treaty. What are the ten "commandments" inscribed on the other side of the tablets, the demands we make of God in this interchange, parallel to the commandments being given to us?

Let's try a first few.

"You are Y-H-W-H our God who brought us forth from Egypt, from the House of Slaves." May Your strength and our faith in You liberate us from all our Egypts, from all the narrow places that constrain us, from every House of Slaves!"

"May we have no other gods alongside You." You have placed us in a world filled with false gods just waiting to be worshipped. Reveal Yourself to us so that we do not turn to false gods and idols. Come out of hiding!

"Do not taken the name of humanity in vain." You created us in Your image and likeness. We are proud of the name *adam*, "human," which we bear. It is made up of the cosmic *aleph*, the oneness of all that lies within us, and *dam*, "blood," representing our flesh-and-blood selves. Do not take our name in vain, either. *Adam* means both "earthling" and "human." Help us to not degrade it.

And the rest? How about you trying to compose them?

5 והלוחות מעשה אלוהים המה והמכתב מכתב אלוהים חרות על הלוחות

"The tablets were made by God; the writing was divine writing, engraved onto the tablets" (32:16). The odd spelling of the word *ḥarut*, "engraved," leads the rabbis to read it as *ḥerut*; "there was 'freedom' on the tablets." They extend that when they say: "Only those engaged with the Teaching are truly free."

How complex and interwoven the divine/human relationship is, a veritable dialectic of intimacy! The ten commandments (or "speech-acts," as I prefer) begin with liberation. "I am Y-H-W-H your God who brought you forth from the Land of Egypt, the House of Slaves." But scripture then also says "For Israel are servants unto Me" (Lev. 25:55). The Hebrew *'avadim* makes no distinction between "slavery" and "service." But it cannot be that we were simply liberated from one form of bondage to enter another! This is what the rabbis understood and chose to comment on here: it says ***freedom*** on the tablets. Not for naught do we thank each morning the One "who has not made me a slave" or "who has made me free." Redemption from Egypt is a redemption of the mind. It was *da'at*, awareness or consciousness, that was in exile, enslaved. That exile consists of a dullness, a passage through life without noticing its beauty, its richness, or its blessings, a ***tyranny of the ordinary***, which is the lot of so many. Liberation opens the possibility of a constantly renewed awareness that the earth is filled with God's glory, shining with divine light. For the ability to see that light we bless God each day for "opening the eyes of the blind."

That light is also the light of Torah. To truly be "engaged with the Teaching" is a quest for the light hidden within it. That quest constitutes liberation from a life of superficiality and indifference, of an inattention that constitutes "the exile of the mind, *galut ha-da'at*. We are filled with gratitude for that liberation, for the understanding that ***there is always something more to seek***. There are endless levels of meaning, in Torah as in life and in the natural world. It is our response to this gratitude that leads us to give ourselves to Y-H-W-H, to ***choose*** a life of service. That is our freely chosen covenant of Sinai, possible only after our liberation from Egypt.

6 פסל לך שני לוחות אבנים כראשונים

"Carve two stone tablets on your own, like the former ones" (34:1). The first tablets had to be smashed. Human beings could not accept a Torah dictated entirely from "above." Tablets made by God and inscribed with God's own writing were too much for humanity to bear; the message of freedom was squashed in them by an excess of awe. God had to learn that from the terrible ordeal of the Golden Calf. Now, convinced by Moses not to give up on Israel, He is ready to start again. "This time," He says: "***you*** make the tablets and I'll do the writing." ***Religion needs to emerge from a joint enterprise between divinity and human creativity.***

Yom Kippur is our annual commemoration of the giving of the second tablets. Moses went back up to Sinai on the first day of Elul. He pleaded for Israel and worked on the carving – and negotiated for Israel's forgiveness – for forty days. He came down with those second tablets on Yom Kippur. That is why there should be lots of singing and joy in a true Hasidic Yom Kippur. "We have been forgiven again!"

Think of it as a celebration of a renegotiated marriage. They got married too young and lived in a world where he dictated all the terms.

She was not prepared to live that way and the marriage failed. But instead of divorcing, they found a great marriage counsellor named Moses who helped them to negotiate the terms anew. Let us join in this celebration of the remarriage of the blessed Holy One and the Community of Israel!

Now we can go on, knowing that God is with us in our shared process of carving and inscribing the tablets, of creating Torah!" "We'll keep carving!" we say in this celebration of forgiveness; "You keep inscribing!" "Write them upon the tablets of your heart" (Prov. 3:3, 7:3).

Yom Kippur clears the path to Simḥat Torah, to a new receiving of Torah.

7 הנה מקום אתי

"Here is a place, with Me" (Ex. 33:21). Sometimes it feels like these are the most powerful and touching words in the entire Torah. The Oneness of all Being says to me: "Yes, I will make room for you in My world. Come, sit by Me. I will make a space for you. And I will protect you as My glory passes by." This seems to be the opposite of the moment (Ex. 40:35) when the tabernacle was so filled with God's presence that Moses was unable to enter.

As small and humbled as we feel by the overwhelming presence of God in our lives, we each need to feel that there is a place for us in this world, a place where we can live the lives and do the bits of good for which we were created. Our instinctive response is to return the favor, to say back to the Presence: ***hineh makom itti*****, "Here is a place, with me**. I will move my ego over and make room for You in my life."

ויקהל
VA-YAKHEL
(Exodus 35:1-38:20)

1 ויקהל משה את כל עדת בני ישראל...ויבואו כל איש אשר נשאו לבו וכל
אשר נדבה רוחו אותו

"Moses assembled the entire community of Israel.... And they came: everyone whose heart had raised him up, and every one of generous spirit, bringing the offering of Y-H-W-H for making the tabernacle" (35:1, 21). The *mishkan* could only be created by the coming together of the whole community. Some may have given because "their hearts had raised them up"; they got some sort of ego satisfaction out of giving. Maybe *nesa'o*, "raised him up" means that he wanted to become a *nasi*, a leader or an important person, through the act of contributing. They came together with the *nadvah ruḥo* people, those of generous spirit.

Yes, Moshe Rabbenu was the first rabbi who had to lead a building drive for his congregation! Without that, how could he have served as a model for Jewish leadership across so many different communities and generations? As everyone – rabbi or communal leader - who has run such a drive knows, giving attracts many sorts of people, who contribute for a wide range of reasons. Even in the holy work of constructing a *mishkan*, we do not stop them at the door and ask "Why are you offering this gift?"

Nor would the answer to that question be simple. Motives combine in the hearts of real people; someone may be giving for the best and worst of reasons at the same time. Perhaps she wants to impress her neighbors by her giving, but she ***also*** wants to honor the memory of her parents. He may want to be asked to join the board precisely ***because*** he feels the warmth of the shul's community. How do we ever know? How much does it matter?

Every leader struggles with these questions. We know that somewhere there are limits. What about the criminal who is giving in hopes of clearing his/her name? Did Moses ask those Israelites who had so much gold and silver how they had gotten it? Later in the Torah we will hear about Datan and Aviram, two wealthy Jews who, as it turns out, had been taskmasters among the slaves back in Egypt. In our post-Holocaust vocabulary, we might call them "collaborators." Were their gifts welcome, until they chose to challenge Moses' leadership? Should they have been turned away earlier?

There are no simple, unequivocal answers to these questions, but they need to be asked. There is a *halakhic* category of things that "acquire impurity." A big building is hard to dip in a *mikveh*. Better to keep it relatively pure in advance.

2 וכל אשר נמצא אתו עצי שטים לכל מלאכת העבודה הביאו

"And whoever had acacia wood with him brought it for the work" (35:24). Here a simple reading of the text is impossible. How could these newly liberated slaves just happen to have had acacia wood – and huge lengths of it, needed for construction – in their backpacks? The sages actually debated this point, some saying that Jacob had planted an acacia forest in Egypt, anticipating this moment. Others (see Ibn Ezra to 25:5) depict Israel as particularly rapacious travelers through the wilderness, having cut down an entire forest for their own use before they even got to Sinai!

Impossible! Our ancestors were better than that. But when it came to this building, they were like any group of Jews setting out to create something. Everyone had their own ideas, most of them pretty foolish. Read עצי שטים here as עצות שוטים, "the counsel of fools." The real skill of Bezalel, whom God had filled with "wisdom, understanding, and awareness" (31:3; 35:31), was to be able to take those *'etsot shotim* and form them into *'atsey shittim*! That's the *da'at* or "awareness" part of what he was given – the power to take bad ideas and turn them around for good. ("Ah, Mr. Goldberg, that's such a good idea! But maybe we could understand it ***this*** way…")

Messiah will undoubtedly have some of that same *da'at.* That's how the new Temple will get built. Meanwhile, all we have on that subject are a lot of foolish counsels. Let us remain wary of them.

3 ויקרא משה אל בצלאל...ואל כל איש חכם לב אשר נתן ה' חכמה בלבו כל
אשר נשאו לבו לקרבה אל המלאכה

"Moses called Bezalel...and every person of wise heart, those in whose hearts Y-H-W-H had placed wisdom, whoever's hearts raised them up to draw near to the work, in order to do it" (36:2). Read this verse carefully. Great skill was required to participate in the building of the *mishkan*. The Torah has just gone through a long list of the various crafts and materials that were involved. But this was also an act of very intimate devotion. Your heart had to be in it, causing you *le-korvah*, to "draw near." The whole project of the *mishkan* is about intimacy. It is the place, after all where *korbanot* will be offered. This word for "offerings" or "sacrifices" bears a sense of "means of drawing near." That same desire for nearness has to be present in the very building of such a place.

But the verse tells us more than that. The wisdom of heart that brings about such an uplifting is itself a gift of Y-H-W-H. ***The desire for intimacy is mutual, in ways we do not fully understand***. Even that which we think arises first within our own hearts, due to various circumstances in our lives, and causes us to seek to draw near, already reflects a ***gift*** that we have been given, a desire that has been implanted within us and that we come to discover. We are given that gift because Y-H-W-H wants us to build – or to become – a *mishkan*.

That is *raza di-mehemanuta*, the secret core of faith. ***Our relationship with the One, the attraction that draws us together, is more mutual than we could ever imagine.***

4 ויצו משה ויעבירו קול במחנה לאמור איש ואשה אל יעשו עוד מלאכה

"Moses commanded, and they passed the word through the camp, saying that no man or woman should do any more work for this holy offering. The people were held back from bringing" (36:6).

What a nice moment for that rabbi running the building campaign: announcing that we are "over the top!"

But telling the people to stop? Preventing them from giving more? Couldn't he have put it into a "rainy day fund," thinking about the need for future repairs to what was, after all, a tent? Surely though purple-dyed curtains would tear one day! There seems to be some wisdom here, a lesson being taught about knowing what is "enough and more," as the next verse goes on to say.

All of us are both givers and receivers as we go through life. Hopefully, we both give love and receive it. We are generous with others, but have also benefitted from the generosity of those around us. The same is true with regard to our relationship to our society, or the community and country within which we live; we give and we receive. When we are on the receiving end, even dependent on the gifts of another, it takes special wisdom to know when to say: "That's enough."

פקודי
PEKUDEI
(Exodus 38:21-40:38)

1 ותכל כל מלאכת משכן אהל מועד. ובני ישראל עשו ככל אשר צווה ה׳ את
משה כן עשו.

"All the work the *mishkan*, the Tent of Meeting, was completed. The Children of Israel did all that was commanded to Moses; thus did they do" (39:32).

The repetition here offers a chance for the eighteenth-century Moroccan Kabbalist R. Hayyim Ibn 'Attar, to make a particularly touching comment in his *Or ha-Ḥayyim*. He says we today fulfill God's commandments in the same collective way that all Israel together built the *mishkan.* Each one had a particular role: some donated gold, other goatskins. Some hammered, some sewed, some forged. But together they completed the work. So it is with *mitsvot*, he says. There is no Jew who can fulfill all the 613 commandments. Some apply only to *kohanim* or levites; others apply only to women and not to men. He says that Y-H-W-H takes all the commandments we fulfill and makes of them a *maḥberet ha-kelalut*, "a joining together into wholeness," thus allowing Torah to be completely fulfilled. He suggests that this is the real meaning of "Love your neighbor as yourself." "[Love your neighbor] because he is like you. His wholeness/fulfillment/being at peace (*shelomo*) will be for your good. It is through him that you are made whole. Therefore he is no other, but you yourself, like a part of you."

This very beautiful sense of all Israel working together to fulfill the Torah, our way of building a *mishkan* for God's presence here on earth, has rich implications for the meaning of Jewish unity. But let us be careful not to abuse it. Too often do we hear: "Oh, I don't need to keep *shabbat* or pray daily, because I'm a generous person. I give to charity and support *tikkun 'olam*." Or, even more dangerous, the opposite equivalent of that! Let us remember that the *Or ha-Ḥayyim* said this to open our hearts to be ***more*** generous and giving of love to one another, not less.

2 ויביאו את המשכן אל משה...וירא משה את כל המלאכה והנה עשו אותה כאשר ציווה ה׳ כן עשו ויברך אותם משה

"They brought the *mishkan* to Moses...and Moses saw all the labor. Behold, as Y-H-W-H had commanded, so had they done. And Moses blessed them" (39:33, 43). The repetition of detail in these two portions has been quite astounding. Hearing them read in the synagogue is sometimes boring, leading one to distraction. But then there comes a sense that the narrative is racing toward a grand conclusion. The Torah has been recognizing the skills and dedication of each man and woman doing a unique piece of the work. There could have been no *mishkan* without each of them. All their labors are important enough that they deserve to be mentioned. But now they all have to be brought to Moses, the only one who has the vision to fit them all together and raise the *mishkan* up.

The individual men and women who contributed to the *mishkan* and made it are like the limbs on the collective body of Israel. Each did his or her part, and without each of these the *mishkan* would not have been complete. But then they all brought all their labors back to Moses, who is called the *da'at* or mind of all Israel. He represents their collective inner consciousness, the embracing over-soul who unites them all. Only he can offer his blessing to the completed project as a whole

The Community of Israel still exists in order to form an earthly *mishkan* for God's presence, as we have said. There are many Jews of all sorts who contribute to this *mishkan* every day through their *mitsvot* and good deeds. Some do it through learning and teaching, some through devotion and prayer, others through generosity or caring for others. Each of these deserves blessing.

But we are a generation without a Moses. We probably wouldn't even want one. How do we see to it that all the pieces of our *mishkan* come together to become one?

3 ויכל משה את המלאכה

"And Moses completed the work" (40:33). The Midrash and the classical commentators (see especially R. Baḥya) have long noted that this chapter reflects the language of the opening chapter of *bereshit*. The *mel'akhah* of making the *mishkan* is the construction of a microcosm, paralleling the making of heaven and earth. Here the same words for concluding and blessing are used, seemingly intentionally. With the *mishkan*, the creation of the world is finally completed and fully blessed. The modern commentator Rabbi Moshe David Cassutto claimed that this was actually *peshat*, that the first books of the Torah were editorially bound together in this way.

We are all participants in God's ongoing work of Creation. When the Torah says "God rested on the seventh day from all His work that God had created *la-'asot*, "yet to be done," the doorway was opened to human partnership in the creative process. We do this partly by ***pro***creation, carrying Creation forward, continuing the chain of embodiments of God's image in the world. But we do it also through all forms of human ***creativity***, paradigmatically employing all the thirty-nine forms of labor called forth in the building of the *mishkan*.

Today we understand ongoing Creation through the lens of evolution. The creative process on our life-bearing planet has brought forth ever new and changing forms of life throughout evolutionary history. Our own acts of cultural transmission and creativity are part of that same process. As we pass the forms of tradition on to new generations, while allowing and encouraging them to creatively enhance and expand those traditions, we are being partners in the ongoing work of Creation and evolution.

Each time we make camp and erect our *mishkan* again, it will look a little different.

4 ולא יכול משה לבוא אל אהל מועד כי שכן עליו הענן וכבוד ה' מלא את המשכן

"Moses was unable to enter the Tent of Meeting, because the cloud had dwelt upon it, and the glory of Y-H-W-H filled the *mishkan*" (40:35).

Sometimes we are overwhelmed by that which we have created – or that which has been created through us – and how it can be filled with the radiant presence of Y-H-W-H. There is a moment when we are forced to stand back and look in wonder. Is this ***my*** Shabbat table – or book of poems – or work of art – or family? Or did it just happen through me? Is this ***my*** inner *mishkan*, or did it happen within me in a way I do not fully understand?

There will be other days, many of them, when we will go in and out of our *mishkan* to do the work we need to do there. There will also be times when we look up and see the holes and patches in our tent, or that the copper vessels have not been polished in a long time. There is always room for maintenance and improvement in our inner lives. But there is also a time to appreciate that *mishkan*, and to see that it is indeed filled to overflowing with the glory of Y-H-W-H, and we can only look upon it in astonishment.

SEFER VA-YIKRA

THE BOOK OF LEVITICUS

ויקרא
VA-YIKRA

1 ויקרא אל משה וידבר אליו מאהל מועד

"...called to Moses, speaking from the Tent of Meeting, saying..." (1:1). The call of the nameless One opening this book has always drawn the commentators. It seems intended to follow directly on Ex. 40:35, the last verse we quoted above in *parashat pekudei*. The tent was so filled with the glory of Y-H-W-H that Moses could not enter it. From out of that glory, the voice spoke to him.

The small *alef* in the opening word *va-yikra* also attracts our attention. Without it, the call would not be complete; one could not be certain of its source. It would be *va-yiker*, debatably drawn from *k-r-h*, meaning "it happened," rather than *k-r-'*, "called." This is said of Balaam's prophecy in Num. 23:3,16; it is a prophecy that just "happened" to him. It is the little *alef*, not in itself audible, representing the "still, small voice" of the One, that makes all the difference. ***Alufo shel 'olam*, the cosmic One, is there in the call**, even if half-hidden by its small size or whispered tone.

Why does the *alef* have to be so small? **Why is the call so faint? That is a question asked by seekers in every generation.** But it has to be - so that we, like Moses, will need to stretch our hearing. Otherwise, it would all be too easy; the adventure of the quest for Y-H-W-H – and the freedom to choose it – would be missing. We should be ***glad*** the call is faint, but should listen carefully.

Shema', yisra'el. ***Listen, Israel***!

2 ויקרא אל משה

"...called to Moses." Another reading, by the *Netivot Shalom*, a recent Hasidic master: It makes no difference who or what called to Moses.

Everything called to Moses! Moses was a person who heard God's voice calling from everywhere. He trained himself to listen to the voice of God that spoke to him from within everything that happened to him. Beyond all the commandments, he says, we are also commanded to listen for that voice, one that speaks to us always.

3 דבר אל בני ישראל ואמרת אליהם אדם כי יקריב מכם

"Speak to the Children of Israel and say to them: 'A person from among you who offers...'" (1:2). This section of *Va-Yikra*, about to be filled with ritual details about animal sacrifice and techniques of purification, begins with *adam*, a person. It is the full human being who feels a need to bring a *korban*, an "offering" that is also an act of "coming near." This book, intended to be read and studied mainly by priests, reminds them that they are not to act as mere religious functionaries, absorbed by getting right all the proper details of the rites they are to perform. They are called to remember that it is all about *adam*, real, whole persons, who need to draw near (*karov*), not just to make offerings (*korban*). The choice of that word here reflects that sense of simple and universal humanity. It recalls the opening of the Book of Chronicles, simply with the word *Adam.*

As this was important to deliver to *kohanim* as they opened their book of laws, so is it true for all those who stand in this sort of "priestly" role today. This begins with *kley kodesh*, religious leaders, but extends to healers of all sorts as well as others with whom people engage initially to resolve a specific "technical" problem. This may include lawyers, financial advisers, and a host of others. The person may be coming to you in the role of "client," seeking your professional help. But never let it be *merely* about that. There is a whole person there behind the question. Notice the person. The question is an opportunity to open a door. Often the question happens because the person asking is seeking a way to get that door open. It is always ***adam*** *ki yakriv*, "the ***person*** who appoaches."

4 ריח ניחוח לה'

"A pleasing aroma, for Y-H-W-H" (1:9, 13, 17). This formula concludes the description of each offering, whether a bullock, a lamb, or a bird. This causes RaSHI to quote the famous line "It is the same whether one gives a lot or a little, so long as one directs one's heart toward heaven (Berakhot 5b)."

But the phrase could also be translated "An aroma **pleasing to** Y-H-W-H." The Book of *Va-Yikra* is quite careful never to tell us that which is said so clearly after the sacrifice of Noah: "Y-H-W-H smelled the pleasant aroma" (Gen. 8:21). The phrasing here remains poised delicately between these two ways of understanding it. Is it something that pleases Y-H-W-H, or it is something pleasing (to us) that we offer in the name of Y-H-W-H?

Prayer is said to come "in place of sacrifice." Try applying the criterion of that same delicate poise to the offering of your lips that we call prayer.

5 וכל קרבן מנחתך במלח תמלח ולא תשבית מלח ברית אלוהיך

"Every gift offering should be salted. Do not omit salt, the covenant of your God, from any gift; add salt to every offering" (2:13). To what "covenant" does this refer? Is there indeed a "covenant of salt?" RaSHI tells us that it goes back to Creation. On the second day, God made the firmament and divided the waters. Because of that division, there is no "It was good" said of the second day. The lower waters (*mayim taḥtonim*), those of the ocean, were salty, while the upper waters, above the earth, were to be fresh. The lower waters wept, saying: "We too want to be near to our Creator!" This is an etiological tale, an explanation of **why tears are salty**. The world's first tears were those of the sea! God recognized the injustice done to the lower waters (like that done to the moon - another classic feminine symbol – in a famous Talmudic tale), and that is why He could not say that the day was "good." He then promised them that one day their time would come. Their salt would be offered on the altar; in that way they would indeed have a chance *le-hakriv*, "to come near."

Every human tear partakes of those original tears of the lower waters. The lowly of this world, the *taḥtonim*, all want a chance. They too want to be close to their Creator. Carry the salt of their tears with you in each offering you give in prayer.

But carry with you also the tears of the sea herself. How must she weep today, being treated by humanity like a huge garbage dump.

6 ואם כל עדת ישראל ישגו ונעלם דבר מעיני הקהל

"If the whole community of Israel errs, in a way hidden from the eyes of the assembly, and acts against one of the prohibitions of Y-H-W-H...the community shall offer a bull from the cattle..." (4:13).

Such an offering is called the *par he'elem davar*. It is good to know that such a prescription exists. We may need it, and for more than one sin of our "whole community." How about the sin just mentioned in the previous teaching? Can we offer a bull, a *par he'elem davar* for that one? How about some other things that we and the whole community of Israel have ignored, including things that have cost an awful lot of human lives? ***The list seems to be growing quickly these days.***

Let's hope there will be enough bulls.

צו
TZAV
(Leviticus 6:1-8:36)

1 זאת תורת העולה היא העולה

"This is the teaching about the rising up: it is *she* who rises" (6:2).

Here in *Sefer Va-Yikra* we are in the heart of Torah as a guide to the devotional life. We have only to learn to read it that way. A few hints that will already be familiar: The Tent of Meeting is our inner place, containing our Holy of Holies. The altar is that of the heart; the fire that burns on it is that of love and devotion.

In the days when sacrifices were the way of worship, it was clear that the fire on the altar seemed to rise, flames and smoke reaching upward. Altars were built on high places, in order to begin that rising from a point closer to the heavens. But here the phrasing hints that it is not the fire itself that rises. Devotion enables the soul – or *shekhinah* within us – to rise, joining to the One that is her Source.

That "rising" is part of the vertical axis on which the ancients saw the world constructed and the spiritual journey taking place. The fact that "ascent" has been understood metaphorically for a very long time has not diminished the power of its image. But we need to remember that there is an alternative metaphor within the tradition, one that may work better in our day: the journey is an ***inward*** one; we are being drawn into the Center, rather than up to the heights. It is ***she, the soul,*** who enters those deepest chambers of the "heaven" that lies within the heart. She goes through the courtyards of our inner Temple, passing through ever more intimate places, until she opens a pathway to unite with her Beloved, the One, the Heart of the World.

2 והוציא את הדשן אל מחוץ למחנה אל מקום טהור

"He shall take the ashes outside the camp, to a pure place" (6:4).

Daily devotion requires daily cleaning out of the ashes. Don't let yesterday's prayer or yesterday's failure to pray keep today's offering from being as fresh and new as though it were the first time you were praying. Even if the words are the same, the moment in which they are being offered is entirely new. That's the point! The Ba'al Shem Tov read the verse *Ḥadashim la-bekarim rabbah emunatekha* (Lam. 3:23) to mean "If it's new every morning, your faith is very great!"

This is not an easy task for those of us, including a great many within the community of religions who live within a liturgical tradition, where the prayers recited are indeed the same nearly every day. How, indeed, do we keep them fresh? The BeSHT also taught that part of the answer lies paradoxically in the distractions that come to us during prayer. They are there, he said, because they seek to uplifted, and that is an essential part of the service of prayer. The words may be the same each day, but the distractions are always different! Work ***with*** them to renew your prayer.

Be-khol yom averkheka, "Each day do I bless You," says the psalmist (145:2). ***By means of each day*** – along with its distractions – I offer blessings. Those are the thoughts that I raise up with me in my prayer.

3 במקום אשר תישחט העולה תישחט החטאת

"In the place where the rising-up offering is slaughtered, there too shall the sin-offering be slaughtered" (6:18).

The role of religion in purification or atonement for sin should not be denied. The same inner "place" from which we ascend to the heights – or to the inward depths – is also the place where we seek to be purified from the sense of contamination by the stains of daily living. This is a part of the spiritual path that we often seek to deny in our times. For good reason, we prefer to leave behind us the sort of religion that bred in us an excess of guilt, leaving us constantly in search of expiation. We want a teaching that liberates us from that cycle.

The religion of the Ba'al Shem Tov was precisely that: a Judaism that sought to lessen the burdens of guilt and remind us to serve Y-H-W-H in joy and wholeness of heart. Regret the sin, promise yourself you will not do it again, but then ***leave it behind you***, was his teaching.

It is the great trick of the Evil One, he said, to make you worry constantly about your sins and to allow this to keep you far from Y-H-W-H, a God of love and compassion.

But the verse here reminds us that the *'olah* and the *ḥata'at*, the "ascent" and the sin-offering, are two faces of the journey; they come from the same inner "place." We are wise not to deny the uncomfortable shadow side of our own spiritual quest.

4 והבשר – כל טהור יאכל בשר

"And the flesh – anyone pure may eat flesh" (7:19). This somewhat strangely written half-verse offers an opportunity to recall some of the Torah's deep ambivalence about consumption of animal flesh.

Humans were created, we will recall, to be vegetarian; we and the other ruminants were given the same plant food to consume, grasses of the field and the fruit of the trees (Gen. 1:30). Only after the flood was the consumption of flesh permitted, perhaps as a concession to the weakness of human nature. But these words, appearing in the middle of the instructions for such offerings, seem to leap off the animal-skin parchment on which they are written and ask us: "Are you pure enough to eat that which required the shedding of blood?

5 ויקח משה משמן המשחה ומן הדם אשר על המזבח ויז על אהרון על בגדיו ועל בניו ועל בגדי בניו אתו

"Moses took of the anointing oil and the blood that was upon the altar. He sprinkled it upon Aaron and upon his garments and upon his sons and their garments, along with him" (8:30). This is the climax of the complex and impressive ceremony that installed Aaron and his sons as priests, alongside the dedication of the tabernacle and the altar. The mixture of oil and blood is found only here. The priests and all their lovely new garments were now immediately to be streaked with oil and blood. What does this mean? If you strive to be a "holy person," you have to recognize these twin dimensions of your role. The oil represents the flow from above, the holy light by which you may be blessed and convey blessing to others. But the blood is there to remind you that you exist to serve mortals, people who are always worried about issues of blood and mortality. Remember that "the blood is the soul" – for humans as well.

שמיני
SHEMINI
(Leviticus 9:1-11:47)

1 ויאמר משה זה הדבר אשר צוה ה' וירא אליכם כבוד ה'

"Moses said: This is the thing Y-H-W-H has commanded that you do, and the glory of Y-H-W-H will appear upon you" (9:6).

The language appears frighteningly formulaic. God commanded Moses to bring the sacrifice to ***celebrate*** the appearance of the glory. But Moses turned it around. "Do this thing in the precisely correct way and Y-H-W-H will appear." Perhaps Aaron's two sons were protesting the transformation of this great spiritual moment into magic.

The tradition struggles mightily with the reason for the death of Nadav and Avihu. Most of the early rabbinic sources seem interested in finding a sin to attribute to them, certain that their deaths were a punishment. But the Kabbalistic and Hasidic sources always see them as spiritual heroes, dying became they came too close to God. This follows the account below in *Parashat Aḥarey Mot* (Lev. 16:1): "as they came close to Y-H-W-H and died." The fire that consumed them from within was the intensity of their own passion.

Nadav and Avihu represent the younger generation. They are not ready to accept any "This is the thing" formula, one that felt to them too conventional and automatic. In their enthusiasm, they want to add something of their own, to do it in a new way. The "alien fire" was that of their own enthusiasm.

What, then, are to learn from their deaths? That one may not change anything? That we must follow the rules exactly as written, or as dictated by the previous generation?

No! Just the opposite! It was because Nadav and Avihu were so holy, even **greater** than Moses and Aaron, according to legend, that they were the chosen sacrifice. The altar was made holy, not polluted, by their deaths. From this we learn that the true fire of the sacrifice

– and of prayer and Jewish living that take their place – is that of the human heart.

2 ויבוא משה ואהרן אל אהל מועד ויצאו ויברכו את העם

"Moses and Aaron came to the Tent of Meeting. They went out and blessed the people, and the glory of Y-H-W-H appeared to all the people" (9:23). In the end, it was not the complex order of sacrifices that brought about the appearance of Y-H-W-H, and not the tragic death of Aaron's sons, but the act of blessing. Moses/Aaron (note the singular verb!) ***went out*** to the people and blessed them. It was their willingness to take the blessing of God's presence they had experienced inside the tent and bring it out to the people that brought forth the glory of Y-H-W-H. This was the moment in which it happened.

Where is the presence of Y-H-W-H to be seen? ***In the act of blessing***, in our willingness to pass on to others the blessings we have received.

3 ויאמר ה׳ אל משה יין ושכר אל תשת אתה ובניך...ולהבדיל בין הקדש ובין
החול ובין הטמא ובין הטהור

"Y-H-W-H said to Aaron: Wine and liquor you shall not drink, neither you nor your children, as you come into the Tent of Meeting… to distinguish between the holy and the profane, the defiled and the pure" (10:8-10).

The placing of these verses right after the deaths of Nadav and Avihu has led some to say that they were drunk when they went in to serve; that was their "alien fire." Others have vigorously denied this, painting them as passionate devotees who just came too close. In any case, the premium placed on priestly sobriety in the face of this event is striking.

The role of priesthood is one of serving both God and people, helping to bring them closer to one another. There is much power in that sacred role, and with it comes great responsibility. Sobriety is needed for the respecting of borders, for knowing which lines not to cross. Sadly, we have seen it too often violated, in all our religious communities. I, too, have been guilty of that.

There is much talk now about the rediscovery of much more powerful substances than wine and their use in a sacred context. They may indeed be of much value in opening our hearts and minds to "the appearance of Y-H-W-H." But this priestly warning needs to stand.

4 ואת שעיר החטאת דרוש דרש משה והנה שורף ויקצוף על אלעזר ואיתמר
בני אהרן הנותרים לאמר מדוע לא אכלתם את החטאת...וידבר אהרן אל
משה...אכלתי חטאת היום הייטב בעיני ה'.

"Moses sought out the atonement goat and it had been burned up. He became angry with Eleazar and Itamar, the remaining sons of Aaron, saying 'Why did you not eat of it?'... Aaron said to Moses...'I ate of the atonement offering. Does that suffice for Y-H-W-H?'" (10:16-19)

Here is a moment of tension between the brothers. Aaron had been silent when his two elder sons were consumed by fire. But now he sees Moses angry at the two others, because they did not eat as instructed. Perhaps they were just not ready to eat after having seen their brothers die! Now Aaron, ever the man of peace, stands up to his brother and says: ***"Enough of your angry God!"*** And Moses backs down.

5 זאת החיה אשר תאכלו

"These are the living things you may eat, among all the beasts that are upon the earth" (11:2).

The middle section of this Book of *Va-Yikra* defines the parameters of Israel's priestly community around restrictions of food and sex. The care taken about eating betokens the sense that all of Israel are indeed "a kingdom of priests" (Ex. 19:6), as was said at Mount Sinai, and these once-priestly restrictions were taken on by all. Ancient Roman writers already accused Jews of being misanthropes because they refused to share in the meals of others.

These food restrictions, and their extension through many generations of rabbinic tradition, are not an easy element for contemporary Jews, living in an open and mixed society. The pleasures of the palate are highly valued in our day, and partaking of cuisines from around the globe is taken as a sign of sophistication and worldliness. To clamp down on that possibility feels like a needless restriction of life's pleasures.

It also just happens, however, that wanton over-consumption is the great sin of our age. ***We,*** the small but privileged percentile of humanity, are laying waste to the world's resources at a pace that threatens to destroy us all. It is clear, in any case, that the least privileged of the human community will be the first to suffer, as is already taking place. The ability of people like us to say "No" to ourselves, to limit our intake, may be the most urgent *mitsvah* of our day.

This is not just about food, of course. But eating is such a basic and powerfully symbolic realm that it makes sense to set the example there. Do the restrictions on our food consumption need to be the same ones that our Torah prescribes? Not necessarily. The same sensitivities that led our ancestors to forbid the eating of blood, or mixing milk and meat, may be there in the large movement toward vegetarianism in our day. Perhaps that is the new *kashrut* that should emerge for a contemporary Judaism. Partial steps toward it, like the avoidance of red meat, also make much sense in an environmentalist spirituality. So too should we reconsider those lovely blueberries or pineapples in mid-winter, if they are shipped all the way from Peru or Hawaii.

A serious Judaism without the element of *kashrut*, raising questions about what food is permitted, is unimaginable. But the nature of those questions may be evolving in our day. Perhaps this will even involve new stringencies, rather than just the loosening of restrictions.

תזריע-מצורע
TAZRI'A / METSORA'
(Leviticus 12:1-13:59) (Leviticus 14:1-15:33)

Introduction to *Tazria* and *Metzora*: It is hard to know what to write about these sections. Our distance from the simple meaning and context here seems to dwarf any attempt at midrash. The Hasidic reading saved *Tazria/Metzora* by posing the *tsaddik* as priest, seeing into the heart's afflictions, hidden behind those of the skin. In itself, this too is hard for us. But perhaps it points a way.

All of us who read these words are survivors. We have lived together through terrible years of a worldwide plague. Many of us lost people we loved or cared about. Readers beyond a certain age are also likely to see themselves as survivors of various other events in the course of our lives: cancers, road accidents, wars, addictions, and lots more sorts of plagues. In the course of this, we have all sought out healers, whether professionals, spouses, or friends. Is there any wisdom for healers or for those needing to be healed (that includes all of us, of course) that might be found in these very obscure chapters of *Va-Yikra*? Let's try.

1 וראה הכהן את הנגע בעור הבשר ושער בנגע הפך לבן ומראה הנגע עמוק
מעור בשרו נגע צרעת הוא וראהו הכהן וטמא אותו

"The *kohen* (read: "healer") shall look at the affliction in the skin of the flesh. Has its hair turned white? Does it appear deeper than a flesh-wound? If so, it is *tsara'at*, (= *'et tsar*, 'a time of woe).' Look at the person and declare it defiling" (13:3).

Dealing with a person in pain requires two sorts of perception, specific and global. Look at the wound itself. Try to see how deep it is. Is it transformative in the person's life? Is it turning her/his hair white (literally or metaphorically)? Does it go deep? Can you be of help in lessening the depth of its effect? This question is one for the counsellor, lover, or friend, as it is for the oncologist or emergency physician. Can I help to keep it from spreading?

But then the verb *ra'ah*, seeing or looking, is repeated at the end of the verse. Look again "See him/her" – this time at the whole person. ***That*** is the one you are seeking to heal.

Now ask yourself that same set of questions about your own wound and your own process of healing. How deep does it go? How can I keep it from spreading, from taking over all of me as a person? Can I heal it, or must I learn to live with it? Or are those the same?

2 ואם בהרת לבנה היא בעור בשרו ועמוק אין מראה מן העור...והסגיר הכהן את הנגע שבעת ימים

"If it is a white spot on the surface of the skin, not appearing to have gone deeper, its hair not turning white, the healer should shut it down for seven days" (13:4).

Sometimes you will see that it is not as bad as you had feared. Then your job is to let the sufferer (or yourself) in on that secret. There is great value in calming the nerves, giving it a cooling-off period. That in itself can be a great step forward. Check in again after a week – or as many days as the situation calls for.

3 צרעת נושנת היא בעור בשרו

"It is *tsara'at noshenet*, 'an old affliction' in the skin of the person's flesh. The *kohen* shall declare it defiling. Do not shut it down; it is truly defiling" (13:11). Recurrence, as we know, can be dangerous – in all sorts of afflictions. If you are called in again as a healer, supporter, or friend, over an ailment you have already seen previously, do not be dismissive. This may indeed be *tsara'at*, "a time of woe." Take the cry seriously.

4 או בשר כי יהיה בעורו מכות אש...וראה אותה הכהן

"If a person has a burn by fire in the skin...the *kohen* shall look

at it. Has the hair turned white in it? Is it deeper than the skin?" (13:24-25)

Here we are talking about an affliction that comes from without, a burn by fire. Let us see it as referring to any sort of wound that has come about due to some external event. Today we call this trauma. Here the healer has to take on something of the role of a burn unit physician. How seriously has this person been "burned?" Is this second or third degree damage to the skin? Or does the hurt dwell in some subtle place in between, one that defies categorization? The healer has to look – perhaps "looking" has to be expanded to ***listening*** – carefully before deciding how to go about helping to heal. There are cases when the healer will then be able to move forward, doing or prescribing something that will help. But there are also cases when that *ve-ra'ahu ha-kohen*, "the healer sees – or hears – the person," is itself a great act of healing. That "seeing" may be all you can do, but in itself it can be a lot.

5 זאת תהיה תורת המצורע ביום טהרתו...ולקח למטהר שתי ציפרים

"This teaching is about the afflicted person on the day of her/his purification…. The *kohen* shall go outside the camp to look. Behold! The wound of affliction has been healed from the afflicted one. The *kohen* shall command that two pure live birds be brought for the one becoming pure, along with cedar wood, scarlet, and hyssop" (14:2-4).

The completion of healing, of announcing and celebrating recovery, is fully a part of the healing process. This moment of being welcomed "back into the camp" is one in which the ancient *kohen* knew exactly what to do, while today's healers, as well as those who are healing, often struggle to find their place within it. But the healer – including the physician – is still needed here, in order to complete the process.

Ritual can play a vital role in this moment. We do not have two prescribed "birds" to offer; words and gestures have to take their place. But the ceremonial quality of this occasion should not be ignored. Orchestrating such a ritual event, involving the healing one plus family and friends in the process, is a skill that today's *kohen* should be able to offer. Like all rituals, it will be more powerful if it contains echoes of antiquity. Here, perhaps, something of our *parashah* might be brought to life again.

אחרי מות
AḤAREI MOT
(Leviticus 16:1-18:30)

1 אחרי מות שני בני אהרן...ואל יבוא בכל עת אל הקדש...כי בענן אראה על
הכפורת

"After the death of the two sons of Aaron...Let him not come at any time into the Holy...and not die, for I appear in a cloud above the ark-cover" (16:1-2). Here, Y-H-W-H warns Aaron against the dangers of coming too close to Y-H-W-H! God is well aware of how dangerous it can be for a person to come too close. This is parallel to the warning given to the people to stay back at Mount Sinai, lest "Y-H-W-H break out among them" (Ex. 19:22), tellingly spoken in the third person. It gives the impression that God is not in control of all of God's own powers. The God of revelation, who seeks to be present and dwell in Israel's midst, is also aware of how dangerous that presence can be. He too has learned from the deaths of Aaron's sons.

What is it that takes place in the divine "personality" in such moments? Why should the desired intimacy turn fatal? The Torah is well aware of the inner rage and fury within Y-H-W-H that sometimes overflow beyond control. We know that wild fury within nature – in tsunamis, earthquakes, and diseases. But why should human closeness awaken it?

We have to turn the question back toward ourselves and ask why we depict Y-H-W-H in that way. We understand that the same wondrous and mysterious power that gave us life will also swallow us up someday. That is the nature of the human condition. But we want to approach it closely to know its secret, which is also the secret of who we are. "Know from where you came and where you are going" – and thus what you are supposed to do between those two. But we are also afraid of it. We do not want yet to be swallowed up, but to live.

All this comes to a head on Yom Kippur. We enter deep into our inner *mishkan* in order to do the work of purification. To accomplish that, we need to come very close to the Great Fire – as close as we can. Hopefully we come forth from that place as did the ***kohen*** in emerging from the Holy of Holies, with a shining face. "The whole house of Israel has been forgiven!" – and we go on to live another year.

2 ונתן את הקטורת על האש לפני ה׳ וכסה ענן הקטורת את הכפורת

"He shall place the incense on the fire before Y-H-W-H. The cloud of incense-smoke will hide the cover that is over the testimony, and he will not die" (16:13). There is some confusion about the "cloud" in this chapter. In verse 2, quoted above, it appears that Y-H-W-H is present in a cloud over the ark, and that is why entry to the Holy of Holies is forbidden. But now the cloud seems to be created by the *kohen*, and it is the cloud that protects him. Could one cloud be protecting him from the other?

The cloud represents the mystery in which divine presence is always shrouded, except, perhaps, in rare moments of grace. We know there is "something there," but we cannot grab hold of it by any definition; it remains a "cloud," hovering over our lives. The forms of religion, mysterious in themselves, are also a cloud; they are our "cloud of incense." We surround ourselves in them, creating a safe opening into that cloudy presence of Y-H-W-H. The two clouds silently flow together, as is the way of clouds.

The One who was in ancient times depicted as *yoshev ha-keruvim*, "seated upon the cherubim" (II Kings 19:16) that were carved above the ark, now comes to be *yoshev tehillot yisra'el* (Ps. 22:4), "seated amid the praises of Israel." **The merging of our cloud and the divine cloud allow for moments like "Moses entered into the cloud"** (Ex. 24:18).

The cloud of ritual and verbal prayer, of which there is so very much on Yom Kippur, serves as a way of bringing us into the greater cloud, in which the One is present. Cloud merges with cloud.

3 וסמך אהרן את שתי ידיו על ראש השעיר החי והתוודה עליו...ושלח ביד איש עתי המדברה...ושלח את השעיר במדבר

"Aaron shall lay his hands on the living goat's head, confessing all the sins...and release it into the hands of a man who happens by,

into the wilderness. The goat will carry all their sins into a forbidden land, and he shall release it in the wilderness" (16:21-22).

A strange moment, indeed. *Ish 'itti* is an unclear phrase, perhaps to be translated "the man of the hour." The Targum renders it by a term that could mean either "someone prepared" or "a passer-by." I prefer the latter thought. ***Anyone*** could do this. Since the goat bears ***all*** of our sins, we are collectively responsible. So any one of us could represent the whole.

Once out there in *erets gezerah*, another odd phrase (Land of Evil Decrees? A cut-off place?), he is to let the goat go. But what happens if the goat refuses to leave him, following him right back home? The goat, after all, is a domesticated animal. Maybe that's why the rabbis changed the practice here. Instead of just releasing the goat into the wilderness, they had this *ish 'itti* push him off a cliff. This change seems to say the sin is liable to wander back unless you destroy it utterly, hearing its bones break on the rocks beneath that cliff.

What do we do to translate all of this into the psychological language of expiating both sin and guilt? Yom Kippur is about both of these. We want to change the behavior, usually something self-destructive or harmful to others, especially those we love. But we also want to relieve ourselves of the torment of failure and guilt. It is important to work on both of these together. This will require working to transform the guilt, using it to see the truth of our sins or "mess ups" and their consequences. To "push them off the cliff" means to work with root causes, not just symptoms, as well as making amends with those we have harmed.

Ultimately, this is not a one-day process. Yom Kippur, or any such ritual, may set us on the path. That in itself can be a big step forward. But it is only the beginning.

4 את משפטי תעשו ואת חוקותי תשמרו ללכת בהם... אשר יעשה אותם האדם וחי בהם אני ה'

"Perform My judgments and keep My statutes, walking in them... the person who does them lives in them. I am Y-H-W-H" (18:4-5). *Mishpatim* or "judgments," are traditionally taken to refer to rationally comprehensible commandment, behaviors needed to maintain the social order. *Ḥukkim* or "statutes" are mysterious; there seems to be no rational reason to do them. These are, in effect, ritual practices.

Hasidic tradition, according to *Degel Maḥaneh Ephraim* on this verse, says that the *mishpatim* protect the outer levels of the self as well as the community. *Nefesh, ruah*, and *neshamah*, the three outer levels of the soul, correspond to our deeds, our words, and our thoughts, three level of conscious activity in the world. The innermost levels of soul (*ḥayah* and *yeḥidah*), those of which we ourselves are often unaware, are given life, nourished, sustained, and healed by the mysterious *ḥukkim*.

They understood something profound about the power of ritual and its ability to nourish the subconscious levels of the human mind. *Ḥukkim* or rituals are addressed to the subconscious, the world of myths, symbols, and dreams. Hence, they speak in its language. We cannot understand them rationally, but we respond to them deeply from within.

The Degel's nephew, Rabbi Nahman of Bratslav, understood this well and built his entire teaching around it. His teachings, and even more so his tales, were addressed to those deeper levels of the human mind and soul.

5 ואת זכר לא תשכב משכבי אשה

"With a man you shall not lie the lying of a woman" (18:22). There is no question that the text says that. But for those of us who recognize the possibility of real love and real lovemaking between persons of the same gender, such a reading is impossible. It would contradict our understanding of the *klal gadol*, the most basic principle of Torah: that every human being is created in the image of God (the view of Ben Azzai in a famous debate with Rabbi Akiva). This has to include the physical expression of their love. That *klal gadol* is meant to define Torah's ultimate message. Nothing in the Torah may contradict or undermine it. If it does, we need to reinterpret.

To recognize that a person is the image of God is to accept him/her as s/he is. The "image of God" includes embrace of the endless differences among humans. "Behold the greatness of God: Every human being is stamped with the image of Adam, and none is like another!" Since love, and the ability to express love in sexuality, is an essential part of our humanity, acceptance means the embrace of a variety of sexual and gender self-definitions. Not because it is the popular view in contemporary liberal society – but because **we may exclude no one from *tselem Elohim***, and the degradation of a person's act of love leads to such dehumanization.

This means acceptance of ourselves, as well as others, as different and unique. Loving partnership, including both sexual expression and responsibility for one's partner, has always been a value in our tradition. "It is not good for a person to be alone" (Gen. 2:18). We believe in family, and the acceptance of multiple forms of relationship leads to stable families in parts of society to whom that right was long denied. Today we understand gender and the varieties of gender attraction in ways the ancients did not, and the *klal gadol* of allowing for, recognizing, and celebrating the full divine humanity of each person leads us to different conclusions.

Then what of the verse? Here, as in several other places in Torah, the *klal gadol* forces us to *midrash*, that which these readings reflect everywhere else as well. The difference is that here we are forced to do so by the ***moral impossibility*** of the *peshat*. In this case, perhaps the text is saying: Know who your partner is; do not transform him/her into another gender – or another person – in your imagination. Do not, in your imagination, expect your partner to become or act like the other gender just because you are sleeping with him/her. A loving relationship between two men or two women is not the same as one between a woman and a man and should not be forced into that box. ***Knowing***, in the biblical sense, also means recognizing your partner for who she or he really is. Allow him or her the right to define themselves, rather than meeting your need or expectation.

6 אל תטמאו בכל אלה כי בכל אלה נטמאו הגויים אשר אני משלח מפניכם

"Do not be defiled by all these [deeds], as were the nations I sent out before you" (18:24). These terrible verses, notably repeated for emphasis in the text, rightly cause us to shudder. But we cannot pass over them without noting that there is indeed such a thing as sexual degradation or defilement, diminishing the image of God in those who engage in them as well as in those who are often sexually "used" in such situations. The Torah wants to remind us of this. ***The act of love, as the Kabbalists so well understood, is a physical act that is also the embodiment of divine mystery.*** It must be done in a way that honors that truth, in the context of a love that enhances the sense of divine image in both oneself and the other.

We live amid a wildly oversexed culture. Today it is the media of popular culture that constitute the "nations" amid whom we dwell. Fantasy, sexual "conquest," violent sex, and adventurism of all sorts are stimulated and endlessly flood so easily into our consciousness. The detachment of sexuality from love, relationship, and responsibility, is rampant. While our categories of what is defiling or degrading are very different than those of the ancient text, it is worth remembering that we do indeed have a strong commitment to values in this regard. Our teaching calls for self-limitation in this vital area of life. A sexual relationship is called a "***knowing***." We have no right to *know* a person only in this way, without *knowing* and caring about who they are, what their needs are, whether they also want to "know" us in these ways, and lots more.

Sexuality is a divine gift. It is given to us to help stimulate feelings of true love within us. That love also contains the love of Y-H-W-H and all of God's creatures. Without all that, it is a shallow imitation.

קדושים
KEDOSHIM
(Leviticus 19:1-20:27)

1 קדושים תהיו כי קדוש אני ה' אלוהיכם

"You shall be holy, for I Y-H-W-H your God am holy (19:2). The commentators have long struggled with this verse. What is the relationship implied here between God's holiness and that expected of us? Is the verse a commandment that we be holy? Can one really command holiness, and what would that mean? That is why many of the Hasidic authors choose to read it not as a commandment, rather as a declaration ***that we are already*** – at least potentially – holy.

Each human being, as a living image of God, is a unique embodiment of divinity; "the soul is part of God above." "***Your*** God" here, as in many readings of *eloheynu*, "***our*** God," in the *Shema'*, is the One present in the human heart. "There is a holy one within you," says the prophet (Hos. 11:9). We are called to a life of holiness because we contain that presence. Discovering it, and fashioning a life in response to it, is our *'avodat ha-kodesh*, our "holy work."

That One calls out to us to protect its holiness. The verse may be read ***more as a plea from within than as a commandment from on high***. In the poignant words of R. Mordechai Yosef of Izbica, the divine soul within you cries out "Wherever you go, I go with you. Please do not take Me to defiled places." It hurts Me too much when we go there.

2 אל תפנו אל האלילים ואלוהי מסכה לא תעשו לכם

"Do not turn to worthless idols, and do not make yourselves gods who mask; I am Y-H-W-H your God" (19:4). Here I choose an original meaning of *elil,* "idol" or "false god," and a later usage of the word *masekhah*, rendering it as "mask," rather than as "molten."

From its biblical origins, Judaism has always been a counterculture. We stood against what we saw as *elilim*, the "false" or worthless gods of the nations amid whom we lived, speaking in the name of a higher and often elusive One, bearer of a name that was hardly a name at all, a word that could not be spoken. If we take *masekhah* as "mask," it becomes an interesting parallel to *elil.* A "masked god" is one that is ***only*** a mask, one with nothing behind it.

But we too believe in a "god who hides." The game of hide-and-seek that lies at the heart of our religious life is sometimes complicated. Our faith is in a hidden God, yet one who is revealed to us everywhere, as we learn to open our eyes to the Presence. What, then, is the mask? It is always there and always ready to be seen through. ***Sometimes masks are there to enable you to see that which would not be visible without them.*** Think of Moses' mask after he descended from the mountain.

Today we all know more about masks than we ever thought we would. We now understand that the intent of a mask can sometimes be precisely the opposite of hiding: to allow us to come close to one who otherwise would have to keep far away. Without our masks, when they are needed, we could not even be together. The same may be true of our relationship with Y-H-W-H.

3 וכי תזבחו זבח שלמים לה׳ לרצונכם תזבחו

"When you offer whole animal sacrifices to Y-H-W-H, you do so as you will" (19:5). This is a rather surprising admission in the middle of *Sefer Va-Yikra*, so concerned with all the rules of proper sacrifice. We can hear an echo in it of what the prophets will say so clearly: it is ***for your sake*** that sacrifices are offered, not Mine. The sacrifices are to fulfill your needs, not those of God.

But the verse can also be read in a completely different (and more typically Hasidic) way: "In order to make a whole offering to Y-H-W-H, you must sacrifice your own desire." Truly giving to Y-H-W-H, *shelamim* and *shelemut*, wholeness, requires giving up our own will. "Negate your will before His" says an early rabbinic adage. A life of spiritual devotion demands submission. This has been difficult for devotees in all times and places, but it is a particular challenge for the seeker in our age, one that so values independence and individuality. "Slaughter your will!" is sometimes as hard a commandment for us as were the words that Abraham heard on Mount Moriah.

But if we say *tefillah bi-mekom korban*, that our verbal prayers take the place of sacrifices, what is the message that comes along with it? True prayer is for the sake of *shekhinah*, the divine presence that peers out at us from within each creature. She longs for us to hear her cry, that of the needs of each of those creatures. But we cannot hear that faint voice if we are still busy listening to the much louder voice of our own needs and desires.

4 לעני ולגר תעזוב אותם אני ה׳ אלוהיכם

"Leave them for the poor and the stranger; I am Y-H-W-H your God" (19:10). The great power of this chapter is the frequent and dramatic repetition of "I am Y-H-W-H." This refrain of God's name is particularly striking in its placement at the center of the priestly book of *Va-Yikra*. We did not find it in this repeated form in description of any of the sacrifices, not amid the lists of forbidden foods, nor regarding the sexual taboos. Notably, it happens repeatedly amid these ethical and interpersonal commandments, culminating in "Love your neighbor as yourself; I am Y-H-W-H" (19:18).

Think of this as a form of emphasis. The repetition of ***ani Y-H-W-H*** is a divine statement that ***these*** are the commandments by which I am truly to be known, in which I am most fully present. Or you may see it as an ancient scribe's form of underlining or boldfacing. This is what Torah, "the teaching," ***really*** comes to teach. No wonder that Rabbi Akiva, one of Scripture's most careful readers of all time, was able to say that "Love your neighbor as yourself" is ***the most basic teaching of Torah***. He understood the special emphasis that this ***ani Y-H-W-H*** gave to that commandment. No wonder also that R. Yitsḥak Luria, the greatest master of prayer among the Kabbalists, opened his morning prayers each day by saying "I hereby accept upon myself the positive commandment of 'Love your neighbor as yourself.'" He too ***heard*** that emphasis in the text, the sense that "***This is what Torah is all about.***"

5 לא תעשוק את רעך ולא תגזול. לא תלין פעולת שכיר אתך עד בקר

"You shall not oppress your neighbor, nor cheat, nor delay overnight paying the wage of one you hire" (19:13). "You shall not oppress" is a very broad prohibition. The Talmud has various opinions about whether the rest of the verse is meant to define it or to add to it.

In our day, when the market system of which we are consumers is so complex and universal, it seems ever harder to observe these commandments. Unless we grow our own food and sew our own garments, everything we consume is likely to be the result of *'oshek*, whether coming to us from industrialized farms in South America or sweatshop garment factories in southeast Asia.

The conscience implanted within us by these verses causes us to seek ways to compensate. We raise our level of *tsedakah* for the poor, we support unions and sign petitions to raise minimum wages, to demand equal pay for all, and more. But it is never enough.

6 לא תחלל את בתך להזנותה ולא תזנה הארץ ומלאה הארץ זמה

"Do not desecrate your daughter by leading her into prostitution, nor may you let the land be prostituted, lest it fill up with wickedness" (19:29). The land on which you live is as much a gift to you as is a child. Treat it with love and respect, as you would treat your daughter. Otherwise, it will fill up with ***zimah,*** a powerful word that combines wickedness, corruption, and pollution.

U-male'ah ha-arets zimah, ***the land filled with wickedness***, stands in contrast to the prophet's familiar *melo khol ha-arets kevodo*, ***"the world filled with God's glory***." Which one it is filled with is up to us.

אמור
EMOR
(Leviticus 21:1-24:23)

1 אמור אל הכוהנים בני אהרון ואמרת אליהם לנפש: לא יטמא בעמיו.

"Speak to the priests, children of Aaron. Say to them, addressing their soul: "Do not become defiled within your people" (21:1). Rabbi Jacob Joseph of Polonnoye, the first published author of Hasidism, spent a great deal of effort on a social analysis of the Jewish people in his day. What was the problem with Jews? Why are so far from actually living the spiritual lives they seem to believe in? Had disengaged or corrupt leaders allowed them to go astray? Or had the leaders themselves been corrupted by the people whom they led? In the end, he decided that both were true. Partly because he himself was a *kohen*, he strongly identified rabbis and scholars with the priests of *Sefer Va-Yikra*, as we have already seen.

In his spirit, we may hear the Torah calling out to leaders, speaking to their souls. "Remember who you are! Remember the ideals that brought you to a life of service to Y-H-W-H, to Torah, and to the Jewish people. Do not let yourself become corrupted by the worst values found among some of those you serve. You are to be a beacon of moral conduct and faithfulness. Do not let its light be diminished by anything you do."

At the same time, do not use "the people" as an excuse to cover up your own failings. Your job is to lead, not to follow. You know how much goodness and desire to learn there is in those you teach. You have been given a great privilege in teaching them. You need the strength to always do it in purity.

2 שור או כשב או עז כי יוולד והיה שבעת ימים תחת אמו...ושור או שה אותו ואת בנו לא תשחטו ביום אחד

"When an ox, a lamb, or a kid is born, it shall stay beneath its

mother for seven days. From the eighth day onward it is fit to be offered as a fire-offering to Y-H-W-H. An ox or a lamb and its offspring you must not slaughter on the same day" (22:27-28). These verses, reflecting a degree of humanity that has to be applied even with regard to animal slaughter, cry out with a special poignancy to any Jew living after the Holocaust. Our mind's eye cannot escape horrible images of these rules being violated, but with regard to human beings. The second verse, written in the male gender (although the *halakhah* strangely changes it to applying only to mothers), calls to this reader's mind Elie Wiesel's accounts of being in Auschwitz together with his father.

How do you pass the caring for the lives and suffering of others, animal as well as human, from one generation to the next? I once heard a senior colleague, Reb Ya'akov Riemer, say that Jewish children learned this more from their mothers checking each egg in the kitchen for bloodspots than they did from long sermons about "Thou shalt not murder."

3 אלה מועדי ה׳ אשר תקראו אותם מקראי קדש אלה הם מועדי

"These are the appointed seasons of Y-H-W-H. You shall call them forth as holy callings; these are My seasons" (23:2, 37). The grand language of this announcement frames the Torah's best-known listing of the festival cycle, at its beginning and its end. This passage also serves as the Torah reading for many of the holidays. It immediately combines the divine and human elements in the fixing of sacred times. They are indeed "My" seasons, but you are to "call" them. The calendar is fixed by the court, originally based on reports of the appearance of the new moon.

The Zohar (3:94a) reads *tikre'u* ("call") as meaning "invite;" the sacred seasons are holy guests that have come to visit us. We prepare a feast in their honor and invite them to join us in it, just as we would for honored and beloved guests. But some of the Hasidic sources read it just the opposite way. They read *mikra'ey kodesh* as "holy callings." The festivals ***call out to us*** to rise into their holiness.

Our relationship with the festival seasons is indeed a mutual one. Each time of year calls us to a special sort of holiness, brings forth from us a *kavvanah*, an inner intent, that can only be expressed through them. Each festival has a special spirit, carried by its description in the Torah, by its prayers, by the aroma of holiday foods, but also by the memories built up in us of all the previous times we have celebrated it and the people with whom we shared it. All of these call out to us. But we also call to the festivals themselves, anticipate their coming, prepare for them, welcome them as guests into our homes and hearts.

4 כי תבואו אל הארץ אשר אני נותן לכם וקצרתם את קצירה והבאתם את עמר ראשית קצירכם אל הכהן

"When you come into the land I am giving you and reap its reaping, you shall bring an *'omer* measure of that first cutting to the priest" (23:10). This ancient offering and the ceremony around it, as well as that taking place fifty days afterward, anticipating the coming harvest, is lost to post-biblical Judaism. It survives only in the form of counting the *'omer* days, now understood in an entirely different context. There were some attempts to revive it in the secular kibbutzim, but these worked only in agricultural settings.

But think of how closely it bound the farmer's work and acts of giving. Suppose we were to imagine applying it to our own lives. The first paycheck of a new job requires a gift to *tzedakah*, a token of gratitude. Fifty days into that new job is a time of checking in. If it is going well, a celebration is in order, and another expression of thanksgiving. Note that on that fiftieth day the grain offering comes in the form of *ḥamets*, a baked and risen loaf (23:17). This is the only place where *ḥamets* is explicitly prescribed for an offering. It seems to anticipate how rich and "risen" the coming grain harvest is likely to be. It is a way of giving blessing to the harvest yet to come.

Might we find a way to re-create these rites in the lives of both individuals and communities?

5 אך בעשור לחודש השביעי יום הכפורים הוא מקרא קדש יהיה לכם ועניתם את נפשותיכם

"Note well: The tenth day of the seventh month is a day of

atonements; it shall be a holy calling for you. You shall afflict yourselves and bring a fire-offering to Y-H-W-H" (23:27).

The word *ve-'initem*, traditionally translated "afflict," is an intensive form of *'-n-h*, to answer or respond. It is also the source of *ta'anit*, "fast." Thus, it might also imply: Do that which makes you ***responsive*** to the call.

Yom Kippur, as we observe it, is so very ritualized, filled with lengthy prayers and repeated alphabetical lists of sins. Perhaps it is time to liberate ourselves from some of those, choosing forms of *ta'anit*, along with fasting, that will better call forth that quality of responsiveness. Remember that Yom Kippur is a day that brings forgiveness and healing as we return to Y-H-W-H. The mystical tradition sees it as a day of joyous celebration of that forgiving. God as loving and embracing Mother (*binah*) appears, triumphing over the forces of judgment, announcing that atonement has been granted to all Her children, and thus a new year may begin. But we cannot open ourselves to that healing message so long as we are burdened with guilt for our past inadequacies.

A new Yom Kippur, a day of fasting and joy, should center around the *'Avodah* service, recounting the ancient Temple rite, climaxing in the High Priest's radiant countenance as he emerged from the Holy of Holies, bathed in divine light. As inspiration for such a Yom Kippur, we turn to a description in the Zohar (3:67a), in Daniel Matt's beautiful translation:

> He enters the place that he enters, and hears the sound of the wings of the cherubim – singing and fluttering their wings, spreading them above. The sound of their wings subsides, and in silence they cleave together.
>
> If the priest is worthy that those above are in a state of joy, so too at that moment issues a rapturous light, scented with mountains of pure balsam above, and it spreads through that place…
>
> The Priest opens his mouth in prayer, fervently, joyously…Then the priest knows that it is a time of favor, of joy for all, and the people know, as is written

"If your sins are like crimson, they will become white as snow (Is. 1:18)..."

Happy is the share of the priest, for through him there is joy upon joy on that day, above and below. Of that moment it is written: "Happy is the people that have it so; happy is the people whose God is Y-H-W-H (Ps. 144:15)!"

6 צו את בני ישראל ויקחו אליך שמן זית זך כתית למאור להעלות נר תמיד... ולקחת סולת ואפית אותה שתים עשרה חלות...ביום השבת ביום השבת יערכנו לפני ה' תמיד".

"Command the Children of Israel to take pure olive oil, beaten for lighting, raising up a constant light.... Take fine flour and bake it into twelves loaves (*hallot*).... On each shabbat set it out before Y-H-W-H, forever, an everlasting covenant by the Children of Israel" (24:2,5,8). This description of the service in the *mishkan* and the Temple is subtly reflected in what becomes the holiness of the shabbat table in every Jewish home. The notion that "one's table is like an altar" is deeply rooted within the tradition. It may be said that the transfer of the locus of holiness from the Temple to the synagogue and the *bet midrash*, but especially to the home, lies at the very heart of rabbinic Judaism. Perhaps unconsciously, this chapter's combination of the lighting of lamps (or candles) and the setting out of loaves, still called *hallot*, sets the scene for the ideal shabbat picture of the Jewish home as a holy place.

בהר
BE-HAR
(Leviticus 25:1-26:2)

1 וידבר יהו״ה אל משה בהר סיני לאמור...ושבתה הארץ שבת ליהו״ה
"Y-H-W-H spoke to Moses at Mount Sinai, saying…the land shall rest in a godly Sabbath" (25:1-2). RaSHI famously opens by asking: "What does the Sabbatical have to do with Sinai?" Why should this, among all the many commandments, be specifically designated as spoken at the Mountain?

The Talmud (b. Sanh. 39a) explains the commandment this way: "Plant for six years and rest in the seventh, so that you will know that the land belongs to Y-H-W-H." But, in the broadest sense, that is the purpose of all the other commandments as well! The earth is filled with God's presence since its creation. That did not begin at Sinai. **Torah was given to provide us with a way to discover that presence, and a path of living in response to it.**

"The world was created by ten divine utterances," says the Mishnah (Avot 5:1). These *ma'amarot* are the ten times God says "Let there be" in the opening chapter of *Bereshit.* (There are only nine, but the word *bereshit* itself is counted as the first.) These utterances live forever; they are the underlying structure of reality, waiting to be discovered. They are present ***in the earth***, as they are in the heavens. At Sinai, they are repeated in the form of the ten *dibrot* (we call them "commandments," but *dibrot* is really another way of saying "utterances" or "speech acts"). These constitute a set of keys for revealing a presence that is already there. They do this by converting the passive sense of presence into a set of imperatives. "Following this path will lead you to a life in which God's presence is revealed." Revealed right where you are, living on earth.

The Sabbatical rule takes Shabbat, the most distinctive practice of

Jewish living, and applies it to the land itself. What better way to teach that "the whole ***earth*** is filled with God's glory?"

It is true that the Torah applies the Sabbatical only to the particular land that Israel is about to be given. But the word *ha-arets* makes no distinction. The prophet's proclamation of God's glory, *melo khol ha-arets kevodo*, does not refer only to the Land of Israel. Neither does the psalmist's "Earth (*ha-arets*) and its fullness are God's" (24:1). Our call to treat our particular land this way is paradigmatic, teaching reverence for the earth as a whole. The Land of Israel, the *Sefat Emet* teaches, became an exception to the category of lands in order to teach us about the holiness of all land, of the very soil itself.

Torah has no more important lesson for our generation. We need to understand that this one comes from Sinai itself.

2 והיתה שבת הארץ לכם לאכלה לך לעבדך ולאמתך ולשכירך ולתושבך
הגרים עמך

"The land's Sabbath, during which you do not eat of it, includes you, your manservant, your maidservant, your hireling, and the stranger who dwells with you. It shall be fodder for your cattle and the wild animals who are in your land" (25:6-7). This very thorough listing means that the land is to be free from any human manipulation, by Israelites or anyone else who is in their charge. It is to revert to its truly natural state, as it was before it was transformed by humans living upon it. One has a feeling that the land itself here is personified. It too has a ***right*** to rest.

The modern return of Jews to the Land of Israel brought about a need to evade the laws of the sabbatical year. It is claimed that a contemporary economy could not survive such periods of abstinence. Various *halakhic* solutions are offered to enable this negation of the Torah's command; only the most strictly pious continue to observe it.

But what ***should*** be kept in the spirit of *shemitah*? A great seventh year dedication to preserving the resources of the earth seems to cry out for fulfillment. We should find a way to extend this beyond the borders of the Land of Israel as well.

3 וקדשתם את שנת החמישים שנה וקראתם דרור בארץ לכל יושביה

"Make the fiftieth year holy and proclaim freedom in the land for all who dwell upon it" (25:10). The jubilee is total, embracing everyone: Israelites, male and female; slaves, Israelite and foreign; strangers, sojourners – everyone. Whom might we include today? Illegal immigrants? Prisoners? Victims of domestic abuse? Victims of cults? Victims of internal enslavement, including addictions? They all need to be set free!

Where does "all those who dwell upon it" end? "***Nowhere***" is the only possible answer. The jubilee is a call for radical liberation, for all who dwell upon the earth. We cannot and will not fully enact it in our world. But the loud *shofar* blast that calls for it should ever be ringing in our ears.

But it is such a liberation for ***you*** as well. The sabbatical returns the earth to Y-H-W-H; the jubilee calls for a return of the ***self*** to its Source. That is the harder task.

4 ובכל ארץ אחוזתכם גאולה תתנו לארץ

"For any land to which you become attached, bring redemption to that land" (25:24).

The word *ge'ulah,* "redemption," has strong spiritual echoes. It is most associated with God's redemption of Israel from Egypt and the future redemption of the world. The idea of redeeming the land is therefore very striking.

The current Zionist appropriation of this verse makes it difficult to read it in any other way. The Jewish National Fund and others have long used it as a slogan to refer to getting ever more of the Land of Israel subject to Jewish ownership (or ownership by the State of Israel), "redeeming" it from the hands of others. But this cannot be all that it means. Ever since *lekh lekha* we have seen Hasidic readings of *erets* as referring to *artsiyyut*, material possessions, "earthly" things. Thus, our verse can be read to say: "***Any attachment we have to the corporeal realm has to be for the sake of redemption.***"

That is the Torah's story as we understand it. We were sent down into Egypt, given an *aḥuzah* in its richest soil, the Land of Goshen, (think of Westchester or Beverly Hills), in order to uplift and redeem sparks of holiness that were trapped there. Those were the shiny vessels we "borrowed" from the Egyptians as we were leaving. We were sent into exile throughout the world for the same purpose. There is a reason why the root ***g-l-h*** means both "exile" and "reveal." The great miracle of the Return to Zion has to mean the same thing, bringing true redemption to that holy place.

Here, I am sympathetic to the views of Rav Kook. The return of the Jewish people to the land, to the body, and to history has been a necessary and positive step. I would like to believe that this whole process may indeed be, as his followers said, *reshit tsemiḥat ge'ulateu*, ***"the beginning of the redemption that we will bring about."*** That redemption will indeed require *tsemiḥah*; it will have to grow out of the land, the way we learn to treat it, and all those who live upon it. That includes the way we learn to share it with others who live upon it. So far, signs of that "redemption" are pretty slow in revealing themselves. There is much reason for disappointment. But "even if they delay, we will wait" for them. We have not given up.

בחוקותי
BE-ḤUKKOTAI
(Leviticus 26:3-27:34)

1 אם בחוקותי תלכו...ופניתי אליכם...ונתתי משכני בתוככם...והתהלכתי
בתוככם

"If you walk in My ways...I will face toward you...I will place My dwelling within you...I will walk in your midst" (26:1, 9, 11-12). The language of blessing in this opening part of *be-ḥukkotai* is particularly rich, preparing the reader for the contrast that is to come. If Israel live well, Y-H-W-H is to be present within them, both community and individual, in a whole way. The divine face, the great source of radiance and blessing, will shine upon them. In response to the *mishkan* or dwelling-place that they have made for Y-H-W-H, He will place ***His*** *mishkan* within them. Thus, the *mishkan* will be erected from above as well as from below. Most striking is "If you walk in My ways...I will walk in your midst."

Hithallakhti, the reflexive form of "to walk," is found very seldom in the Torah. We immediately recall (Gen. 3:8) Adam and Eve hearing Y-H-W-H *mithallekh*, "walking" in the Garden. One has a sense there that God is present in a wholly natural way, just "strolling about" in Eden.

For those of us who know Y-H-W-H chiefly as an inward presence, these promises are particularly touching. "Walking in My ways," living as we should, awakens the divine presence within us. We come to feel it in that natural way; we need no great miracles to testify that it is there. Y-H-W-H just "walks about" within us.

But how do we know when we are walking in God's ways? The traditional answer, of course, is *halakhah*. That is precisely what it is supposed to mean. The norms of tradition are supposed to guide us in the path. But we also know that it is not enough of an answer. Too much is outdated, too much that was decided in a different age just doesn't work for our times. We still seek to find Y-H-W-H strolling about in our inner garden. We still need the tradition's guidance in creating a path for that presence. But *halakhah,* indeed like *aggadah*, has to become more of a living and growing vehicle to make that happen.

The "proclaim liberty" of *be-har* comes before the "Walk in My paths" of *be-ḥukkotai*. The *halakhah* needs to learn to keep walking as well.

2 ואם לא תשמעו לי ולא תעשו את המצוות האלה

"But if you do not listen to me and do not perform all these commandments" (26:14).

The *tokhaḥah*, or "reproof" that constitutes a large portion of this *parashah,* together with its longer counterpart in *parashat ki tavo*, are among the most difficult sections of Torah. They describe the most terrible horrors that the ancient Israelites could imagine, perhaps written in living memory of awful battles and sieges, taking them as divine threats. First, blessings are listed; these are the rewards of keeping God's law. They are followed by the much more fully described horrors that will ensue as a result of violating it.

We read them today in an age still close to living memory of human-inflicted horrors even worse than those described in this chapter. The suffering endured by the Jewish people, and many others alongside them, during the years of the Holocaust, exceeds those of the human imagination. I find it impossible, when hearing these chapters read, not to think of accounts of the death camps or of the terrors endured in Warsaw, Leningrad, and so many other places.

I find myself caught between two impulses when confronted with this *parashah.* My faith is far from one that affirms the wrathful and destructive God depicted here. Religion by intimidation has itself caused a great deal of pain in the lives of so many. It has also driven large numbers of Jews away from the tradition, and with good reason. Who wants to live with such an angry and punishing Parent-God? It is time to be done with such religion! The *tokhaḥah* also fiercely blames the victims for their terrible fate, a view that I, along with most post-Holocaust Jews, firmly reject.

At the same time, the call to human responsibility is powerful and attractive. "If you walk according to My statutes and keep My commandments by doing them, I will give rain in its season; the land will give of its produce and the trees of the field will bear fruit.... But if you do not listen to Me..." (26:3-4, 14). How can we who live in an age when human misdeeds indeed threaten our very existence turn our backs on the dire warnings of passages like these? That which seemed, in the childhood religion we rejected, like the wrath of a punishing Parent, now looks like a warning about the consequences of human deeds.

In particular, the placement of this difficult chapter right after the Sabbatical laws, as well as the joining of these two sections in most years' Torah readings, calls us to read the *tokhaḥah* here as referring to the consequences of the way we treat the earth. Perhaps we had better learn to hear it in a new way.

3 אלה החוקים ממשפטים והתורות אשר נתן ה׳ בינו ובין ישראל בהר סיני ביד משה.

"These are the statutes, judgments, and teachings that Y-H-W-H has placed between Himself and the Children of Israel at Mount Sinai, by the hand of Moses" (26:46).

This verse feels like it was meant to be the closing of the section, or perhaps even of the Book of *Va-Yikra*, the final chapter about evaluations for the jubilee something of an addition. The wording of "placed between" is interesting. The same phrase is familiar to us regarding Shabbat: "a sign between Me and the Children of Israel," but it is otherwise rarely found.

Torah indeed serves as an intermediary, "placed between." Living in accord with Torah is our way of becoming close to Y-H-W-H. That is what Judaism is all about. The mystical tradition sees Torah as a verbal incarnation of the divine self. (I have invented the word ***inverbation*** to describe it.) In the Hasidic sources this is described by means of a re-read Talmudic interpretation of *anokhi,* the opening word of the Ten Commandments. The Talmud reads it as an acronym for *Ana Nafshai Katvit Yahavit*, "I Myself wrote it and gave it." They saw this as a hidden "author's signature" in the Torah. But the Hasidic masters read it as "I wrote and gave Myself!" The Torah is God's presence, given to us in verbal form.

Our ability to open our hearts to such an understanding does not have to rise and fall with literal belief in verbal revelation. How the divine word or presence enters the text is too subtle a process for us to grasp, but our faith in Torah attests to it. Despite all the difficulties we may have with aspects of the test, we sense a divine presence that remains within it. This reality is affirmed for us by many generations of Jews who have loved Torah and lived by its word.

4 "ואף גם זאת בהיותם בארץ אויביהם לא מאסתים ולא געלתים לכלותם להפר בריתי אתם כי אני יהו"ה אלוהיהם."

"Even when they are in the lands of their enemies, I have not rejected them or been so repulsed by them as to destroy them, to break My covenant with them, for I remain Y-H-W-H their God" (26:44). Why "Even," using the feminine form of ***af gam zot***? For the Kabbalists, this hints at *shekhinah* – My presence is still within them (but not ***only*** or exclusively within them!!). That has not changed. Because of ***zot, shekhinah's*** presence that they accepted to carry within their midst, I cannot abandon them. "For I am Y-H-W-H ***their*** God" – the God who dwells within their hearts. In redeeming humans, God redeems Godself from exile.

SEFER BE-MIDBAR

THE BOOK OF NUMBERS

במדבר
BE-MIDBAR
(Numbers 1:1-4:20)

1 בשנה השנית לצאתם מארץ מצרים

"...In the second year of their coming out (*le-tsetam*) from the Land of Egypt" (1:1). Two years have passed and they're still "coming out!"

Reading it this way serves as a reminder that coming out of any "Egypt" that enslaves us is not a onetime event, but a long process. In this book called "In the Wilderness," we are going to be reminded that it took the Israelites forty years. Patience and persistence are both essential elements in the course of this process – and they were not always present in Israel's long journey. So too is the ability to recover from failures, to get up and try again. We have to recognize the need for these, both in the way we treat our own processes of liberation and in the way we relate to others engaged in the same ongoing struggles.

This truth applies to individuals as well as to communities. Although this book of *Be-Midbar* is mostly the tale of the people's struggle with God, think of it with regard to your own trek through the "wilderness" as well. Just as each of us has an inner *mishkan*, we each have an inner wilderness as well. We are all on journeys to our Promised Land, the place of peace and fulfillment, and we each have to survive and cross through a wilderness – or more than one – to get there.

It is not an easy journey; *Be-Midbar* is not an easy book. There will be more than one point when you will say: "Let's turn around and go back to Egypt!" But you won't do it. A little later in this book (14:19) we will read: "As You have borne this people from Egypt unto here..." meaning that "If we have come this far together along on the journey, we will manage to go the rest of the way." That can only be called a statement of faith. You will persist together, you and the divine spark within you.

2 ויתילדו על משפחותם לבית אבותם

"They proclaimed their birth-origins by families, according to their parental households" (1:18). The unusual verb form *va-yityaldu* emphasizes the importance of families of origin. We come into this world not as lone individuals, but as the products of the combined families that gave birth to us. As we look into our family roots, it is a marvel to behold that each of us is the child of two parents, four grandparent, eight great-grandparents, sixteen great-great grandparents, and so forth. The DNA of each of them is within us, and we will pass it down, together with our partners, hopefully in the same radiating circles. Each of us is a meeting-point of generations past and future.

This is true of cultural as well as genetic legacy. We live in an age that tends to glorify the lone journey; it is the figure of Abraham, leaving his father's household, that we find attractive, especially in the years of young adulthood. We are a culture that loves tales of youth and youthful journeys. But as we mature, bringing forth our own future generations, many of us turn back and try to find out where we come from, sometimes turning up memories – or even living cousins – from branches of the family tree that had long been left behind. We find we have developed the same instincts our parents had – and we had perhaps once rejected – to root new generations in the soil from which they emerged.

Read the verses quite literally: "They ***birthed themselves*** according to their families." Sometimes the discovery of family can lead to a sort of rebirth. There is a rebirth in youth that consists of emerging as an individual, breaking some of the bonds that in childhood tied you too closely to your parents and their ways. Finding your own path in life becomes the only goal. But there is another rebirth that takes place in mid-life, as your parents age and your children grow, when you want to "birth yourself according to your family."

3 ואלה תולדות אהרון ומשה ביום דבר ה' את משה בהר סיני

"These are the generations of Aaron and Moses on the day when Y-H-W-H spoke to Moses on Mount Sinai" (3:1). After this grand opening, there follow only three verses listing the sons of Aaron, repeating the account of the death of Nadav and Avihu. Moses' sons are very notable by their absence, almost as though their names have been excised from the text.

We have offered one explanation of this above in *parashat tetzavveh.* But here the absence is very strong, missing in a place where it was announced as coming. Is there some "family secret" here that was hushed up in the tradition? What might the masters of *aggadah* in our own day make of this?

4 ואני הנה לקחתי את הלויים תחת כל בכור פטר רחם בבני ישראל...כי לי כל בכור ביום הכותי כל בכור בארץ מצרים

"I have taken the Levites from amid the Children of Israel instead of the firstborn, openers of the womb...For all firstborn are Mine since the day when I smote every firstborn in the Land of Egypt" (3:12-13). Here we have the origin of one of the stranger rituals that still exists among Jews, the Redemption of the Firstborn. The broader context of this sense that the firstborn belongs to God is quite complicated in the Torah. Here it is attributed to the slaying of the firstborn in Egypt. Earlier passages in the Torah (Ex. 22:28, 34:20) do not make this connection. There it seems more connected to the ancient agricultural cycle. The firstborn belongs to God among humans and flocks alike. The human firstborn and that of the donkey have this in common; they both need to be "redeemed." We also associate it, of course, with the command to Abraham to offer up Isaac, "your son, your only, whom you love."

As any parent will tell you, there is indeed something especially miraculous and wonderful about the birth of one's first child. If the child emerges alive and healthy, we are filled with gratitude, perhaps more so than at any other moment in the regular course of human life. ***Of course***, it becomes a time of wanting to give in return. But the tale of Isaac tells us definitively that God does not want us to take that life, that there is another way to give, instead. That ram in the thicket now gives way to the Levite, offered as a servant to Y-H-W-H instead of our firstborn children.

As the times changed, so did the way of expressing that gratitude.

Think of how we might do it today. ***This is a ritual form that begs to be renewed in a meaningful way.*** Given who we are in the world, we need to offer more than five silver dollars on the birth of a first child (of either gender, of course).

Adoption of an unwanted child might be the strongest way to express it. There are children in this world who thirst for parental love. But not all of us are capable of going that far. Perhaps a regular commitment to giving to a child-centered charity, or even financially "adopting" one of the millions of needy children among our planet's poor, might be a way of truly "redeeming" the gift of our first birth.

5 ולא יבואו לראות כבלע הקדש ומתו

"They shall not come to see the disappearance of the holy, lest they die" (4:20). There is a mysterious power to this detailed description of the need for the *kohanim* to cover each sacred object in its special case before Israel could set out on each of its many journeys. The Kehatite family among the Levites were charged with carrying these objects, but they could only approach them once they were fully hidden from view. To see them before they were covered, or even in the moment when they disappeared (literally: were swallowed up) into their goatskin bags, would have been a fatal desecration.

The fragility of this moment of hiding reveals the truth that even the most sacred of objects, those we most venerate and love, are in themselves merely ***things***. Their holiness lives in the way we see them, the way we open our inner eye to them. It is that way of seeing, itself a precious gift, that needs to be protected.

In our own Jewish practice, the passage reminds me of the closed coffin at Jewish funerals. The living human face is a sacred object, containing within it something of divine light, the *me'or panim* of the face of Y-H-W-H. Many people report seeing that light shine with special brightness just before their loved ones pass. We should not let that vision be diminished by seeing the face as it is swallowed up by the earth, as we all one day will be.

נשוא
NASSO
(Numbers 4:21-7:89)

1 נשוא את ראש בני גרשון גם הם למשפחותם

"Raise up also the heads of the Children of Gershon, according to their families" (4:22).

The choice to begin the *parashah* here makes an important statement about the dignity of labor and respect for those who do it. The Kehatites, described above, have the privileged role among the Levitical families. They get to carry the ark, the menorah, and the altars as Israel wander through the wilderness. The Gershonites get to carry only the curtains and outer accessories of the Tent of Meeting. That is why the *gam hem* ("also") of the verse is significant. Their mention and counting in the Torah is no less important than that of their Kehatite cousins.

We are a community very much marked by much professional and economic privilege. We have worked hard for that status and take some degree of pride in it. But we should remember those around us, Jews and non-Jews alike, who "carry the curtains of our tent" and do all the other things that make our lives possible. ***Gam hem, "they too,"*** deserve to be treated with a full measure of dignity and to be included in our own *Sefer Torah*.

2 איש או אשה אשר יעשו מכל חטאות האדם למעול מעל בה'

"A man or woman who commits any human sin, rebelling against Y-H-W-H, is guilty" (5:6).

The text is talking about robbery, a sin against another person, and goes on to prescribe repayment. Note the phrase *ḥat'ot ha-adam*, "a ***human*** sin," which indicates a transgression within the human community. But the text here undermines the notion of a complete separation between transgressions against people and those against God. Robbery, conceived in the broadest sense, is a defiance of God, using our God-given powers to act against another of God's children. The gift of life on this earth is one we all share. Using it to violate the rights of others is an act of blasphemy against Y-H-W-H. Just as God is present in every *mitsvah* that we do, so is any intentional act against another an attempt to remove Y-H-W-H from that portion of our shared human lives. To use a more Kabbalistic metaphor, all of us are twigs or leaves of the single Tree of Life. To harm one another is to disturb the Tree itself, with its roots in heaven. It is a transgression against *melo khol ha-arets kevodo*, "the whole earth is filled with God's glory."

There is no ultimate distinction to be made between the spiritual and ethical realms. Seeking to live in the presence of Y-H-W-H has built into it a demand that we enable others to do the same.

3 ולקח הכהן מים קדושים בכלי חרש

"The priest shall take holy water in an earthen vessel" (5:17). In the midst of describing this terrible trial-by-ordeal ritual for the suspected wife, the term "holy water" appears, occurring only here in the Torah. RaSHI explains that it is made holy by being placed in the tabernacle's basin. The basin, he reminds us, was made up of the polished copper mirrors that the women had used in Egypt to beautify themselves to attract their husbands, leading them to mate "beneath the apricot tree" (Cant. 8:5).

The crime of which the *sotah* is suspected is thus a violation of a pattern set up by Israel's women themselves. The water is "holy" because it was placed in this basin, made up of those mirrors. Sexuality within marriage, including attempts to make oneself attractive in order to encourage it, is completely affirmed. The basin formed out of these mirrors means that she is to examine herself in the light of those standards, those of the women of Israel.

In that sense, it is ***the community of women*** against whom the adulteress, has sinned, not just the authority of the husband and the priest.

4 איש או אשה אשר יפליא לנדור נדר נזיר להזיר לה׳

"If a man or woman does something so wondrous as to take on a Nazirite vow for Y-H-W-H" (6:2). The literal meaning of *yafli* is unclear, but the root is the same as *pele*, "wonder." In our morning *berakhot*, we refer to Y-H-W-H as *mafli la-'asot*, "acting wondrously (based on Jud. 13:19)." The Torah sees it as a wonder that an ordinary flesh-and-blood human being can find the inner strength to fulfill this voluntary vow of abstinence and purification.

In our day, we too stand in awe of certain spiritual feats or acts of voluntary dedication that others take on. Like the ancient Nazirite, who was given no special privilege or reward for his/her act of special devotion, they stand as a challenge and inspiration to the rest of us mere mortals. Think of doctors and nurses serving in the midst of a pandemic, firefighters and rescue workers daily risking their lives to save others, and many more. There is indeed something ***wondrous*** and magnificent to be seen in the human ability to do such things. Let us remember to take notice.

5 יאר ה׳ פניו אליך ויחונך

"May Y-H-W-H light up your face and be gracious to you" (6:25). A midrash (*Sifrey Zuta*) says: "*Vi-yeḥuneka* means 'May He grant you the consciousness **to be gracious and merciful toward one another**, as Scripture says: 'May He grant you mercy and make you merciful (Deut. 13:18).'"

We are given the light of the divine face to shine in our own faces in order to be able to pass it on to others. That is our great privilege as beings who live in the divine image. We must learn both to share that light with others and to see *shekhinah*'s light in the face of others. That should help to turn us into *ḥonenim zeh et zeh*, people who treat one another with compassion and grace.

6 ישא ה׳ פניו אליך וישם לך שלום

"May Y-H-W-H lift His face toward you and place peace before you" (6:26). The Ba'al Shem Tov reads an old rabbinic tradition to say that *shalom* is the vessel we need in which to contain God's blessing. It is not enough to pray for blessing; divine blessing is pouring forth upon us in every moment that we exist. But without a proper vessel in which to hold it, that blessing just washes over us and vanishes.

Shalom means "wholeness" as well as "peace." It means being whole with ourselves, accepting who we are in the fullest sense. It means being at peace with family members, with our neighbors, with the very unpeaceful world in which we live. This is not an easy challenge, but without it our vessel is not whole and cannot contain blessing.

The verb used in this blessing, *ve-yasem*, says it all (We re-state it in our prayer that responds to the blessing, *sim shalom*). All God can do is to place the opportunity for peace before us. Only we can choose it, placing it within the vessel of our own inner peace.

בהעלותך
BE-HA'ALOTEKHA
(Numbers 8:1-12:16)

1 בהעלותך את הנרות אל מול פני המנורה יאירו שבעת הנרות

"When you raise up the lamps, all seven flames should shine toward the face of the menorah" (8:2). Read *be-**he**'alotheka et ha-nerot*, "as you are raised up **along with** the lamps." The "face" of the menorah represents the "face" of Y-H-W-H, the great source of light from which blessing shines forth, as we just read in the priestly blessing (6:27). The seven lamps, say many of the Hasidic authors, represent the seven *middot* or moral qualities of the person. These must all be part of our "ascent," our journey upward (***or inward***!). You cannot make that journey unless they are all facing toward the great Source of Light.

This is a good place to review a contemporary reading of those *middot*. Really, they are five:

חסד

Ḥesed: Love and compassion for God's Creation and all within it, each creature imbued with the spirit of Y-H-W-H;

גבורה

Gevurah: Strength of character; good judgment; holding back when necessary;

תפארת

Tif'eret: The beauty and dignity of being a person who attains the proper balance between *ḥesed* and *gevurah*. For the *ḥasid* (remember always that the word derives from *ḥesed*!), this means ever being pulled toward the right, placing compassion above all, but without getting out of balance;

נצח

> ***Netsaḥ***: A sense of triumph, accomplishment, but without triumphalism. Overcoming the pride and self-satisfaction that can derive from all that balancing, realizing that the battle is never fully won;

הוד

> ***Hod:*** The grace of submission – recognizing how much lies beyond us - and gratitude for all we have received,, ***hoda'ah*** and ***hod****ayah*. (Neither word ***really*** derives from *hod*, but that's how they read it!)

The final two are:

יסוד

> ***Yesod***, the firm "foundation" or personal stance that you create within the self by joining all these together, and

מלכות

> ***Malkhut,*** the dwelling or tabernacle you build on that foundation, allowing *shekhinah* to dwell within you and within the community you build in ever expanding circles around you.

It is with these that we turn toward the Face of Light, reflecting back the light that we have been given. Think of this as a bit of Hasidic *mussar*. If you want to "rise up along with the lights," you've got to take these seven with you. Otherwise, you're just "getting high," not "rising up."

2 על פי ה׳ יסעו בני ישראל ועל פי ה׳ יחנו

"By the mouth of Y-H-W-H did the Children of Israel journey, and by the mouth of Y-H-W-H did they camp" (9:18). The repetition and detailing of this statement (9:15-23) seems to reflect an insistence on it. One wonders why. Might there be a concern lest someone think that Israel's wanderings were aimless, that they were simply "lost" in the wilderness? One remembers Pharaoh's words shortly after they had left Egypt: "The wilderness has closed in upon them" (Ex. 14:3).

This description precedes the extension of the period in the wilderness to forty years, marking the passing of the generation that had come out of Egypt, which will come about only in the following *parashah*. It is hard to imagine how difficult the changes in anticipation must have been, and how much hope must have been raised every time the cloud lifted, only to be dashed again when it stayed in place for long periods of time. "Sometimes the cloud would be there from evening to morning. As it rose in the morning, they would travel on…But it might be two days, or a month, or a year that the cloud would remain in place over the *mishkan*" (9:21-22). How can one live that way, not knowing if we are breaking camp and moving on today, tomorrow, or perhaps not for a year?

How different or how similar are our own wanderings? How do we know when it is the right time to make a move, perhaps a life-changing one? Is there an inner voice that tells us when to stay put for a long period of time, accepting our lot, or whether it is time to move on? How do we learn to listen to it? Or to find the strength to overcome it, when we must?

3 וארון ברית ה׳ נוסע לפניהם שלושת ימים לתור להם מנוחה

"And the ark of Y-H-W-H's covenant travelled three days ahead of them, seeking for them a place of rest" (10:33). RaSHI quotes a midrash that says this was a special ark that was used in battle, and that it contained the broken tablets. This tradition offers a unique view of Israel's wanderings. ***Every place they went, every battle that they fought, they had the broken tablets out there before them.*** All their journeys were about following the broken tablets, the grand truths that had been shattered. Perhaps they (like us!) could no longer relate to the perfection projected from and demanded by the whole tablets; they could trust only the broken fragments.

In our own battle for the relevance and survival of Judaism, as we wander through the postmodern wilderness, we too can only follow the ark with the broken tablets. We once thought we knew the whole truth, enough to provide answers for all our questions, but that proved not to be the case. The tablets have to be smashed over and over again by our inner Moses, the one who knows that is the only way to keep us from worshipping the next Golden Calf that might come along. They are always out there in front of us. This is, after all, the ark of the covenant we made with the ever-elusive One, Y-H-W-H., who likes to be called "I will be whatever I will be." The only authentic way to worship such a God is by constantly breaking the tablets.

We wander through the wilderness, on our way to the Promised Land. Leading us are pieces of the broken tablets, ever reminding us how much we do not know. We ***rejoice*** in the honesty of that truth. Only with it can we be ***'am ḥofshi be-artsenu,*** "a ***free*** people in our land."

4 וישמע משה את העם בוכה למשפחותיו איש פתח אהלו ויחר אף ה׳ מאד
ובעיני משה רע

"Moses heard the people weeping by families, each at the entrance to its own tent. Divine anger was kindled greatly; this was bad in the eyes of Moses" (11:10). Here we see the relationship of God, Moses, and Israel in all its complexity. Just above (11:1-2), Moses cried out to Y-H-W-H as the people began to seek meat, no longer being content with the manna. There he was playing the classic role of intercessor, as he had following the incident of the Golden Calf. But now he sees that the divine wrath is unabated. The verse leaves us just a bit unsure as to what "was bad in the eyes of Moses." Was it the people's complaint or God's reaction? He had already played out his ability to intervene and protect them from divine anger. What else could he do? And where did this leave him?

This is the first in a series of similar events that characterize the narrative of *Be-Midbar*. Y-H-W-H and Israel are "in a wilderness" together in their relationship. The pattern is that they rebel and God bursts out in anger. Moses, whose life is all about keeping this relationship together, must see that these outbursts do not help the situation.

How is God doing in the task of keeping ***His*** *middot* in balance?

What are we – as parents, spouses, and humans created in the image of God – supposed to learn from this account? What can we today make of all this divine anger? A Hasidic master, R. Yitshak of Radvil, read the *shema*'s words *ve-ḥarah af Y-H-W-H ba-khem* to mean "Divine wrath will break forth ***within you***." Y-H-W-H is ever loving and unchanging in that; only in us does that love get hidden and distorted.

5 אספה לי שבעים איש מזקני ישראל...לאהל מועד...וירדתי ודברתי עמך
ואצלתי הן הרוח אשר עליך ושמתי עליהם

"Y-H-W-H said to Moses: Gather for Me seventy men from among the elders of Israel...to the Tent of Meeting...I shall descend and speak with you there. I will spread forth the spirit that is upon you and place it upon them...and you shall not bear it alone" (11:16-17).

This is the divine response to Moses' desperate outcry "Did I conceive this people or give birth to it?... How shall I bear alone?" (11:12-14). The voice of God seems to be saying: "I know this is too much for one person. I was wrong in placing the burden upon you alone. At Sinai, you were there with the elders, but they all stood back and you approached Me alone. Perhaps even then I should have asked them all to come forward into the cloud with you."

In thinking about Hasidism for a new era, the question of the *tsaddik* immediately comes to mind. The only model that existed in Eastern European Hasidism was that of a single leader, upon whom the spiritual lives of his flock depended to varying degrees. This model was also that of the surrounding society: the king or tsar ruling over his people. For us, raised on the values of democratic society and responsible citizenship, submission to a single leader or teacher is a much less attractive model. We also know too many stories about the abuses of such leadership.

But can the intensity of spiritual life that the *ḥasid* seeks exist without faith in the leadership of a single *tsaddik*? Those of us involved in the shaping of a future Hasidism should read this chapter carefully. Perhaps we need both the charismatic leader and the council of "elders (but including both young and old, men and women)," who guide that leader's hand.

שלח לך
SHELAḤ
(Numbers 13:1-15:41)

1 שלח לך אנשים ויתורו את ארץ כנען אשר אני נותן לבני ישראל...כולם
אנשים ראשי בני ישראל המה

"Send yourself men, and they will spy out the Land of Canaan that I am giving to the Children of Israel. One man from each tribe of his fathers shall you send, all princes among them. Moses sent them from the wilderness of Paran, according to the word of Y-H-W-H, all of them men, leaders of the Children of Israel" (13:2-3).

Read these verses carefully. When Abraham was told *lekh lekha*, RaSHI commented that it meant "for your own sake, for your own good." Is the same true of *shelaḥ lekha* here? Is this another response to Moses' feeling of inability to lead his confused and wayward flock? Is it ***for Moses' sake*** that they are being sent? Did he need them to vindicate him, to testify that the land of milk and honey really existed, and was not just a figment of his imagination?

The repetition of the word *anashim*, "men," is also striking. This refers to more than their gender; it means that they were strong figures, indeed leaders of the people.

Who are the ***anashim*** that we send forth to look for ***our*** Promised Land? What sort of future do we look toward for the Jewish people, half a century or a century from now? Who are those who go ahead of us, those toward whom we should look to help shape that future? How do we step beyond being dominated by the demographers and their dire predictions? "The future looks bleak," they say. In Israel, they tell us, there are two ***giants*** standing before us: demographic bombs threatening the future. The Palestinian population will overwhelm us politically and the Haredi growth will threaten the economy. In the diaspora, the ***giants*** are intermarriage and assimilation, and "we look like grasshoppers before them."

But without vision, our people will indeed perish.

And what is the Promised Land that we want them to spy out? What are the great clusters of grapes we want them to bring back, attesting that such a "land" really exists? Surely a copy of the final peace treaty that Israel will sign with its Palestinian neighbors, agreeing to live side by side as equals. How about a picture of an Israel that uses its high-tech skills to export water purification and agricultural advances, saving human lives, rather than weapons and spy technology? How about a strong and proud diaspora community, contributing the wisdom of its tradition to improve human life and helping to save the earth from destruction?

Yes, there are "giants" out there, fighting on the other side. Some of them are even internal. But the Torah keeps telling us not to fear them. We have been around for a very long time and we have seen worse than these. We need some Joshuas and Calebs who, while not denying the truth, will help assure us that there indeed is a way forward, and that it is worth the effort.

2 ויאמרו...הארץ אשר עברנו בה לתור אותה טובה הארץ מאד מאד
"They [Joshua and Caleb] said to the whole community of Israel: the land which we passed through to spy out is a very, very good land" (14:7).

A midrash for our generation: We need to read "**very, very** good" in this verse to mean that it is good enough to sustain both us and those who dwelt there already. We do not accept the alternatives of "defeat them over and over again," in the hope that they will disappear, or else they will do that to you. A "***very, very*** good land" is one that can be ***shared.***

Yes, this is a very different reading that that of the biblical text. But we need to declare, clearly and openly, that we have grown beyond the ethos of conquest and slaughter that characterized our people's vision more than two thousand years ago. ***We need to learn from having been victims of the largest genocide and "ethnic cleansing" in human history.*** We read passages about the destruction of our enemies in order to remind ourselves to stand up in witness against them.

3 ויאמר משה אל ה': ושמעו מצרים...מבלתי יכולת...ועתה יגדל נא כח ה'
לאמור ה' ארך אפיים ורב חסד...ויאמר ה' סלחתי כדבריך

"Moses said to Y-H-W-H: The Egyptians will hear that this people whom You brought forth...They will say.... Because Y-H-W-H was unable to bring this people to the land He promised them.... May the Lord's power be such as You declared, saying: Y-H-W-H is long-suffering, greatly compassionate.... And Y-H-W-H said: I have forgiven, as you say" (14:13-20).

These verses are clearly parallel to those we read in Exodus 33-34, where God forgave Israel after the sin of the Golden Calf. Are these two separate events, or two versions of the same account, with God ready to destroy, Moses arguing on the basis of "What will the nations say?" followed by a declaration of divine compassion and ending with God's forgiveness? In either case, the parallel calls for a comparison of the two seemingly very different occasions for this outburst of divine wrath: the Golden Calf and the spies' report.

What the two events share is the people's fear. They ask for the Golden Calf because they are afraid that Moses won't return from the mountain and they will be stranded in the wilderness. Here they are afraid of fighting the nations of the Promised Land, who they now discover live in fortified cities and have giants fighting on their side. Both of these stories seem to illustrate the weakness and insecurity of the tribes that have come out of Egypt, and the long-term debilitating effects of their enslavement. Recovery from human degradation is neither immediate nor automatic. It takes a long time and demands great patience. Not for naught do the divine qualities begin with ***erekh apayim*****, "long-suffering" or "patient."**

The Jewish people is still suffering from the after-effects of the Holocaust's trauma. We need to recognize this in ourselves and work toward slow and patient healing. Those who deal with us – whether our neighbors in the diaspora or Palestinians in Israel – need to know this about us and keep it in mind. They were not responsible for our suffering and indeed it is not fair that they should pay the price. But this is who we are; it does no good to deny it. So too must we be aware of the trauma-based fears and hurts of others, supporting them in their own long journeys of healing. ***None of this is easy, and both the terrible events of October 7 and the ensuing destruction of Gaza have made it even more difficult.*** But there is no choice. Both our trauma and that of the Palestinians need to be healed.

4 ויאמר ה׳ סלחתי כדבריך. ואולם...
"Y-H-W-H said: I forgive according to your word. However..." (14:20-21). There is no escaping the harsh and ugly language of some of the following verses. "Your corpses will fall in this wilderness. Your children will be herdsmen in the wilderness for forty years, bearing the burden of your whoring until the end of your corpses in the wilderness" (14:31-32). The Israelites experience their lot as one cursed by an angry and vengeful God, one who has lost all patience with them.

Then what is the "forgiveness" that Moses has achieved? The *ve-ulam*, "however," following the forgiveness seems to render it meaningless. What value was there to his pleading and argument, naming God as "long-suffering," when He continues to be just the opposite? This question does not apply to Moses alone.

The positive point in this very difficult and painful chapter is that Y-H-W-H has not given up on this project called the people Israel, those named for their ancestor's wrestling with the angel, those he called forth to be "a kingdom of priests." They turn out to be a very tough bunch, as Y-H-W-H keeps learning throughout this book, more insecure, needy, and rebellious than He had bargained for. He is tempted, time and time again, to give up on them. But He won't. ***The project is just too important.***

We too are tempted to give up. The task of existing through history as a people whose very identity is tied to a universal sacred message, to the truth that Y-H-W-H is one, that divine presence flows through all that is, and that every person is God's living image, is no small burden. A history of persecution and terrible suffering has indeed made us insecure, needy, and rebellious – just like our ancestors in the wilderness. If we gain some bit of privilege (as in America, where people hate blacks more than Jews, or France, where Muslims are lower that Jews, or Israel, where we seem to enjoy dominating over others), we cling to it too fiercely, forgetting our mission. We are tempted to give up on it, time and time again, retreating into the world of our own self-interest.

But we can't. ***The project is just too important.***

5 והיה לכם לציצת וראיתם אותו ועשיתם את כל מצוותי

"It will be a fringe for you. You will see it and remember all My commandments and do them" (15:39). Both the Midrash and the Hasidic sources read *oto* in this verse as referring to God, translating it as "You will see '***Him,***' rather than 'it.'" They derive the word *tsitsit* from the verb *le-hatsits*, "to peer" or "peek," and connect it to a well-known verse in the Song of Songs: "Here he stands, behind our wall, looking through the windows, peering through the lattice" (2:9). As Y-H-W-H our Lover peers through to us from behind "our wall," that of our defenses and our well-protected individuality, so do the *tsitsit* give us a moment of peering back at the One, that deeper level of reality that embraces us all.

It is in this sense that *tsitsit* serve as a paradigm for all the *mitsvot.* They are moments, occasions, or objects through which we are offered a glimpse at the ray of divine light that is ever shining into our lives. Take a peek.

6 אני ה׳ אלוהיכם אשר הוצאתי אתכם מארץ מצרים להיות לכם לאלוהים

"I am Y-H-W-H your God who has taken you forth from the Land of Egypt *to become* your God" (15:41). The Hebrew *li-heyot le-* means "to become." This relationship is constantly in a state of becoming. We are redeemed from all our Egypts in order to get us ready for it, ***to make us free enough to become engaged with Y-H-W-H.***

Just as the liberation from Egypt, as we have seen in these chapters, is a long and slow process, so too is the building of that relationship. We work on it throughout our lives, ever learning (despite our famous stiff necks) to become openhearted, trusting, less demanding, more giving – all the things you learn in a relationship of love.

קרח
KORAḤ
(Numbers 16:1-18:32)

1 ויקח קרח

"Korah took" (16:1). The surprising choice of this verb, not followed by any object, opening the Korah narrative, says it all. Korah was a taker. The Midrash depicts him as a man of great wealth, much of it acquired by acts of taking that which was not his. In Yiddish, the phrase "as rich as Korah" is used to describe the rich and stingy, those who never tire of taking. Moses is the opposite. In the Shabbat service we say *yismaḥ Moshe be-**mattenat** ḥelko*; Moses' greatest joy is in the act of giving back that which had become his.

Torah exists to teach us to be givers. In the language of Kabbalah, we who ***receive*** all the blessings of life are training to become ***givers***, both to God and to those around us. For forty days on Sinai, the midrash says, Moses kept learning and forgetting, learning and forgetting. Finally, Torah was ***given*** to him as a gift. ***Mattan** torah,* the ***giving*** of teaching, is an act that never ceases. Witnessing and being receivers of that constant flow of teaching is meant to turn us into givers as well. This is the very process of "tradition," each generation giving to the next.

Onkelos, author of the *Targum Onkelos* in c. 110 CE, translates the "taking" of Korah as *itpallig*, "he separated himself," but it can also be understood as "he became divided." There is a Korah, along with a Moses, who lives within each of us, one who wants us to cut ourselves off from the life of giving, to take what is ours (and perhaps even more) and hoard it. A teaching in *Pirkey Avot* tells us that the one who says: "What's mine is mine and what's yours is yours" bears the quality of Sodom, the place where no one would give to strangers in need. That's also the quality of Korah.

Religion's best quality is that it cultivates ***generosity of spirit*** and the ***spirit of generosity*** in the faithful. Without these, it's hardly worth the effort.

2 כל העדה כולם קדושים ובתוכם ה׳

"The whole community – all of them – are holy; Y-H-W-H is within them" (16:3). Here Korah gains our sympathy for the moment. He is onto something; there is indeed divinity within each person. But this is the most pernicious point of Korah's "taking." He has latched onto the idea of equality, trying make it the steed on which he will ride to glory. This is what the sages meant when they used Korah's argument as the prime example of "a controversy not for the sake of heaven." He was using the idea of equality as a means of self-promotion. We have seen people – and politicians – like that. They are particularly dangerous because they have latched onto a certain truth.

Be wary of populists, those who claim to speak in the name of "the people."

3 וישמע משה ויפול על פניו

"Moses heard and fell on his face. He said to Korah.... In the morning Y-H-W-H will declare who is His and who is holy and will draw near (*hikriv*) the one He chooses...take yourselves firepans, Korah and all his assembly" (16:4-6).

Moses falls on his face, as though in prayer, but no words of his prayer follow in the text. He tries to call out to God, but he has nothing to say. His arguments in defense of the people have been fully exhausted. Even with his newly appointed seventy elders, he no longer has the strength to stand as an intermediary between the people and the explosion of divine wrath that he knows is sure to come. The near-magical test that he sets up is a statement of his exasperation. We hear in it echoes of Nadav and Avihu and of the future trial between Elijah and the Priests of Baal. Essentially, he is saying: "You deal with it, Lord! Pull off some supernatural trick if You choose to. Draw them near or burn them up, whatever You like. I have nothing left to give."

But then the test actually comes. They take their pans, set them afire, and fill them with incense. God tells Moses and Aaron to step away from the sinners (6:21) so that He might destroy them. Suddenly, Moses and Aaron find the power to speak, crying out "O God, divine spirit of all flesh! ***Shall one person sin and You become enraged at the entire community***?" The immediacy of the threat has restored their voice, which they had lost earlier. Now we hear again the very human cry of Abraham at Sodom: "***Will the judge of the whole earth not do justice***?" You are the God of all ***flesh***, not just of the righteous few or the people of "spirit!"

What are we to learn from this account? Perhaps it is that even the greatest among us reaches a breaking point, thinking we have nothing left to offer. But then a moment of true crisis comes, calling forth resources we didn't know were there within us. The followers of Korah are all destroyed, along with him. The divine judgment was that they bore responsibility for following a wicked leader. But the nation is saved.

We are waiting for the new strength of resistance, and the new leadership, to emerge out of our current crisis. Which crisis? You name it.

4 אמור אל אלעזר וירם את המחתות מבין השרפה...כי קדשו...ועשו אותם רקועי פחים צפוי למזבח

"Speak to Eleazar the son of Aaron the priest. Have him lift the firepans out of the burnt area, casting out the fire, because they have become holy. The pans of these mortal sinners shall be hammered into sheets that cover the altar, since they brought them near to Y-H-W-H and they became holy. They shall be a sign for the Children of Israel" (17:2-3).

The pans were declared holy, surely not only because they had touched the altar. This incident is to become part of the story, present in every future offering (and "prayer that replaces offerings") that the Israelites were to bring. But of what, exactly, was it to be "a sign?" What were they to recall when they saw that hammered covering around the altar? Was it just the dangers of following a wicked leader who tries to the don the oh-so-holy mantle (the all-blue *tallit*) of saying "All the people are holy?" Or was there some spark of holiness in their claim that needed to be redeemed, perhaps adding to the altar a "covering" that it had lacked?

Our times have seen bad leaders in many places who have spoken in the name of "the people." They, as well as those who follow them in doing evil, deserve the bad end to which they ultimately will come. But the message that holiness is found in everyone, not just in the anointed, needs to be added to our altar, especially because religion so easily tends toward patriarchy and hierarchy. The covering made up of those beaten fire-pans rings out and says over and over again: ***"The whole community – all of them – are holy; Y-H-W-H is within them."***

5 עבודת מתנה אתן את כהונתכם

"I will make your priesthood a gift of service" (18:7). The *Degel Maḥaneh Ephraim* notes that worship itself is at its best when we see it as a gift. This is what the Talmud means when it says: "If a person makes his prayers fixed, they are not supplications" (Ber.27b?). If you think it is ***you*** alone who are "fixing" what your prayer will be, you have not yet opened your heart to true prayer. Understand that the ability to pray is itself a gift, that the words of prayer are being spoken ***through*** you. We open our *'amidah* by saying "*Adonai,* open my lips that my mouth might speak ***Your*** praise" (Ps. 51).

The same is true of other aspects of our "priesthood." We should not seek credit for our willingness to serve others and do good in the world. The desire to serve is itself a gift, ***'avodat mattanah.*** We should be grateful for it.

חוקת
ḤUKKAT
(Numbers 19:1-22:1)

1 זאת חוקת התורה

"This is the statute of the Torah" (19:2). The commandment of purification through the ashes of the red heifer is understood by the tradition as the ultimate absurd ritual. There is no explanation possible for it, and you are not even supposed to try to find one. One tradition says that its meaning was known to Moses alone, but he was not allowed to pass it on.

Why a cow? Bovine sacrifices are always male. This is not a sacrifice, but why should it be the ashes of a female animal that purify one from contact with the dead? Interestingly, the ritual of *'eglah 'arufah*, a community's washing its hands of an unsolved murder, to be described in Deut. 21, also requires the slaughter of a female calf. Might there be a hint here that the female, the one who gives birth, can renew life in the face of death? Is there an implicit recognition here that females have a deeper connection to the mysteries of birth and death?

And why the strange recipe for the ashes, adding cedar, hyssop, and crimson (19:6) to the mix? It seems, as the sages inferred, intended to mystify. Most strange is the paradoxical effect of the rite. All those engaged in preparing or administering it are ***defiled*** by contact with the ashes, those same ashes that are used to ***purify*** anyone who has come into contact with the dead.

The word *ḥok* or *ḥukkah* is understood by the tradition to refer specifically to ritual acts, the part of the *mitsvot* that one would never think to fulfill had they not been commanded. The term derives from the root *ḥ-k-k*, meaning "carve" or "engrave." Most of the commentators read this to mean that they are "carved in stone," unchangeable and unquestionable. But some of the Hasidic sources see them as ***carved into the hearts of Israel***, meaning that their powerful impression is never quite forgotten and can always be retrieved, even after generations of neglect. "Inscribe them upon the tablet of your heart" (Prov. 3:3).

For a ritual to work, it needs to be embraced in all its absurdity. Tying little boxes to your arm and head each morning, waving palm branches and citrons in all directions, blowing into a ram's horn, eating a specific form of quick-baked crackers on a certain evening in the spring – all of them could seem quite insane to the visitor from Mars to whom you were trying to explain this human phenomenon called "religion." They would have to be from Mars, of course, because real earth-bound human beings all understand that ritual is a part of life.

It is this absurdity itself that gives transcendent meaning to the ritual deed. Its truth eludes us; it is beyond our understanding, taking the act into the realm of mystery. Hopefully, it is taking us there along with it. That is precisely its power.

2 זאת התורה אדם כי ימות באהל

"This is the teaching: a person who dies in a tent" (19:14). In attempting to limit the halakhic scope of requiring the use of red heifer ashes, R. Shim'on ben Yoḥai formulated that *adam* here refers only to Israelites and not to others (b. Yevamot 60b). In a wide array of later sources, his phrasing ("You are considered *adam*, but the nations of the world are not") was taken out of context to serve as the banner of what can only be called a racist version of Judaism, claiming that Israel alone were fully human, or were somehow "more human" than others. While this was an understandable reaction to centuries of bitter persecution and victimization, in which the full humanity of Jews was often denied by our oppressors, it cannot be allowed to stand in our day. Shamefully, it does in some circles. That understanding of Judaism, based on an almost racial superiority of Jews, is still bandied about. It has become a pernicious force, particularly within the religious politics of Israel.

In sharp contrast to that, we may choose to read the verse as the Kotzker rebbe might have suggested: *zot ha-torah: adam* – **"this is the teaching: be a *mensch*!** Torah exists to underscore and support our humanity, in the highest sense of that term. The relatively rare phrase *zot ha-torah* (it appears only here and twice in *Va-Yikra*) seems to say: "***This is what Torah is all about.***"

We are engaged in a great struggle for the living soul of our tradition, both in Israel and in the diaspora. Much of it may be seen in these alternate readings of this seemingly obscure verse. Is Torah to be read as a teaching about our universal humanity, showing us a uniquely Jewish way to live out the truth that every person is the image of God? Or is it about our difference from all others, with a strong whiff of implied superiority?

The gap in values between my friends in the embattled small religious left in Israel and the Kahanists and Hilltop Youth on the right is as wide as any in Jewish history. Most Israelis, and too many diaspora Jews as well, try to avoid taking a position with regard to it. But a day of reckoning has come, when we will all need to stand up and be counted.

That is the meaning of the phrase *ki yamut be-ohel*, "who dies in a tent" in this neo-Kotzker reading. The "tent" is the House of Study. Our universalist reading of Torah is engaged in an uphill struggle. We need to dedicate our entire lives to asserting its truth, recognizing that it is a matter of life and death.

3 ותמת שם מרים ותקבר שם ולא היה מים לעדה...וירב העם

"Miriam died and was buried there. There was no water for the assembly to drink, and they gathered around Moses and Aaron, and quarreled" (20:1-3). With Miriam's death, the miraculous well that had accompanied Israel through the wilderness, giving them water whenever they tapped into it, suddenly went dry.

The word *be'er*, "well," can also refer to a verb meaning "explanation." *Miriam ha-Nevi'ah*, "the prophet," was the first ***commentator*** on her brother's Torah. The *be'er* she provided was a wellspring of wisdom. His teaching came from on high, received at the mountaintop. Her wisdom came from the well, deep within the earth, undercutting the hierarchy by the very fact that it was taught by a woman. That gave a new voice, softer and more internal, to the words of Torah. The Kabbalists identify the ongoing process called Oral Torah with *shekhinah*, the feminine voice that speaks from within, ever reinterpreting – and thus renewing – the eternal divine Word.

Perhaps Miriam's death represents the disappearance of *shekhinah* from Israel's midst. Without romanticizing the past too much, there was once a sense that all of Israel were "on the same team," not only members of the same tribe. All of us were at least theoretically committed to a way of holy living, to fashioning a spiritual and moral "place" where *shekhinah* might dwell on earth. When we lost that shared sense about one another, when our Miriam died, we turned to quarreling.

4 קח את המטה והקהל את העדה...ודברתם אל הסלע

"Y-H-W-H spoke to Moses, saying: Take the staff…and speak to the rock" (20:7-8). Moses' sin at the Waters of Merivah is very difficult to understand. If Y-H-W-H wants him to speak to the waters, what need is there for the staff? R. Ovadiah Seforno suggests that God wanted to create a super-miracle here, one that would bring an end to all the complaints of Israel. The waters were to flow forth from the rock by the influence of speech alone. This would be a miracle of the divine word, parallel to that of Sinai. The staff was then to be used to divide the waters among the tribes. But Moses and Aaron didn't believe the people were ready for this new miracle, and Moses just repeated something they'd already done back at Marah (Ex. 17:6), striking the rock with his staff.

Perhaps the staff is there to remind Moses, the faithful shepherd, of the two sorts of power he has. A skillful shepherd should be able to call to his flock and get them to follow his voice. Only one who fails at calling, perhaps out of exasperation, has to strike them. Moses can no longer perform the true miracle of the wilderness journey – that of leading the people – by words alone. He feels that he has failed too many times and that his patience for trying to convince them is at an end. He can only use his staff. Y-H-W-H sees this and understands that Moses cannot be the leader to take them into the Land.

5 וימת שם אהרן בראש ההר...ויבכו את אהרן שלושים יום כל בית ישראל

"Aaron died there, at the top of the mountain…. And they wept for

Aaron for thirty days, the whole house of Israel" (20:28-29). RaSHI tells us that this included everyone, women as well as men. But when Moses died, the mourning was only by ***beney*** *yisra'el*, there referring to the men, but not the women. He explains (on Deut. 34:8) that Aaron, as a peacemaker, often brought about peace between husbands and wives, and was especially beloved for that.

Who knew that so much of Aaron's priesthood was devoted to marriage counselling?

Moses lived as a celibate for the forty years following Sinai. He may have needed to do this (it was his choice, not God's command), but it did not make him a good role model for family living. The absence of women from mourning him says a great deal.

6 וישלח ה׳ בעם את הנחשים השרפים...ויאמר ה׳ אל משה עשה לך שרף
ושים על נס...ויעש משה נחש נחושת

"Y-H-W-H sent fiery serpents into the people and they bit them. Many of the people died...Y-H-W-H said to Moses: Make yourself a Seraph and place it on a staff.... And Moses made a brass serpent" (21:-6-9).

The change in terminology is significant. Were the fiery serpents (*ha-neḥashim ha-serafim*) just fierce snakes? What does the word *serafim* mean here? Were they perhaps supernatural figures, destructive angels in the form of serpents? Then Y-H-W-H tells Moses to make a *Seraph*, perhaps an image of a fiery but healing angel, like those who stand above the divine throne (Is. 6:3). This was supposed to have healing power. But Moses instead makes a *naḥash*, a brass serpent-figure, and the people are healed by looking at it. This is all very strange.

Aaron has just died, following the death of Miriam. Moses sees his own mortality and knows that he will not be the one to lead Israel into the Promised Land. His powers are waning. Now it turns out that he cannot make a Seraph. That possibility depended on Aaron, the leader of Israel's cult. While he was alive, it was possible to fashion cherubim that would appear to embrace over the ark, showing God's love for Israel. A healing Seraph, burning out the sting of the serpents' bite, should have been something that the brothers together might have fashioned. But now Moses feels old and alone. All he can manage is a brass serpent. The healing works, but it is magical, rather than divine. It comes from the earth where the snake crawls, not from the heavens. That is all he has left in him.

It is no coincidence that "the Children of Israel journeyed to Ovot" appears in the very next verse. This is a place of the forbidden spirit-world (Lev. 20:7; Deut. 18:11), representing a corruption of their faith. Trust in the One who had brought them out of Egypt was failing, so they turned instead to faith in spirits and healing serpents.

The line that divides religion from magic is not always easy to detect, but it is an important marker to keep in mind.

בלק
BALAK
(Numbers 22:2-25:9)

1 ויגר מואב מפני העם מאד כי רב הוא...עתה ילחכו הקהל את כל סביבותינו
כלחוך השור את ירק השדה

"Moab feared the people greatly because it was so big (*rav*); Moab detested the Children of Israel.... 'That assembly (*kahal*) will lick up everything around us like an ox licks up the grass of the field'" (22:3-4).

After all these accounts of Israel's complaints, arguments, and rebellions, it is hard to believe that they were such a frightening enemy. Couldn't Balak have found a way to prey on the divisions among the Israelite tribes? Perhaps by a disinformation campaign? Spreading a rumor that Moses and his God really do want to wipe them out in the wilderness? That shouldn't be too hard. Half of them already believe it!

This makes me want to suggest a counter-reading of the passage. Word had indeed leaked out of the bickering among the Israelites. They were people that were constantly arguing (read *rav* here as derived from *riv*, "quarrel," as in 20:3) and ganging up (*kahal* as in *va-yikahalu*) on their leaders, challenging their authority. "What will happen to my Moabites, who follow me like sheep," thinks Balak, "if they are surrounded by people like these? These ornery, stiff-necked Jews are ***really*** dangerous to a regime like mine." My tribe might learn from them and start asking tough questions.

Before you say that this is just a retrojection, remember that Jews have been a countercultural element ever since Abraham was called *ha-'ivri*, "the whole world standing on one side and Abraham on the other." How did he pass that quality on to his descendants? ***By talking back and arguing, even with God***. He created for them a ***religion*** where you can talk back and argue.

Balak – and those like him – are indeed right to be afraid, even though the view from ***within*** the Israelite camp looks very different. "The power of Israel is in their mouths," says an old adage. It lies precisely in the fact that we are trained to speak so freely.

2 וישלח מלאכים אל בלעם בן בעור

"He sent messengers to Balaam, son of Be'or" (22:5). No biblical figure is treated as badly by the rabbinic tradition as Balaam. Even Esau – like Balaam often having *ha-rasha'*, "the wicked," added to his name – is depicted with a certain humanity. But not Balaam, despite the fact that in the text he does all that Y-H-W-H asks of him, and blesses Israel assiduously.

In fact, there are two pictures of Balaam presented in the tradition. One always calls him "Balaam the Wicked." He is a magician who cynically turns to evil forces in order to distort the truth. The other says that he is a true prophet, one even as great as Moses, and in some ways even greater. Often these two views are found in combination. It is the latter view, of course, that is much closer to what the text really says.

The second view was often neglected in the past, but is an important one for us to hear. Its neglect, or intentional avoidance, took place in the context of religion as a zero-sum game: for my prophet to be true, yours needed to be utterly false.

We cannot dismiss Balaam so quickly. It means that there is indeed prophecy outside Israel, that we do not have the only channel to hearing the divine word. Once we recognize that truth, our task is one of separating the true prophecy in the words of those prophets from the worldly elements with which they have been combined in the various traditions that stem from them. On what basis can we do this? How do we distinguish a true prophet from a false one, as an upcoming *parashah* will ask? Only in retrospect, by looking at the ***effect*** of their words, both on individuals and societies. What kind of community has been created in response to this prophecy, what values emerge from it, including both the good and the bad?

Once we raise that question about non-Mosaic prophecies, however, we need to respect the right of others to judge our Torah in the same way. What are the good and the bad, they might ask, that have come out of the prophetic path we Israelites have followed?

Perhaps that is why we are given this prophecy of Balaam in the Torah, as well as its location right here, after all the quarrels and dissention within Israel. Perhaps this prophecy of Balaam is given to us as a mirror to be held up opposite the prophecy of Moses, one that we should not be afraid to look into, an opportunity for ***reflection***. How does our behavior as a community supposedly following Moses' teaching appear in the mirror of Balaam's prophecy? Is this a real problem, or just one that can be solved by our public relations department?

3 אם לקרוא לך באו האנשים קום לך אתם ואך את הדבר אשר אדבר אליך אותו תעשה

"If those people came to call you, arise and go with them, but do only what I tell you" (22:20).

Why does the divine strategy change between the first and second sets of messengers? First God tells him to refuse to go with Balak. Then he allows him to go along, but reminds him to do only what He commands. If Balak here is the real enemy and Balaam is sincerely trying to follow the will of Y-H-W-H, what are we to learn from these two approaches that the inner voice suggests to the prophet? And then why does the angel stand in Balaam's way when he tries to follow what God has told him to do?

Sometimes our attempts to "just say no" are not going to work. Simply refusing to go along with the "evil urge" or the demonic forces in the world will not work, either because we will fail at it or because such a gesture is ultimately ineffective. Instead, we try to go along with them a certain part of the way, precisely to use the power that gives us for the sake of the good. Think of all those old films you've seen about the young woman who takes the job with the Vichy regime in order to spy for the French underground. Or, for that matter (with a *le-havdil*, if you choose), of the "leakers" or whistleblowers from within the halls of what they see as unjust governments?

It takes an awful lot of courage to follow that course. In the first example, even a willingness to die. Perhaps the voice of Y-H-W-H to

Balaam represents a high-minded intent, an ideal that will be hard to fulfill. The angel or messenger of Y-H-W-H, who has lived in this world among real human beings, does not believe he'll be able to stand the test.

How does this work within our lives as individuals? How dangerous is it to follow this second counsel? Do we trust ourselves enough? Or should we listen to our faithful ass and just stop in our tracks?

4 ובגויים לא יתחשב עם לבדד ישכון

"A people that dwells alone, not counted among the nations" (23:9).

This definition of Jewish identity, first proclaimed here by the prophet of the nations, survived for nearly 3000 years, until the twentieth century. But does it today? Does the collective decision of the Jewish people to create a nation-state nullify this form of identity? Today we are proud to have a Jewish state "counted among the nations." We rejoice in seeing the Israeli flag fly at the United Nations. But does that mean that we are just a nation, like all others? Isn't that what the prophet Samuel warned us against when we first asked for a king? And where does that leave the half of the Jewish people living in the diaspora? And what does it say of the citizen of Israel who is not a Jew, but bears a different national identity?

But the State of Israel is not identical to the Jewish people. We Jews are still the ***Children of Israel*** (as distinct from "citizens of the State of Israel"), that lone people that chose to follow the ever-elusive Y-H-W-H, in our own unique wilderness-born way. No matter where we live and to which state we owe loyalty, we remain the seed (spiritually more than biologically) of Abraham and still affirm the covenant of Moses (with all our questions and challenges). We remember that we were slaves in Egypt and know that "freedom" was inscribed on the tablets; we are obliged to help all who struggle to be free. We stand up against the many idolatries amid which we live, including that of nationalism, no matter which color flag it waves. We still seek a life of holiness, decency, and respect for every person as a living image of God.

Jewish statehood has not brought this existence to an end. We are still seeking to survive as a minority throughout the diaspora, as well as seeking to learn how to turn a long exilic tradition into the basis for a modern state.

We need to do both of these in ways that reflect our most basic values – awareness of divine presence, a life of holiness, freedom, and respect for humanity. These are great challenges and our future depends on them. In seeking to fulfill them, we are still "***a people that dwells alone***."

5 והנה איש מבני ישראל בא ויקרב אל אחיו את המדינית לעיני משה ולעיני
כל עדת בני ישראל והמה בוכים פתח אהל מועד.

"A man from amid the Children of Israel brought that Midianite woman near to his brethren, before the eyes of Moses and the whole community. They were weeping at the entrance to the Tent of Meeting" (25:6).

A very strange verse. Who is weeping, and why? RaSHI quotes the sages as saying that Zimri challenged Moses, saying to him: "Is this woman permitted to me or forbidden? And if you say 'Forbidden,' who permitted you to marry the daughter of Jethro (a "Midianite priest")? Moses remained silent; "The law (or maybe *halakhah* as 'a pathway out of this') escaped him." Then Pinhas rose up and did the deed.

This interpretation remains unsatisfying. Is Moses silent because he knows that Zimri is right, that he has caught him? He does not know what to answer. But then do he and the whole community break out in tears? What is the nature of that weeping?

But we might try another reading. Suppose it is Zimri and Kozbi who are in tears. Yes, the contact with the Midianite women began on the lowest level. But these are two respectable young people, children of tribal leaders, "from good families." They fell in love and want to be accepted, living together as a couple. Moses responds to their weeping and seeks to find a solution. But he hesitates. Does he dare to permit it on the basis of his own example?

Then Pinhas jumps in and kills them. We have no escape from denouncing him as a fanatic, trying to prevent Moses from giving in. His deed opens the path toward the most horrid and shameful passage in our Torah, the killing of the Midianite women and children.

But let us go back to Zimri and Kozbi, weeping at the place of judgement, the entrance to the Tent (Might we think of it as "the rabbi's study?"). What shall we do for them? The solution of Pinhas is not for us.

פינחס
PINḤAS
(Numbers 25:10-30:1)

1 הנני נותן לו את בריתי שלום

"I hereby give him my covenant of peace" (28:12). The protest against this verse begins in the Torah text itself. Look carefully in the Torah scroll and you will see that the word *shalom* here is written with a very rare broken line in the *vav*. It seems that someone quite early in the chain of transmission (these Masoretic notations are eighth-ninth century) needed to find a way to say that the "peace" of this covenant was not quite whole. Or at least that he was not quite "at peace" with it.

Pinhas is one of the hardest biblical heroes for Jews in our age. The tradition that he was reborn as Elijah perhaps also indicates an understanding, already in ancient times, that he was in need of a "makeover." Elijah is a harbinger of universal redemption. Tribal vengeance must be conquered before that redemption can come. Elijah has to turn not only "the hearts of fathers to their children and the hearts of children to their fathers," but the hearts of Midian toward Israel and the hearts of Israel toward Midian. Only then can he announce the messiah. It seems appropriate that Pinhas, reincarnated as Elijah, should be the one to deliver this message. Even ***he*** has to be convinced.

2 ויהי אחרי המגפה

"It was after the plague" (26:1). Here occurs another rarity in the Torah text. The reader is instructed to pause in the middle of the verse. Only then do we go on and read about the new census of the people. It seems as though a moment of silence has been injected into the text in memory of those who died, as though we shouldn't pass over them too quickly.

But why is the verse interrupted here and not after all the earlier plagues that fill this book about the wilderness journey? Perhaps "the plague" here refers to the whole extended "plague" of this narrative, that of Israel's constant rebellion and the divine wrath that results. From chapter 11, back in *parashat be-ha'alotekha,* until now, this has been the essential story of the Book of Numbers. From here on there are no more rebellions, no more bursts of anger, no more divine curses. It is the whole pattern that has ***plagued*** Israel's history in the wilderness that is said to end here.

That's worth a deep breath, at least.

3 ובני קרח לא מתו

"And the children of Korah did not die" (26:11). This odd little notation, constituting a verse all by itself, is intriguing. It is usually understood in connection with the psalms attributed to them by later generations, noting that the family had not died out. Then it becomes a way of asserting the important lesson that a once disgraced family name can be rehabilitated.

But it might also mean something like "People like Korah never disappear!" In every generation there will be those who are like him, speaking in the name of "all the people" while really being interested only in self-aggrandizement, accumulating endless power and wealth. Sadly, we have known such "leaders" even in our own generation. We should be on the lookout for them and learn to guard against them.

4 יפקוד ה' אלוהי הרוחות לכל בשר איש על העדה...ולא תהיה עדת ה' כצאן אשר אין להם רועה

"May Y-H-W-H, God of the spirits of all flesh, appoint a *mensch* over the community...Thus will this community of Y-H-W-H not be like a flock who have no shepherd" (27:16-17).

Moses sets a high standard for leaders who will come in his wake. I choose the Yiddish *mensch* to translate *ish* because it is not about either gender or physical strength, but about the virtues of caring about others and their needs. Such a leader is like the good shepherd, the one who knows and cares about each one of his flock.

The choice of the phrase "God of the spirits of all flesh" is also interesting here. As Moses draws near to the end of his life, he seems to be reaching toward a more universal human vision, extending beyond the borders of his own community. "***All flesh***" here reminds us of the boldly universalist use of the same phrase at the conclusion of the familiar *ashrey* psalm (145:23): "May all flesh praise His holy name forever." Is Moses, as he is about to "go the way of all the earth," looking beyond his national mission and seeing again, as he learned back at the burning bush, that Y-H-W-H is indeed God of all?

We ***need*** to find a hint of this Moses here, partly to steel us against the horrifying picture of him to come in next week's reading.

5 אשר יצא לפניהם ואשר יבוא לפניהם ואשר יוציאם ואשר יביאם

"One who will go out before them and come in before them, who will lead them forth and bring them in..." (27:17).

Who is a leader? One who has the courage to be ahead of her or his community. "***To go out before them***" means to be ready to try things that they might not dare, to gently push them forward in a direction the leader thinks is of value. But that same leader has to "***come in***" before them as well. If they are going too far or too fast, doing things that might threaten the essential values of the community, a leader needs to know how to pull them back, to remind them of what they stand for and where they need to draw lines.

A good leader needs to be able to do both of these, sometimes even at the very same time.

6 עולת תמיד העשויה בהר סיני

"The regular offering ('*olah*, also "ascent"), as done at Mount Sinai" (28:6). What is the verse talking about? There is no record in the Torah of a regular daily offering given at Mount Sinai!

Rabbi Barukh of Miedzybosh, the Ba'al Shem Tov's grandson, reads it this way: "Why do Jews constantly *(tamid)* want to 'ascend?' Because they've already done so at Mount Sinai!"

This special desire for experiences of "ascent" or self-transcendence is, of course, not limited to Jews. But it is hard to deny that it seems to be found with great frequency among us. Some of us have to go on long journeys to India, Thailand, or the jungles of South America in order to find a path to fulfill it. Others are fortunate enough to be able to do it closer to home. For many today, psychedelic aids are a helpful tool in such a quest.

But there is also an "ascent" that fulfills itself simply in purity of spirit and doing good in the world. This too can be a recreation of "the ascent done at Mount Sinai."

מטות
MATOT
(Numbers 30:2-32:42)

1 ואשה כי תדור נדר לה׳

"When a woman vows an oath to Y-H-W-H..." (30:4). This chapter begins with the statement that a man's vows and oaths must be kept. But almost all of it then turns out to be about the vows of women. While as contemporary readers we will surely deplore the ability of fathers and husbands to undo women's vows, there is a sense throughout that women's words are real, have power, and need to be taken at face value. It is not coincidental that this chapter almost immediately follows the account of Zelophahad's daughters. Both were significant statements, in the ancient world, of respecting the rights of women. They could own and inherit property, and their word was to be taken seriously. The Torah is not locating women as a class together with children and slaves, as do some later legal formulations.

There should be a way, in our reading of this chapter, to find a basis for equally accepting women as witnesses in rabbinic courts. If the vows of independent women have full validity, as seems to be the intent here, the legitimacy of womens' testimony under oath should be obvious. This is especially important in matters of abuse and sexual misconduct, where women are the main victims, but then should apply to women serving as witnesses altogether. **Why does it not seem to work that way?**

2 וידבר ה׳ אל משה לאמור נקום נקמת בני ישראל...וידבר משה אל העם לאמור...לתת נקמת ה׳ במדין

"Y-H-W-H spoke to Moses saying: Avenge the vengeance of the Children of Israel against the Midianites...Moses spoke to the people saying.... Deliver the vengeance of Y-H-W-H upon Midian" (31:1-3).

The entryway into this terribly dark and difficult chapter, perhaps the most painful to read in the entire Torah, sets out a dilemma. God speaks of it as ***the vengeance of Israel***. They have a mortal enemy, one who has attacked them in a vile and defiling way, and they seek to take vengeance. God does not forbid it. But when the word goes out from Moses, it becomes "***the vengeance of Y-H-W-H***." Surely God is on our side; an attack on us is an attack on Y-H-W-H. Killing Midianites has become a religious duty.

Priests and leaders blessing their troops have spoken this way to armies all over the world as they set out to kill, maim, and destroy. "This war is the will of God. God will help us win it and protect ***His*** troops." Chaplains on both sides of two world wars in the last century said so with fervor. So, too, did those who blessed American troops in Vietnam, Iraq, and Afghanistan. In the latter two cases, imams on the other side were even more fervent in their blessings, sometimes endorsing killing of civilians as well as enemy troops.

This is not said in support of an absolute pacifism; there have been wars that indeed had to be fought. But we need to evaluate carefully and honestly how much they are about our own (including Israel's) national self-interest, often including greed and "honor," and not the will of the Giver of all life, who loves all creatures equally.

Perhaps this call for the "vengeance of Y-H-W-H" is here to remind us of what we too are capable. For that reason, it is particularly important that we read this chapter and cringe while hearing it. It is too easy for us Jews – who have been victims rather than perpetrators for so much of our history – to say that "ethnic cleansing" and genocide are things that other people do. We need to pay attention.

With Aaron and Miriam gone, Moses has been left alone to interpret the word of God. We miss the presence of his brother, the "pursuer of peace," who might have held him back, and of his sister, who translated his words from the commanding "mountaintop" to the deep well. They might have helped him to find another way of interpreting the divine voice. With them gone, Moses stands all alone. Here we suddenly recall that he was chosen after he killed that Egyptian.

3 כל דבר אשר יבוא באש תעבירו באש...וכל אשר לא יבוא באש תעבירו במים

"Anything that goes through fire, you shall pass through fire to purify it. Purification by water shall be for all that cannot pass through firc. Pass it through water" (31:23).

After this terrible slaughter of the Midianites, Eleazar the priest tells Israel's warriors how to purify the booty. The camp will feel defiled if you just bring in all those blood-stained possessions of the people you have just slaughtered. But the rabbis who read this had no use for such an instruction. Instead, they transferred it to the realm of kashrut, and it still stands as the basis for our way to render objects fit for use in a kosher kitchen.

Fire and water are the two agents of purification. They are the two elements that both bring us life and threaten death. They thus bespeak the liminality of our situation. We stand between them, needing and fearing both.

How remarkably unchanged that situation is! In ancient times, the sages spoke of Y-H-W-H as the great Peacemaker, bringing together *esh* and *mayim*, fire and water, to create *shamayim*, the heavens. That is the meaning of "May the One who makes peace in the heavens" at the end of each *kaddish* and *'amidah*. In the centuries of martyrdom in the Middle Ages, we called out: "Save us for the sake of those who went through fire and water for the sake of Your name!" **And today we wonder about whether our civilization will be destroyed by the fires of nuclear holocaust or will be washed away by the rising seas.**

Using these elements to purify, to protect and delineate the little sanctuary of our kosher kitchen, reminds us of their great power and of all the good we can do if we use them well, as well as of the opposite.

4 ונפש אדם ששה עשר אלף

"And of human souls, sixteen thousand. Of them, the payment to Y-H-W-H was thirty-two souls" (31:40). These were the half of the thirty-two thousand surviving virgins who were given to the soldiers. The other half (31:46) were the property of all Israel, presumably available for sale on the open slave market. These “human souls” are listed in the booty following the sheep, the cattle, and the donkeys.

Let us remember what we did there, in its full horror.

5 ויבואו בני גד ובני ראובן ויאמרו...אל תעבירנו את הירדן

“The children of Gad and the children of Reuben said to Moses... Do not have us cross the Jordan” (32:2-5).

This chapter feels like it exists to assert an Israelite claim to the East Bank of the Jordan as well as the West. The listing of all those “fortified cities” that these tribes built, just before crossing the Jordan to fight, seems bizarrely exaggerated. How many fortified cities can a group of shepherds construct in their final year of wandering, while still fighting off their enemies? It sounds much more likely that they inherited existing cities conveniently emptied of their inhabitants and declared them their own. Such things take place in our own day as well.

Let us beware that no neo-Reubenite or “Bnai Gad” movement emerge among Jews amid the strange and dangerous times in which we live.

מסעי
MASSA'EY
(Numbers 33:1-36:13)

1 אלה מסעי בני ישראל

"These are the journeys of the children of Israel as they went forth" (33:1).

If there is a new Kabbalah to be revealed among Jews in our age, I have long suspected that its biblical basis will be these seemingly obscure concluding chapters of the Book of *Be-Midbar*. The *parashah* will go on to list the various stopping places in the course of Israel's forty-year journey through the wilderness. The Torah reading tradition, as practiced in the Ashkenazic synagogue, recognizes a mysterious quality in these place names, chanting them in a special lilting tune that is used only here and at thc Song of thc Sea.

Imagine Moses writing them down as he completes the Torah, just before giving his great final speeches. He knows that he is not to enter the Promised Land, that he will have no part in what lies ahead. Instead, he chooses to leave his people with a list of all those places in which they had camped along the way, back when they were still just wanderers. But this record of travels, seemingly meaningless and perhaps confused meanderings around the desert wasteland, is not written down just as a memento for future generations. There is something sacred in the list of place names – a secret yet to be revealed.

They journeyed from Elim and camped at Yam-Suf. They journeyed from Yam-Suf and camped at Midbar Sin. They journeyed from Midbar Sin and camped at Dofkah. They journeyed from Dofkah and camped at Alush. They journeyed from Alush and camped at Rephidim, where there was no water for the people to drink. They journeyed from Rephidim and camped at Midbar Sinai. They journeyed from Midbar Sinai and camped at Kivrot ha-Ta'avah ("the Graves of Desire").... (33:10-16).

Journeys, wanderings. We Jews have been wanderers for a long time. How did Moses know that this was to be the fate of his people, thousands of years into the future, wandering from place to place? He gave us a zigzagged, back-circling map of forty-two places where we had camped.

Some of the old desert place names seem to have meaning, and might be translated that way. They journeyed from Community and camped at Mount Beauty. They journeyed from Mount Beauty and camped at Trembling. They journeyed from Trembling and camped at Choirs. They journeyed from Choirs and camped at the Bottom (or maybe at "The Rear End"; anyway, it was a terrible place). Others still puzzle us, but the new Kabbalah will undoubtedly find in them sublime secrets, not yet revealed.

Perhaps there is similar meaning to be found in the names of all the other places we have been in the course of this long and sometimes confusing journey. Pumbedita. Fez. Saragossa. Strasbourg. Worms. Prague. Berdychiv. Odessa. Scarsdale. Ann Arbor. Pardes Ḥannah.

I used to think this applied only to diaspora Jews, still eternal wanderers. But now I see that Israelis are among the great world travelers, even seeking out and going to places most diaspora Jews never dreamed of reaching.

Does it ever end? Pardes Hanna. Dharamsala. Katmandu. Ecuador. Bet Shemesh. Casablanca. Netivot. Jerusalem. Los Angeles. What does it all mean? How can there ***not*** be some secret here?

2 ויכתוב משה את מוצאיהם למסעיהם על פי ה' ואלה מסעיהם למוצאיהם

"Moses wrote down the goings forth of their journeys by the mouth of Y-H-W-H; these are their journeys according to their goings forth" (33:2). The forty-two journeys about to be listed here have a mystical meaning, according to the Ba'al Shem Tov. They correspond to the hidden forty-two letter name of God. They seem to represent the totality of human journeying. Just as all forms of labor are said to be found within the thirty-nine listed in constructing the *mishkan*, so are all of life's journeys to be seen here, if we learn how to look.

"**By the mouth of Y-H-W-H**." Does that mean that God decides where we are supposed to go, that we are just unknowing followers? Or might it mean that everywhere we choose to go is nevertheless *'al pi ha-shem*, right next to the mouth of God. ***Wherever it is, Y-H-W-H is speaking there***. We can hear the unique word in that place, if we learn how to ***listen.***

3 ויסעו מרפידים ויחנו במדבר סיני. ויצאו ממדבר סיני ויחנו בקברות התאווה

"They traveled from Refidim and they camped in the Wilderness of Sinai. They traveled from the Wilderness of Sinai and camped in the Graves of Desire" (33:15-16).

In this list, it seems like "Wilderness of Sinai" is just another stop along the way, with nothing special about it. But above in *Shemot* and soon again in *Devarim*, we will read about it as the center of the journey, the very reason we were taken out of Egypt. This is even more so in rabbinic and later sources.

Could this list represent a counter-tradition, in which Sinai was indeed just another stop along the way? They encountered Y-H-W-H in all forty-two places, each a holy letter. They learned Torah all along the way. Their journey didn't need a climax.

What does this say about our own journeys? Is there a "mountain-top moment" somewhere along the way? Does there need to be?

4 ואם בכלי ברזל הכהו וימת רוצח הוא...ואם באבן יד...רוצח הוא...או בכלי
עץ יד...רוצח הוא

"If he strikes him with an iron vessel and he dies...or with a hand-sized rock...or with a wooden bat...he is a murderer" (35:16-18).

And with an automatic rifle?

What might this teach us about the handy availability of deadly weapons?

SEFER DEVARIM

THE BOOK OF DEUTERONOMY

דברים
DEVARIM
(Deuteronomy 1:1-3:22)

1 אלה הדברים אשר דבר משה אל כל ישראל

"These are the words Moses spoke to all of Israel..." (1:1). As Moses prepares for his death, he gathers the entire people, now a new generation, and tells them the story of their forty-year trek through the wilderness.

The opening verses of *Devarim* mark the beginning of ***Judaism*** in two distinct ways. This is the first: ***Judaism is storytelling***. We recount the past, ever passing it on to new generations. Like this one, the story as told is somewhat different from the prior chronicle, perhaps even different than the way things "really" happened. But that is part of the storyteller's privilege, perhaps even obligation. The tale needs to be reshaped so that new generations can receive it.

Think of the most widely observed of all Jewish rituals, the Passover *seder.* The essential *mitsvah* of that night is telling the story. We use the *haggadah*, or "narration," to fulfill the commandment of *ve-higgadeta le-vinkha*, "Tell your child." There too, if the narration is well done, it will change and grow from year to year. "The more you embellish the story (***marbeh*** *le-sapper*)," says the Haggadah itself, "the better it is."

Here in *Devarim*, the story notably does not begin with Egypt, but in the wilderness. Here the formative experience of the people is that of the wilderness journey. Moses is addressing the younger generation, those who grew up in the course of that journey. He wants to frame ***their*** story for them, and to make it no less significant that the story of their parents. In the next *parashah* it will be about the Sinai revelation itself. But Moses as narrator here seems to want the new generation to move on from the memory of Egypt, to see itself as forged anew in the course of these very difficult forty years.

"Moving on" is a value we need to consider sometimes. We expend a great deal of effort on recalling the past, telling the old story. That is as it should be. But Moses may have come to feel that his Israelites were too enthralled with their own version of remembering Egypt. All those good things we had to eat there! Maybe now they needed to be liberated from ***their memory of*** Egypt.

Does this happen to us as well? How do we strike the balance?

2 הואיל משה באר את התורה הזאת לאמור

"Moses was willing to explicate this teaching, saying…" (1:6). This is the second beginning-point of Judaism: commentary. Oral Torah, the need to explicate that which has been given, begins with *Devarim*. Moses opens the door to this process by repeating the narratives and teachings of Torah in slightly different words. This is true even of laws and forms of practice. We then need commentary to reconcile the differences, to decide which version is binding or how they fit together. *Devarim* thus forms the seamless link between written text and oral tradition.

The word used for "explicate" here is *be'er*. The Hasidic commentators note that this word also means "well." It is the act of interpretation that turns Torah into Judaism, making of it a wellspring of ever-renewed meaning that never runs dry. That's exactly the point! It is **bi'ur,** the ability to reinterpret forever, that keeps Judaism bubbling up (or "***welling forth***") as a fresh-flowing stream.

3 פנו וסעו לכם

"Turn and get yourselves moving" (1:7). "***Turn***" is the first word of Moses' instruction to the people. The Hebrew *penu* is an opening that leads in many directions. Is it leading *le-fanim*, "go forward?" Or toward *panim*, the "face?" Or is there an inward turn demanded here, as in *penimi?* Note that the following two words *u-se'u la-khem* are the same rhetorical form as the *lekh lekha* said to Abraham, which we often read as "go into yourself."

The first thing that Moses' Torah, now being explained to the new generation, demands of its hearers is an ability to ***turn***, to change your life. ***Penu u-se'u la-khem*** means "Make the turn to understanding that life is a journey. You are not just here "hanging out," waiting for it to be over and having some fun along the way. It is all about something, a journey of discovery, that of the self and that of the Promised Land, that never quite ends. ***Make the turn and get yourself going.***

4 ואומר עליכם בעת ההיא לאמור...הבו לכם אנשים חכמים ונבונים וידועים לשבטיכם

"I said to you at that time.... 'Take for yourselves wise, understanding, and recognized people in each of your tribes, and I will appoint them your leaders'" (1:9-13).

This is the beginning of a new sort of leadership for Israel. The choice of leaders is to be made on the basis of wisdom and understanding, not heredity. It would have been natural for Moses to appoint the sons of each of the deceased tribal elders to take their fathers' roles. Priesthood was heredity in Israel, and the future kingship would be as well. Why not tribal leadership also?

Here, too, we may see a beginning of what later came to be called Judaism. Leadership was to be based on wisdom and understanding, not heredity. Note also the qualification of "listening among your brothers (1:16)." Being a leader requires the ability to listen well.

It is also noteworthy that the appointment of judges is now linked to the account in *Be-Midbar* 11, not that in *Shemot* 18. In doing so, the *Devarim* account changes the nature of that event. Instead of the charism of shared prophetic spirit that poured down upon them (*Be-Midbar* 11:17), the tribal leaders are called upon to judge by their own understanding. In the generations following that of Moses, we have no more prophecy. All we are left with is the teaching and our own wisdom in trying to understand its message for us. Eventually we come to learn, of course, that such wisdom is itself a divine gift.

5 לא תכירו פנים במשפט כקטן כגדול תשמעון. לא תגורו מפני איש כי המשפט לאלוהים הוא

"Recognize no faces when judging; listen alike to the small and

great. Fear no person, for judging belongs to God" (1:17). Do not give special privilege to the "great" or powerful when they come before you in judgment. They expect that their faces will be recognized for special favors, and impartiality is essential. This also means giving no special privilege to people of your own tribe, nation, or race, those whose faces you might "recognize" more readily. But take care of over-favoring the "small," or the underprivileged, as well. Their moral position can draw us toward favoring them unfairly, and as judges it is not our place to do so. "Fear no person" includes the small as well as the great. Judgment is a sacred process, ultimately in the hands of God.

We seem to need a special reminder about this matter these days, in at least two countries we know.

6 וייראו מכם ונשמרתם מאד. אל תתגרו בהם

"They are afraid of you; be very careful not to challenge them" (2:4-5). This is an important reminder. Yes, you are the stronger party. They have reason to fear you. But that does not mean that you can do whatever you want. If you act like an aggressor and push them around just because you can, things can still go badly, for you as well as for them.

This is a part of the "purity of arms" that does not get enough attention. But we have seen examples of people who think that just because they are stronger they have a free hand to do whatever they want. History will not judge them well. As I write these words, the Russians are failing in Ukraine. More important, they are turning the whole world against them.

We should be paying close attention to this lesson. You can't get away with things just because you are stronger. And not only in Ukraine.

ואתחנן
VA-ETḤANAN
(Deuteronomy 3:23-7:11)

1 עלה ראש הפסגה ושא עיניך...וראה

"Go up to the peak of the mountain; lift up your eyes...and see..." (3:27). Moses does so only at the very end of this Book of Devarim (34:1). All that comes up to there are the words of Moses, long speeches to Israel that somehow delay his ascent up the mountain. Think of this as the last act of an opera, that long aria before the hero dies. Or perhaps compare it to the Book of Job, with a framing tale at the beginning and end, enclosing the true content of the book's dialogues.

Moses is indeed a great leader, but one who has failed near the end of his days. Was his failure that of striking the rock at Merivah? Or was it perhaps his failure to stand up against God (as Abraham would have!) and protest the command to slaughter all those Midianite women and children? In any case, we no longer see in Devarim the living, dynamic relationship between Moses and Y-H-W-H that filled the pages of the earlier narrative. He only speaks to the people in the name of Y-H-W-H, but we never see him turn toward heaven. After he is told "Do not speak to Me any more ***about this matter*** (his impending death – 3:26), he in fact never speaks to God about ***anything***.

Is the One who will take his soul simply waiting respectfully until Moses completes his charge to the people? Or is He hoping that His faithful servant will turn toward Him and speak once again? But he never does.

2 ואתם הדבקים בה׳ אלוהיכם חיים כולכם היום

"You who cleave to Y-H-W-H your God *are fully alive* this day!" (4:4) This verse, plucked wholly out of its original context, plays a key role in the emergence of Jewish faith. It is the first source for the notion of *devekut*, "cleaving" or "attachment" of the soul to Y-H-W-H. This is the language most used for mystical devotion and union throughout later Judaism.

Prior to this verse, the root דבק is best known from its usage in Gen. 2:24: "Therefore a man leaves his father and mother and cleaves to his wife, and they become one flesh." Only here in *Devarim* is it used in several places to refer to attachment to Y-H-W-H. That means that the word always carries with it an erotic edge, a sense of ***intimate*** attachment to the One. The same is true of the word *yada'*, used for "***knowing*** Y-H-W-H," since that verb first appears in Gen 1:4: "Adam knew his wife Eve."

My teacher, Abraham Joshua Heschel, in his masterful ***Heavenly Torah***, discusses the controversy between the schools of Rabbi Yishma'el and Rabbi Akiva over the meaning of this verse. Moses will say later in this same chapter that "Y-H-W-H your God is a consuming fire (4:24)." The students of Rabbi Yishma'el asked: "Can a person cleave to a consuming fire and live?" They answered: *Devekut* means attachment to God's ***ways***. Just as He is compassionate and merciful, so should you be. Or it might mean "Cleave to the sages, the masters of Torah." Rabbi Akiva disagreed. The verse means what it says, he argued. "Cleave to the fire of Y-H-W-H!" *Devekut mamash* – ***really*** cleave!

Rabbi Akiva's reading is the beginning-point of Jewish mysticism; Rabbi Yishma'el's is foundational to Jewish ethics. As Heschel's own life demonstrated, one does not have to choose between the two. "Both these and those are the words of the living God!" "Hold fast to this one," the wise king says, "but do not let go of that other one, either."

3 וידבר ה׳ אליכם מתוך האש. קול דברים אתם שומעים ותמונה אינכם רואים

"Y-H-W-H spoke to you from the midst of the fire. You hear the sound of words, but you see no image" (4:12). The shift into the present tense in this verse is striking. Moses is recounting the events at Sinai for a new generation born in the wilderness, about to enter the land. But he wants to retain the vividness of the present tense. So too is he saying it to all generations. Our Torah is one that reveals itself to those who love it through the living word. "A great sound that never ends" (5:19), echoing through all the ages. The revelation of Torah is a living, life-giving, and never-ending process. "You ***hear*** the sound of words," in the ever-present tense.

"But you see no image" – even though Exodus (24:10) says that the elders "saw the God of Israel!" But Moses here wants to distance them from the visual element in revelation. The commandment "You shall make no graven idol or image" will be stronger if there indeed was no image seen, even at Sinai.

But then what of "All the people saw the thunderbolts and torches" (Ex. 20:15)? That's just the point, says the BeSHT's grandson, rabbi of Sudilkow. They were busy looking at the side-show, all the "special effects" that accompanied the revelation! Had they truly heard those first two commandments as powerfully spoken by Y-H-W-H, we never could have forgotten them.

4 ויוציאך בפניו בכוחו בגדול ממצרים

"He brought you forth from Egypt by His face, by His great power" (4:37). This verse often goes unnoticed amid the rich prose of this chapter. At first it seems to contrast with the verse we have just explained. At Sinai there was only a voice. But did Israel see the face of Y-H-W-H as they were redeemed from Egypt? Doesn't "face" imply a visual sort of revelation? Were they redeemed "by the face?"

But the face of Y-H-W-H is not seen, even by Moses. "You may see My back, but My face will not be seen" (Ex. 33:23). The human encounter with God's face is not one of seeing. It is one of receiving its light, in which our own faces becoming vehicles for the transmission of divine light. "May Y-H-W-H cause His face to shine upon you" (Num. 6:26) does not mean that you will "see" God's face. It is a blessing to help us receive that light without ever looking directly into it. ***"May the light of God's face shining into you make you into a person of grace"*** is its meaning, enabling you to pass that light on to others. It is by the light of that face shining through us that we are redeemed from all our Egypts.

5 וידעת היום והשבות אל לבבך כי ה' הוא האלוהים...אין עוד

"Know the day and set it upon your heart that Y-H-W-H is Elohim in heaven above and on earth below – there is none other" (4:39). Three great lessons emerge from this verse, and their coming together is not coincidence.

Ve-yada'ta ha-yom, "Know the day," takes us back to our reading of the first day of Creation. It is not called "first," but "***one*** day," note the commentators. Light and darkness, daylight and dark night, combine to form a single day. So, too, with joy and suffering, blessing and loss, life and death. Together they form a single day. "Know the day" – understand that you need both constitute a single whole day in the reality of this world in which we live. Accepting this truth will guide us through many hard days, even those "in the valley of death's shadow."

Y-H-W-H *is Elohim*. This too takes us back to *Bereshit. Elohim* is that plural-form name for the singular God. As soon as Creation happens, there are bound to be multiple ways of experiencing the One. Not only do religions and symbol systems vary; so too do individuals and their ways of encountering that One. Even within a single person, the way we meet God will vary from one day to the next. ***Ve-yada'ta ha-yom*: recognize that this day, too, is one in which you can find another of the many faces of *Elohim*.** All those faces are one; Y-H-W-H may be present in all of them, if our hearts are open to the breath that flows into them and gives them all life.

Eyn 'od. The *Tanya* (2:1) insists on translating these words as "There is ***nothing*** else." This means that everything we encounter is potentially a face of *Elohim*, and all of them are Y-H-W-H.

Put these all together and you have a teaching to live by, a *torat ḥayyim*.

6 שמע ישראל יהו"ה אלוהינו יהו"ה אחד. ואהבת..

"Hear, O Israel…And you will love" (6:4-5). *Shema' yisra'el*, says the Zohar, refers to "the upper unity," the realization that all is one in Y-H-W-H. This is the consciousness that sees beyond Creation and back before it. "You were the One before the world was created, and You are the One since the world has been created." Unchanged. We add in a whisper "Blessed is the name of God's glorious kingdom forever" – referring to a "lower unity," in which Y-H-W-H remains One ***in and through*** all creatures.

The commentators have long struggled with *ve-ahavta* as a commandment to love. How can love be commanded? Love arises from a spontaneous movement within the human heart! Therefore, says the Maggid of Mezritch, see it as an assurance, rather than a command. When you really take the truth of the *shema'* into your heart, the result will be love. You will love all that exists, all that emerges as the manifestation of the One. Hence the English translation as "will," rather than "shall."

The rest of the paragraph continues from there. You will be so excited by that love that you will be talking about it all the time: when you lie down and when you get up, from the time you leave your house in the morning until you return at night. You'll keep trying to drum it into your children! You'll write your Lover's name on your arms and between your eyes, so you won't forget it! You'll be scribbling it on your doorposts and on your gates!

That's what it means to be in love with Y-H-W-H, ***your*** (in the singular) God. None less than the very sober Maimonides describes that love for us:

> What is that proper love? One should love Y-H-W-H with an exceedingly great love, very powerfully, until one's soul becomes bound to Y-H-W-H. One is thus intoxicated by it constantly, as though sick with love-sickness, one's mind never being free of the love of that woman.... All the Song of Songs is a parable of this. (*Mishneh Torah, teshuvah* 10)

עקב
‘EIKEV
(Deuteronomy 7:12-11:25)

1 כל המצווה אשר אנכי מצווך היום תשמרון לעשות למען תחיון

“Take care to perform *kol ha-mitsvah*, the entire *mitsvah,* that I place before you today, *so that you come alive*” (8:1).

Each day has its own *mitsvah*, unlike that of any other. The day is waiting for you to discover and fulfill it. Indeed, it for that purpose that the gift of this day has been given to you. It takes great discernment to figure out what is the special *mitsvah* of the particular day in which you stand. It is possible to do lots of *mitsvot* in the course of a day, yet still to miss the crucial one.

Once you find that *mitsvah*, make sure to examine it carefully, understanding how to fulfill it in its wholeness. ***Kol ha-mitsvah*** often demands much more than you had expected. How will you know when you have found it and done in that complete way? You will feel the ***le-ma‘an ti<u>h</u>yun***, “so that you come alive,” the surge and renewal of life that doing ***the whole mitsvah*** brings you.

2 כי לא על הלחם לבדו יחיה האדם כי על כל מוצא פי ה׳ יחיה האדם

“A person does not live by bread alone; a person lives by all the comes forth from the mouth of Y-H-W-H” (8:3). We have here the first echo of what the prophet will call “a hunger, but not for bread; a thirst, but not for water, but to hear the word of Y-H-W-H” (Amos 8:11).

A person’s spiritual needs are no less real than those of the body. While we may no longer believe, as did the Hasidic masters, that there is inner “limb” of the soul calling out for fulfillment of each of the 613 commandments, the experiential reality underlying that teaching remains true. Our spiritual limbs, too, need their sustenance.

Torah provides us a language that serves as a set of keys for unlocking the doorways to the inner life. For those of us who are both blessed and afflicted by facing questions like "Why do I exist? What am I to do with these years I have been given? What is it all about?" the urgency of finding such keys, and being sustained by what lies behind them, is no less great than that of finding food and water to sustain the body.

"I rejoice over Your spoken word like one who has found a great treasure!" (Ps. 119:162)

3 כי ה׳ אלוהיך מביאך אל ארץ טובה ארץ נחלי מים מעיינות ותהומות יוצאים בבקעה ובהר

"For Y-H-W-H your God is bringing you to a good land, a land of streams of water, of wellsprings and depths that emerge from both valley and mountain" (8:7).

Even in our age of a very concretized *erets yisra'el*, it is still permissible sometimes to spiritualize the notion of Promised Land. To follow Y-H-W-H through your personal wilderness truly does lead to a good land. This is our statement of faith. There will be streams of water that flow forth from mysterious depths within us, wellsprings that we did not know were there.

We have to understand, however, that these wellsprings are to be discovered both in the mountains and in the valleys. Sometimes the waters flow as we expect they will, gushing down from the heights of a "peak experience" and sustaining us in its glow. But at other lines we will find the waters only in the low places, the ***valleys*** of our journey. There, too, we must learn that it is possible to dig for water.

4 ועתה ישראל מה ה׳ אלוהיך שואל מעמך כי אם ליראה את ה׳ אלוהיך ללכת בכל דרכיו ולאהבה אותו ולעבוד את ה׳ אלוהיך בכל לבבך ובכל נפשך

"Right now, Israel, what does Y-H-W-H your God ask of you? Only that you be in awe of Y-H-W-H your God, walking in all His ways, loving Him, serving Y-H-W-H your God with your entire heart and soul" (10:12). Here is the classic Jewish definition of the life of service. It requires a joining together of *yir'ah*, "awe," and *ahavah,* "love."

Neither is whole without the other. We are filled with awe and wonder as we stand in the presence of the One. "How many billion years old did you say this planet is? How many galaxies are out there? How did we evolve from such primitive forms of life?" We are overwhelmed and dwarfed by our sense of astonishment. That is *yir'ah ila'ah*, a sense of awe at the majesty of existence.

But then we add the assertion that this underlying One of the cosmos called Y-H-W-H knows you, loves you, calls out to you, specifically, in a unique way. Otherwise, why were you brought into existence? The One desires to be manifest in each of its creatures. *Yismaḥ Y-H-W-H* ***be-ma'asav. Divinity rejoices in each form of existence that it brings forth*** (Ps. 104:31).

To this we can only respond by opening our hearts to receive that love and to respond to it. Now we are ready to serve.

5 הוא תהילתך והוא אלוהיך

"He is your praise and He is your God" (10:21). This is the place to quote the teaching of R. Pinḥas of Korets that I have tried to make famous. "People think that you pray ***to*** God," he said. "But that is not the case. Rather prayer ***itself*** is truly of the divine essence."

God is not just the addressee of prayer, the One to whom we are speaking. The presence of divinity is found in the act of prayer itself, in the opening of our hearts. In prayer we are discovering and revealing the presence of that One within ourselves. In ancient times, God was described as "dwelling upon the cherubim" (Ps. 80:2). Today we understand that Y-H-W-H is "dwelling within the prayers of Israel" (Ps. 22:4). **"He is your praise; He is your God!"** They are one and the same.

6 והיה אם שמוע תשמעו אל מצוותי אשר אנוכי מצווה אתכם היום לאהבה
את ה' אלוהיכם ולעבדו בכל לבבכם ובכל נפשכם

"If you truly listen to My enjoinments by which I join Myself to you this day, loving Y-H-W-H your God and serving Him with your entire heart and soul..." (11:13).

I take this second paragraph of the *shema'* to describe the great journey that is the life of faith. Once you know in your heart that Y-H-W-H is one, you are ready to set out on that journey. Know in advance that it is going to be is a bumpy ride. It contains moments of seemingly boundless spiritual fulfillment and reward. But there are also times of fear, loneliness, and disappointment. They are all part of the roller coaster called life. But our faith is that Y-H-W-H is present in all of them, binding them together. Perhaps that is why this passage begins with the word והיה, which is nothing other than Y-H-W-H in hidden form. Sometimes you just have to turn the letters around to rediscover the name – and the Presence.

The passage begins with *Le-AHAVAH et Y-H-W-H eloheykhem.* It appears as though a noun has replaced the verb: it is not *le-ehov*, "to love" in the usual verbal form, but *le-ahavah*, to be in the state that can only be described as "love." There is a hidden warning here not to take this second paragraph of the *shema'* too simplistically. The simple or childlike reading of this passages tells us that if we really love God, lots of good things will come our way. If we don't, "better watch out." That is the faith of childhood; it doesn't work for adults, who have seen that the world isn't constructed that way.

But we adults have something else; we have an understanding of *le-ahavah*, of the state of being in love, as something that has the potential to transform our vision. The experience of being in love has the power to change the way we approach life's journey. If we learn to look through the eyes of love, *le-ahavah*, we may see our world – the same world, with the same pain, the same losses, the same arbitrariness – in a different way. We will learn to ***accept*** life, and the world in which we live it, with all its faults, as only longtime lovers can. How much we learn to accept in those we love! So too the "One" we love. When we do that, we can receive the real reward this passage promises, at its very end (as our teacher R. Zalman translated it), *ki-yemey ha-shamayim 'al ha-arets*, "heavenly days, right here on earth!"

This paragraph describes a journey that lasts through the course of an entire human life. "Yes, let yourself dare to love! Be in that state of loving Y-H-W-H, which means loving All that is! Be ready to serve, with all your heart and all your soul. You will *love* doing it; you will fill up on the rewards of all that love: inner versions of wine, corn, and oil. But watch out; these things don't last forever. Constant joy is no joy at all, as the Ba'al Shem Tov taught. One day, when your heart just isn't paying attention, you will find yourself distracted, "turned aside," and worshipping something else. The heart is always worshipping something. When we turn aside from Y-H-W-H, there are countless other preoccupations lined up to take that place, to become our "gods" for the moment. False gods, of course.

But then you look around and "the heavens will shut up and there will be no rain." You will get angry. "Divine wrath will break out ***in you***." How quickly you will feel that you've lost your moorings upon the land! All of a sudden you will feel that faith has abandoned you, that all is lost, that there is nothing left. Yes, these moments happen in the life of every religious person.

What is the life-raft you hold onto in such a moment? Here the Torah turns sharply from *de*scription to *pre*scription. It is now that you need to take My words to heart, quite literally. Now those once spontaneous responses to the discovery of oneness, of Y-H-W-H filling all and being expressed everywhere, need to be turned into ritual. "Tie them on your hands! Bind them between your eyes!" "Write them on your doorposts!" Then you will be more than thankful that you have the wherewithal to do that. It is in these moments of feeling totally lost and without moorings when we most need the reassurance of ritual, of familiar religious forms. Those simple and down-to-earth things will bring you back to life, helping to hold your faith in those moments of doubt and despair that happen in every religious life. Trust in them and they will carry you over to the place where you and your offspring will indeed enjoy those "heavenly days right here on earth."

Trust me. I know.

ראה
RE'EH
(Deuteronomy 11:26-16:17)

1 ראה אנוכי נותן לפניכם היום את הברכה ואת הקללה. הברכה אשר תשמעו
למצוות ה' אלוהיכם...והקללה אם לא תשמעו.

"Look! Today I place before you blessing and curse. The blessing is that you listen to the *mitsvot* of Y-H-W-H your God by which I join Myself to you this day. And the curse is if you do not listen…" (11:26-28).

Seeing and hearing are joined together in these verses, just as they were at Sinai, when we "saw the audible and heard the visible." The "today" of this verse is that of the reader; every day is such a day, if you will both look and listen.

Note that the positive part of the passage does not use the word "if." The blessing is ***that*** (*asher*) you listen. Learning to listen with one's inner ear to the *mitsvah* of each particular day is itself a tremendous blessing. The day calls forth with its ***enjoinment*** (understanding *mitsvah* derived from *tzavta*). "This is how you may be joined to Y-H-W-H on this day!" We need only to be there to listen. The blessing does not come about ***because of*** our listening; the privilege of listening itself is the greatest of blessing. Perhaps this is what our sages meant by "The reward of a *mitsvah* is a *mitsvah*;" such inner listening bears its own reward.

The curse, on the other hand, come upon us only "***if*** you do not listen." Listening means engagement; not listening is to become disengaged, and that leaves a day of emptiness. "Nature abhors a vacuum" – we have left a space for all sorts of "curses" to enter our day.

2 ושמחתם בכל משלח ידכם אתם ובתיכם אשר ברכך ה' אלוהיך

"You shall rejoice with everything that your hand reaches, you and your household with which Y-H-W-H blesses you" (12:7). The verse is said about pilgrimage to "the place God chooses" and offerings there. These are immediately followed by the call for a total rejoicing, involving everything your hand can reach. The ideal of *'avodat ha-shem be-simḥah*, serving God with joy, which we so associate with Hasidism, is in fact an imperative of the Torah itself.

The phrase *mishloaẖ yad*, "That which your hand reaches," also means "profession" or "trade" in rabbinic Hebrew. It is that which you set your hand – or your talent – to do. The verse then means that the shoemaker should rejoice with fine leather, the farmer with bounteous crops. The teacher should rejoice over a great class s/he's taught, the doctor with success in healing a patient. Whatever is your "occupation," you should be able bring it to your inner Jerusalem, a way to celebrate the divine presence that uplifts and transforms your life.

3 כי ירחיב ה' אלוהיך את גבולך...כי ירחק ממך המקום...

"When Y-H-W-H widens your border...if the place is too far from you...you may eat meat as you desire" (12:20-21). This is a very interesting example of a change in the Torah's law, a compromise with a new situation. *Va-Yikra* (17:1-4) allowed only the consumption of sacrificial meat. Here in *Devarim*, with its insistence that sacrifices be permitted only in a single place, it became impossible to demand that meat be eaten only in Jerusalem. A new ruling was thus issued. Yes, you could slaughter domestic animals for food, eating them just as you would a deer or a wild goat (they must have still been hunting!). All was permitted, as long as you let the blood run out.

New circumstances required a change in the Torah. The religion of Israel seems to have survived that change. What might that tell us about changes in our own day? Were these verses considered as precedent when the Conservative rabbis permitted driving to *shul* on Shabbat, now that "the place is too far from you?" The synagogue, the *midkash me'at*, is too far away for you to walk. Was that a fair application of them? Many people, including some from within that movement, now regret that decision. Others think it was truly necessary, given Jews' pattern of living. These days, there are many who want to "attend" services via Zoom. Should this be permitted only for the sick or elderly shut-ins?

Or should it be either completely forbidden, or an option for anyone? How do we know when to apply a halakhic principle like "A decree that people can't live up to" to help allow for changes in *halakhah*?

We understand how very fragile *halakhah* is, especially because it is a "law" that has no means of enforcement. We therefore think more than twice before we allow for changes in it. But it is important to note that the Torah itself here seems to have permitted a major change due to "***If the place is too far from you***."

4 מקץ שבע שנים תעשה שמיטה

"At the end of seven years, you shall declare a release (*shemitah*). This is the content of the release: every lender shall open his hand to release his neighbor" (15:1). Here again we see a great change. The *shemitah* of *parashat be-har* was all about giving ***the land*** a chance to rest. It seems to have been created for an agricultural society. Here in *Devarim* it is all about the human community, a matter of borrowing, lending, and proper treatment of the poor.

Behind the text here is a historical change. The Israelites have become a more urban and business-centered society. The old rule about letting go of the land for the year is now being applied to releasing the poor from debt. One cannot but think of Marx's analysis of the switch from the land-based to the capital-based economy. The "means of production" is no longer the soil, but the capital one needs to borrow in order to undertake a new venture, to "bring something forth." Therefore, the rule of *shemitah* comes to be applied in an entirely new way.

But perhaps the most telling verse in this section comes a bit later: "For the poor will not stop existing from within the land" (15:11). This is an admission that the *shemitah* of loans, or any other do-good device we might create, will not solve the problem. Marx's classless society is in fact a dream, one that turned out to be a nightmare. There will always be people at the bottom of the ladder, and they will need you to "open your hand to ***your*** brother, to ***your*** poor, to ***your*** needy, in your land." If the land is yours, so too is responsibility for the poor and needy who live within it, all of them. They too are ***yours***.

5 ושמחת לפני ה׳ אלוהיך אתה בנך בתך עבדך והלוי אשר בשערך והגר
האלמנה והיתום אשר בקרבך

"You are to rejoice before Y-H-W-H your God, you, your son, your daughter, your servant, the Levite within your gates, and the stranger, thc widow, and thc orphan within you (*be-kirbekha*)" (16:11). This passage is speaking of the festival of *Shavu'ot.* Three verses later, when speaking of *Sukkot,* the widow, orphan, and stranger are also included as "within your gates." This difference allows us to think that here these three are perhaps internal "widows, orphans, and strangers, ***be-kirbekha***, '***within you.***'"

Many of us have parts of ourselves who feel eternally like victims or outsiders. They refuse to join into the celebration when we are happy, standing off by the side and not allowing us the wholeness of our joy. Rabbi Nahman knew these parts of the psyche well; he insisted that we not leave them as "wallflowers" at the party, but chase after them and force them into the circle of our dance. Yes, all of us carry lots of unhealed pain within us and will throughout our lives. But there are times of true joy as well, when we need to let go of those feelings of alienation and hurt, to bring our whole selves into the moment of celebration and joy.

Shavu'ot, when we stand again each year before Mount Sinai, is surely such a moment, a time to make our whole selves join into the dance.

שופטים
SHOFTIM
(Deuteronomy 16:18-21:9)

1 שופטים ושוטרים תתן לך בכל שעריך

"Place yourself judges and guards at all your gates" (16:18). The verse sounds so tough and restrictive! But then we recall a well-known Zohar passage that reads *she'arim*, "gates," as the gates of the imagination (from *le-sha'er* as "to imagine"). This becomes a piece of spiritual counsel: Keep your fantasy life under control. The inward journey is one that thrives on cultivating a rich imagination. That is mostly for the good. But there are places where it can lead you astray, especially if you lose the sense that it is an imaginative creation.

Where are we to place those "judges and guards? Where do you need to exercise judgement and watchfulness over your imagination? I cannot tell you, because they are different in each person's journey. But they exist. This *mitsvah* in the Torah will come in use some day.

2 צדק צדק תרדוף למען תחיה

"Justice, justice shall you pursue, so that you live" (16:20). The only values linked in traditional Jewish language to the verb "pursue" or "chase after" are justice and peace. Here we are told to pursue justice, and elsewhere "Be of the disciples of Aaron, who was a lover and pursuer of peace."

An old midrash (BR 8:5) says that justice and peace argued before humans were created. Justice said "Let them be created," because of all the acts of justice they will do. Peace said: "Let them not be created, for they are all about conflict." The tale is based on Psalm 85:11, which reads "Compassion and truth *nifgashu*; justice and peace *nashaku*." The midrash follows what was probably the original meaning of the two verbs: they met in conflict and did battle, *nashaku* as related to *neshek*, "armament." But *nifgashu* can also refer to meeting in love, and *nashaku* can mean "to kiss." (See the comment above in *parashat shemot* about the meeting and kiss of Moses and Aaron.)

"Justice, justice" here says we should not give up on humanity. Yes, humans are full of conflict, often leading them to do terrible things. But listen to the insistent voice of Justice in this debate. We ***need*** people, for the sake of all the justice they can do. Eventually, we believe, justice and peace will get to meet and kiss.

Think about this tension next time you hear "No justice, no peace!" chanted at a rally for justice. We need them both.

3 כי יפלא ממך דבר למשפט...דברי ריבות בשעריך וקמת ועלית אל המקום אשר יבחר ה׳ אלוהיך

"When a matter is too wondrous for you to judge…[causing] controversies in your gate, rise up and ascend to the place which Y-H-W-H has chosen" (17:8).

The Hasidic readings (TYY *va-yeḥi*, 247; DME Shoftim) say that in order to resolve conflict, you need to go up to a higher place. The seven *middot* within the self exist in intentional tension with one another, giving rise to differing views. We live in the world that they have created. We need love, awe, pride, triumph, submission, and all the rest in order to live our daily lives. But sometimes they stand in conflict with one another. We need to recall that in their source, *binah*, the "Higher Place," the womb in which they were all conceived, they are all one. Take them there. "Rise up and ascend *el ha-makom*, to Y-H-W-H, who is called the cosmic "place."

This truth works on an internal axis just as well as a vertical one. It applies to internal conflict as well as to those between parties. To resolve a conflict, go deeper, closer to the Source. The self-humbling involved in taking that journey will in itself become the first step toward resolution.

4 רק לא ירבה לו סוסים ולא ישיב את העם מצרימה למען הרבות סוס

"He shall not have many horses, and shall not take the people back to Egypt for the sake of having many horses" (17:16). This strange rule for the future kings of Israel stands out in the text. Why would he "take the people back to Egypt" in order to acquire many horses? Might it refer to an alliance with the Egyptians, something the prophet Jeremiah was to rail against? Or is "take the people back to Egypt" to be read in a metaphorical way? He should not enslave the people, nor overburden them with taxes, for the sake of his own grandeur. "Beware of kings," perhaps the Torah is saying, as they have a tendency to sell the people out.

What would these "kings" and "horses" be in our own day? Governments and their desire for tanks and fighter jets? Or grand presidential mansions? Expensive gifts given to presidents and prime ministers? Or even more valuable "gifts" of national resources that the ruler distributes to his various friends?

The preceding verse (17:15) says to choose a king "from among your brothers," not a "foreign" ruler. But *nokhri* can also mean "distant" or "alienated." Beware of what power can do to people. Even those who arise from within the people can get into that nasty habit of collecting horses. Then they become "foreign," even to those who elected them.

5 והיה כשבתו על כסא ממלכתו וכתב לו את משנה התורה הזאת על ספר...
והיתה עמו וקרא בו כל ימי חייו

"When he is seated on his royal throne, he shall write this second teaching in a book, before the priests and Levites. It shall be with him, and he shall read in it all the days of his life" (17:18-19).

Can we imagine a democracy where "the first thing I'll do when I get into office" will be copying out the constitution, in longhand, a document that will then remain on the president's desk throughout her term? It might be a bit humbling to some of the people who have held that office.

A favorite Hasidic reading (*Tif'eret Shelomo*) sees the "king" here as the rebbe. In order to be a true rebbe for others, you need to have the teaching with you (i.e. "***within*** you") at all times, and be able to read all the days of your life in it. This means not only that you read it each day, but that you must be able to use Torah to ***as a way of understanding everything that happens in your life***. You must "find" each day of your life in the Torah.

The training of rebbes thus parallels that of psychoanalysts. It is having undergone your own analysis that most qualifies you to work with others. Only when you can find "all the days of your life" within Torah are you truly ready to "say Torah" to others.

כי תצא
KI TETZE
(Deuteronomy 21:10-25:19)

1 כי תצא למלחמה על אויבך.

"When you go forth to war against your foe" (21:10). The Hasidic readings almost always take these "battlefield" passages as referring to the inner battle, the person's ongoing struggle against the evil urge. One is reminded of the way the Sufis speak about ***jihad***, as the constant war within the heart. The human soul is a battlefield, site of an ongoing struggle between good and evil.

Of course, the Hasidic sources had the luxury of being able to read these passages just in a spiritual way. They did not yet have to think about questions of "purity of arms," what sort of conduct is to be permitted of soldiers in a real war. We read these passages today with very different eyes. The situation demands that we do. But even when facing the frenzy of real battle, the fighter must ask him or herself "Who am I? ***How can I be true to myself in this moment?"***

Can we ever win the inner struggle against evil without convincing ourselves that both we and the person opposite us, our enemy, are both holy souls, part of the same living God? Or dare we not allow ourselves to think such a thought, lest it make us freeze up and not shoot?

2 כי תצא למלחמה על אויבך.

"When you go forth to war against your foe" (21:10). This model of the divided inner self, caught up in the struggle between our two urges, reaches back into the earliest rabbinic sources. But it is first found in the book of *Devarim* itself, with its great emphasis on moral alternatives, the need to choose good over evil and the results of that choice. It stands in contrast to a different model, one that is perhaps best articulated in the daily morning prayer "My God! The soul You have placed in me is pure." This becomes more central in the mystical tradition; the pure soul, "a part of God above," struggling to emerge from behind *kelipot*, outer shells that it needs to break through in order to become most fully itself.

The second model, that of soul and "shells," is more optimistic than the first. The person, as soul, is essentially good, a goodness that is struggling to burst forth. But the first, the sense of ongoing battle within the self, defends itself as being more "realistic." But which of them will be more useful in controlling our behavior, whether on the battlefield or in daily civilian life? This is an old question, forming the essentially different approaches to the person of the Hasidic and traditional Mussar traditions. Therapists of various schools still debate and struggle with approaches that are nothing other than modern versions of this question.

3 ואם לא חפצת בה ושלחתה לנפשה ומכור לא תמכרנה בכסף. לא תתעמר בה תחת אשר עיניתה

"If you do not want her, send her forth on her own. You may not sell her for money or mistreat her, since you raped her" (21:14).

Here we have a woman taken captive, considered a part of the booty. That was understood as legitimate in biblical times. She was given no choice in the matter. But then you get her home, your urges settle down, and things look different. You see her again after she is all cleaned up, and you realize it is not going to work. How will she get along with your mother? With your other wives? Will she ever master the food taboos of your crazy Israelite kitchen?

You realize you made a mistake, and you want out. Understand that you cannot simply discard her. She is a human being, not a piece of property. Whether physically or emotionally, you forced yourself upon her. Even if you observed all the rules – waiting for her to mourn, to cut her nails, and all the rest – it is still considered rape.

Might this passage be helpful to us in our current discussion of what we mean by sexual abuse?

4 כי יקרא כן ציפור לפניך

"If a birds' nest happens before you" (22:6). The rabbis originally objected to a reading of this verse that demonstrated God's mercy. "If someone says," they taught, that this means 'Your mercies reach even unto a birds' nest!' they should be silenced (Berakhot 33b)." Divine decrees are not to be reduced to anything, not even to mercy.

But the Kabbalists outdid the rabbis' wildest dreams. The 'bird" here, they claimed, is none other than *shekhinah*. Her "nest" is this world, the place where She has chosen to dwell. If you should happen upon that reality "along the way," you must learn to recognize it. *Shekhinah* is the mother bird; the eggs and chicks are human souls. We are that fragile, and the divine spirit hovers over us, seeking both to feed us and to protect us. The remaking of "God," from the all-powerful father-figure in so many people's imagination, into a mother bird, hovering over her chicks and feeding them, is in itself a worthwhile exercise.

But in other places the Kabbalists offer a "higher" reading. Here, the bird is *binah*, the "upper" divine Mother, surrounded by the emerging *sefirot*. Then you send Her off into the upper world and take the "baby birds," the lower *sefirot*, which are the seven *middot* or moral qualities, and the eggs, unborn souls, and live through them. ***Our mental trap will never catch the free-flying bird that is Y-H-W-H. But we can still "walk in God's ways*.**"

5 כי תצא מחנה על אויביך ונשמרת מכל דבר רע

"When you go encamp against your enemy, be on guard against any evil thing" (23:10). This verse stands alone, coming without any further explanation. RaMBaN's commentary unpacks it well. ***"It is well known that camps going out to battle eat all repulsive things, steal, and act violently. They are not even ashamed of sexual transgression and mistreating corpses. Even a person of upright nature comes to be garbed in cruelty and wrath as that camp goes forth against the enemy."*** Already in the thirteenth century it was clear what war does to those who fight it. "Beware of any evil thing" is a very broad warning, recognizing the grave danger of what happens to people in this situation. Nothing much has changed, it seems, in the intervening centuries.

The warning applies to our interpersonal battles as well. We hear stories of "road rage" where someone without a prior record of violence beats someone terribly because he cut him off in traffic. We know stories of terrible divorce battles, where two usually decent people do things that are vindictive and ugly. News coming from the West Bank in recent months shocks us, but belongs to the same genre, the result of the uncontrollable passion of rage. "Battle mode," if allowed to run rampant, can lead us into terrible places.

The same can be true of internal battles. There may be something you don't like about yourself, even a quality you define as your "evil urge," against which you feel you need to do battle. Still, "***beware of any evil thing***." Fight it in a way that will not destroy you as a person. Always remember the great power of kindness and compassion, in dealing with others and in the way you treat yourself. As the Torah says a few verses later (23:15), "***Let your camp be holy.***" Even the camp of battle.

6 לא תסגיר עבד אל אדוניו...עמך ישב בקרבך במקום אשר יבחר באחד
שעריך בטוב לו

"You shall not hand a slave over to his master...He shall dwell in your midst, wherever he chooses, in one of your gates, where it is good for him" (23:16).

Yes, the Torah was written in an age that still accepted human slavery. We cannot escape that. But there were limits; the slave was still a human being. That meant that s/he was essentially entitled to freedom. Once a slave had gained it, even by flight, you could not help take it away.

American Jews who were here already before the Civil War should have been obligated to join the underground railroad, but not many did. How can we still get onto that train?

Read the verse carefully. The former slave should be able to live anywhere he wants, "wherever he chooses." No restricted neighborhoods. No "redlining." No participating in clever arrangements that keep certain suburbs "lily white." Or Galilee towns that do not allow Palestinians to move in.

"In one of your gates." I think about those "***gated communities***" in which so many people are choosing to live these days. Does the verse mean that we are being called upon to allow immigrants, fleeing from slavery, as well as descendants of slaves, to live "within our gates?"

כי תבוא
KI TAVO
(Deuteronomy 26:1-29:8)

1 כי תבוא אל הארץ אשר ה׳ אלוהיך נותן לך

"When you come to the Land that Y-H-W-H your God gives you" (26:1). This refrain, heard so frequently throughout the Book of *Devarim*, hearkens back to the call to Abraham in Gen. 12:1: "Go forth from your land…to the land that I will show you." There we followed the Hasidic reading of the word *erets*, "land," as referring to *artsiyyut,* meaning "earthliness" or "corporeality." The call to Abraham is one of leaving behind his former attitude toward earthly things and learning to see them through a new perspective, that of Y-H-W-H. This refers to the presence of godliness throughout all of earthly existence; "the whole earth filled with God's glory."

But there is a difference. For the Hasidic masters, that meant mostly a leaving behind of asceticism, a rejection of this-worldly concerns, and especially of the human body, as inherently defiled. They were emerging from a kabbalistic worldview that sought to create pure souls by training people to detach from the corporeal world, punishing the body until it would lose its attraction to earthly desire. The "land" belonged to the Gentile peasants around them; they should have as little to do with it as possible. "No, that is not the way," the Ba'al Shem Tov taught. ***The land, meaning the corporeal world, including the body, belongs to Y-H-W-H.*** Find and uplift the holy sparks that lie ***within*** the corporeal world and all its beauty. You will do this best by appreciating this world and ***finding it worthy*** of uplifting.

We come from a different place. The former "land" or attitude toward material things that we are called upon to leave behind is that of hedonism and reckless consumption. We live with levels of creature comfort and luxury, without regard for the destruction we cause, and still we long for more. (Just think: What will you ***order*** from ***Amazon***

– think of it as the grim reaper of rainforests – today?) Yes, the Torah is calling us to leave that way of living, that *erets*, behind us and to enter the new "land" of discovering the divine glory in each place and each moment as it is.

When you get there, you will want to "put the first fruits of your land" in a "basket," bringing them up (or "in?") to "the place where Y-H-W-H your God chooses to make God's name dwell." That may be a private inner place or a communal place, one where you come to express your gratitude over this gift of transformation.

Understand that this new "land," this new *artsiyyut,* that shines through with divine light, is a ***gift.*** It is not you who have either discovered or invented it; it is "***the land that I will show you***."

2 ארמי אובד אבי

"My ancestor was a wandering Aramean" (26:5). Hear the utter humility of this formulation. There is no "You loved Abraham more than anyone else" or "You chose us at Sinai as Your special treasure." We were just an ordinary wandering tribe, descendants of some lost Aramean. The Egyptians oppressed us terribly, and we cried out to You, the God of our ancestors. You heard us and redeemed us, bringing us to this place. That why I am bringing You my first fruits. The lack of grandiosity here is astounding.

The singular form of this declaration (*avi* rather than *avinu*) hints at its applicability to each person and his/her redemption from a particular "Egyptian bondage."

Try telling the story of your own enslavement and liberation just that simply, with the same lack of pretense. Go ahead. Give it a try. Then bring your "first fruits" as a gift of gratitude.

3 ושמחת בכל הטוב אשר נתן לך ה׳ אלוקיך

"Rejoice in all the good that Y-H-W-H your God has given you" (26:11). Here we need to pay attention both to "rejoice" and to "good."

"It's a *mitsvah* to be happy always!" says Rabbi Nahman of Bratslav, a man who struggled so hard to do so. God loves happiness and wants us to find it. And at what should we be happy? "In ***all*** the good" – in the gift of life itself that we receive every day, in all that sustains us, in both body and soul. We are surrounded with reasons to be happy.

But *tov*, "good" can also be read as "goodness." We are happy that God made us caring and compassionate, that much goodness is deeply implanted within us. Yes, we have to cultivate those qualities, both in ourselves and in our children, but their roots lie deep within our hearts. The capacity to share God's goodness with others is also a divine gift.

4 את ה' האמרת היום...וה' האמירך

"You caused Y-H-W-H to speak...and Y-H-W-H caused you to speak" (26:17-18). This is how the *Sefat Emet* reads it, based on an interpretation ascribed to Yehudah Ha-Levi.

We, Israel, caused Y-H-W-H to speak. Moses was the one who was able to translate divine thunder-speech into words of human language (Ex. 19:19). We preserved that mystery of divine speech and have expanded and expounded upon it over many generations. The core message, the one "we heard from the mouth of that Power," still echoes within us: "I am Y-H-W-H, liberating you from bondage. Therefore, worship nothing else as God." The rest is all our verbal expansion of that truth, ever continuing to bring Y-H-W-H further into language.

But in this same process, Y-H-W-H has transformed ***us*** into language. Our story, our way of life, is a tale told throughout humanity about a people redeemed and seeking to live in that Presence. ***Becoming Torah*** is the role for which we are chosen.

5 וכתבת על האבנים את כל דברי התורה הזאת באר היטב

"Inscribe upon the boulders all the words of this teaching, carefully explained" (27:8).

The words *ba'er heytev* may just mean "clearly written." But in the context of Jewish culture, they refer to the endless rounds of commentary that are offered on each word and letter of the text. Picture these two great stones erected at the entrance to *Erets Yisra'el* as written like a Talmud page. The text is in the center and the commentaries surround it. But surrounding them are more commentaries, and around them still more. All the understandings of these verses, throughout all the generations, are there on those boulders. They keep expanding and growing as the generations go on.

In fact, *Ba'er Heytev* is the title of a well-known commentary on the *Shulhan 'Arukh*. You will find it down on the bottom of the page, surrounding those earlier commentaries that already surround the text.

6 ארור האיש אשר יעשה פסל ומסכה תיעבת ה'...ושם בסתר

"Cursed is the person who makes a molten idol, that which Y-H-W-H reviles...and places it in secret" (27:15). Why is there a special prohibition against those who keep their idols hidden? Hidden from others, or even from themselves?

What is a "secret idol?" Do we have any?

נצבים
NITZAVIM
(Deuteronomy 29:9-30:20)

1 והתברך בלבבו לאמר שלום יהיה לי כי בשרירות לבי אלך

"He will feel contented in his heart, saying "I'll be fine!" using that tough heart muscle" (29:18). This description of the individual who refuses to see him/herself as belonging to the covenant is well known to us. "I'm fine" is the way people say "No" these days. It means, "I don't need whatever it is you are offering," as though everything were a question of consumerism and buyer appeal. This person doesn't see the consequences that appear in the next verse: **"Y-H-W-H will separate him for the worse**." He has already separated himself out of indifference; it is going to turn out badly.

To see yourself as belonging to a covenant is to live responsibly. "I understand that my actions will affect others, even the shared situation of us all. I will therefore live in accord with that understanding." You are part of a community, a covenanted partner.

We Jews have been born into two covenants: that of the Jewish people, reaching back to Abraham and Sinai, and that of all humanity, even all living creatures, going back to Noah. Both of those covenants are in bad shape today for the same reason: people who say "No, thanks. I'm fine."

2 פן יש בכם שורש פורה ראש ולענה...למען ספות הרווה על הצמאה

"Lest there be within you a man, woman, family, or tribe…a root that bears the fruit of wormwood and gall. He will bless himself in his heart, saying 'I will follow my own tough heart,' adding the quenched on to the thirsty" (29:17-18).

The final phrase seems to be an idiom the meaning of which has been lost. It must have made perfect sense to ancient desert wanderers.

Some interpreters refer it to the land, meaning that the rich fields will become as wasted as the dry deserts. Others see it as referring to the sins the wicked will commit, adding unnecessary misdeeds onto those for which they really thirst.

Both readings combined seem to fit our generation. We are so filled up with our own version of "wormwood and gall," the fossil fuels that we have spouting forth from under the ground and beneath the sea, that we are about to turn our earth into a heat-stricken wasteland. We do so not because we ***need*** the endless levels of creature comfort and convenience that dependence on them has brought us, but because we do not know how to wean ourselves off our addiction to them.

3 ושב ה׳ אלוהיך את שבותך

"Y-H-W-H will return along with your return, having mercy for you" (30:3). This seems like the proper translation for *shav*, rather than the expected *heshiv*, at the opening of this verse. The verse wants to avoid the sense that God causes our return. Our freedom requires that the return to Y-H-W-H be at our own initiative.

But then the verse only makes sense if one changes the meaning of *et*, reading it as "with." *Teshuvah* is a mutual process; our return to Y-H-W-H creates an opening from "above" or "within" for a sense of merciful presence that embraces us. "Open for Me a space like the eye of a needle, and I will open for you a broad corridor."

It feels hardly accidental that this chapter is always read during Elul. The *Sefat Emet* finds the same message in the tradition that this month's name may be read as an acronym for *Ani Le-dodi Ve-dodi Li*, "I am my beloved's and my beloved is mine" (Cant. 6:3). Why, he asks, isn't the name *Dalul*, after the verse *dodi li va-ani lo,* "My beloved is mine and I am his, which occurs earlier in the Song of Songs?" (2:16)

The process of *teshuvah*, which defines this month, he says, has to begin with us.

4 לא בשמים היא לאמור מי יעלה לנו השמימה...אלא בפיך ובלבבך לעשותו

"It is not in heaven, saying 'Who will ascend to heaven for us,

taking it for us and letting us hear it, so that we might do it...The word is very near to you; it is within your mouth and your heart to do it" (30:11-14).

This does not sound like Moses is saying: Torah ***used to be*** in heaven, but I brought it down for you. This is a different voice speaking in the name of Moses. If you choose, you may say that he sees things differently in these moments before his death. The teaching does not dwell in heaven, but in the human heart. Its spoken word is not one that comes out of the heavens, but out of your own mouth.

These verses open the doorway to an understanding of the journey to Y-H-W-H as an ***internal*** rather than a ***vertical*** one. Such an undercurrent has existed in Judaism since ancient times, though often garbing itself within the garments of verticality. In our time, I believe, that reading has to "come out of the closet" and serve as our primary metaphor for understanding religious experience and the life-path that embodies it.

These verses come immediately after the Torah's only use of the image of the circumcised heart: "Y-H-W-H your God will circumcise your heart and that of your children to love Y-H-W-H your God with all your heart and all your being, so that you might live" (30:6). Circumcision of the heart is a very powerful and graphic metaphor. It means cutting away that which hides the heart's opening, the place of its vulnerability, removing its defenses. Then the "journey" to loving Y-H-W-H becomes one of going into that newly open place, rather than traversing the heavens.

Of course, "up" and "in" are ***both*** metaphors. "Heaven," my great teacher insisted, exists within the human heart.

וילך
VA-YELEKH
(Deuteronomy 31:1-31:30)

1 וילך משה וידבר את הדברים האלה אל כל ישראל

"Moses went (or 'walked') and spoke these words to all Israel" (31:1). Where did he go? Why does the verse begin with this seemingly needless and unexplained detail?

Moses kept going, even at the end. Tradition describes the human being as a *mehalekh*, a walker, as distinct from the angels, who are *'omdim*, standing in one place. Walking signifies personal growth and spiritual striving, never being satisfied with what you have done or whom you have become until that moment. Even as he is about to announce in the next verse his inability "to go in and out" any longer, he was still walking. That, too, is a form of growth.

2 ויכתוב משה את התורה הזאת ויתנה אל הכוהנים בני לוי...ואל כל זקני ישראל

"Moses wrote this teaching and gave it to the priests, sons of Levi, those who carry the covenantal ark of Y-H-W-H, and to all the elders of Israel" (31:9).

This is the beginning of tradition. Moses hands over a written text to be passed on to the next generation. Notice that he gives it both to the priests and the elders. The priests were probably interested in all the details, getting every sacrifice right, every stricture of ritual purity, and all the rest. But who were the *zekenim*, the elders of ***all*** Israel, at this moment? Remember, everyone over forty, except for Joshua and Caleb, had died out during the years of wandering. There were no physical elders in the camp! Therefore, "elders" has to mean something else here. These were people with lots of life experience, those who would know what it means to live with this teaching in the real world. They were to serve as a counterpoint to the priests, wise leaders who came from within the people. They would know how to apply the teaching to the lives of ordinary human beings.

Each of us who lives within a religious tradition carries such a "priest" and "elder" within us. Living the life of Torah requires constant negotiation between them.

3 ועזבתים והסתרתי פני מהם

"I will leave them and hide My face from them" (31:17). What is this hiding? Why does Y-H-W-H hide the divine face from humans? Some read it as punishment; evildoers are not worthy to be in God's presence. But it may be read in the opposite way as well. The face of Y-W-H-H emanates a bright, shining light. Were God to allow that light to shine on evil deeds, it would bring them out in all their horror, for all to see. Those who perpetrate them would be utterly shunned and disgraced. The hiding of God's face is an act of *hesed*, giving them a chance to repent of their own accord.

Or perhaps the face is hidden because there are moments when Y-H-W-H simply cannot bear to look at these creatures of His and the way they are destroying His world.

In our daily *shaharit* prayers, we say: "He shines light upon the earth and upon those who dwell upon it in compassion." In order to be worthy of seeing God's light, we first need ***"to dwell upon it in compassion."***

4 ואנוכי הסתר אסתיר פני ביום ההוא

"I will hide, hide My face on that day" (31:18). This verse is quoted and interpreted on the first page of commentary on *bereshit* in the *Toledot Ya'akov Yosef*, the very first Hasidic book to be printed. He says that the doubling of the word "hide" refers to two levels of hiding. In the first, you know that something is hidden or lost, and you look for it until you find it. But there is a second level of hiding, indicated by *haster astir*, where you do not yet know that you are missing anything, and thus cannot even begin to search.

Why is this quoted on the first page of the first Hasidic book? He is saying to his readers: "After you read this volume, you may not yet have found the treasure you seek. You may not have all the answers. But you will surely know that there is something missing, and you will forever be a seeker."

The author of these teachings would be happy with the same result.

האזינו
HA'AZINU
(Deuteronomy 32:1-32:52)

1 האזינו השמים ואדברה ותשמע הארץ אמרי פי

"Listen, O heavens, and I will speak; may earth hear the words of my mouth" (32:1).

"Listen, O heavens" immediately calls to mind the opening of Psalm 19: "The heavens declare the glory of God." Our relationship with the heavens, it appears, is a mutual one. We listen to their (silent) testimony and we expect them to hear ours as well. But "heavens" here can be understood in various ways. Moses could be speaking just to the vast expanses of skies as he ascends the mountain, looking out toward the Jordan that he will not cross. But *shamayim* is also used as a name of God, as in King Solomon's *ve-atah tishma' ha-shamayim*, "May You hear our prayers, O heaven" (I Kings 8:) or "May heaven help you!"

Or, perhaps it is indeed the people he is addressing, and "heaven" and "earth" are ***modes*** of hearing. "Listen to me with the heavens within you as well as the earth!" May the angel and the beast who dwell within your heart both hear my words! Listen to me with your deepest soul and your coarsest impulses! Both you***r shamayim*** and your ***erets*** need to listen.

2 כי שם יהו"ה אקרא הבו גודל לאלוהינו

"As I call out the name Y-H-W-H, ascribe greatness (*godel*) to our God" (32:3). The act of calling out a name is one of great power. In choosing to use this name of God, the one revealed to him at the beginning of his journey, Moses is closing a circle. He has learned over the course of these forty years what it means to call out the name that includes all of being: past, present, and future, including but transcending all of time and space, as a single One. It contains all that is, both mortality and eternity, striving and acceptance, bounteous blessing and wrathful destruction. In this prototype of what will later be rendered as *yitgaddal ve-yitkaddash* ***shemey rabba*** ("May His ***great Name*** be exalted and holy"), he has learned to embrace them all.

3 כי חלק ה' עמו יעקב חבל נחלתו

"The people of Y-H-W-H is His portion, Jacob His inherited lot" (32:9). The Hasidic sources regularly invoke this verse to mean that Israel are part of divinity, that there is no separation between Jacob's descendants on earth and the heavenly prototype of the patriarch, the blessed Holy One, Source of all blessing.

The very same sources teach that "the soul is a portion of God above." This must be taken to include every human soul. We are a continuum with the Holy One from the moment when God breathed that first divine breath into the nostrils of (the still undivided) Adam/Eve. That must include all humanity; it is not unique to Israel. In bad historical circumstances, there were Jews for whom this truth became blurred or confused. Today we need to stand up and clearly proclaim that Judaism is not a tradition that may be understood as based on a claim of spiritual superiority, making it a sort of spiritual racism.

Then what does our verse mean? It refers to the collective, not the individual. Each human being is indeed a part of Y-H-W-H, in an equal way. But we Israelites ***as a people*** have declared ourselves to belong to Y-H-W-H; our ***national and historic*** existence is dedicated to embodying and proclaiming divine truth.

The following verses go on to say how much God delights in this desert foundling, protecting them like an eagle hovering over her nest, then carrying the young amid her pinions as she flies, feeding them the very best the fields below have to offer. Most of the rest of the poem, however, is a bitter outcry against Israel for betraying this trust, for not living up to the great hope that Y-H-W-H had pinned on them.

In our day we have lived through a great rebirth of the Jewish people, following the most wretched destruction the world has ever seen.

Everyone who gazes upon this process sees it as something of a miracle. In this moment, we have been given a chance to reclaim that role, to make ourselves worthy to be called a people of Y-H-W-H.

How are we doing so far?

4 כי לא דבר ריק הוא מכם כי הוא חייכם

"It is not an empty matter for you; it is your life" (32:47). The well-known midrashic comment goes "If it is empty, it is so because of you," meaning that you have not put enough of yourself into it. That emptiness is filled up only when the Word and the person meet.

What do we mean when we say that Torah, the teaching, "is your life?" Our approaching the end of this volume offers a good moment to reflect on that. ***It is quest for meaning that makes living worthwhile.*** That is what ***torah*** or "teaching" is; we engage with this ***teaching*** as a guide in that process, seeking the resources within it – a religious language, symbolic deeds, daily opportunities (called *mitsvot*) to become closer to the One who is at the core of all being. The ongoing process of creative reinterpretations helps to express and constantly enrich that meaning. Torah has served as a never-failing spring to nourish that quest for Jews and others over the course of several thousand years.

Even in struggling with the text, even when we feel forced to reject its outer meaning and to dig deeper, we are engaged in that work. That is why the blessing over Torah study is worded ***la-'asok*** *be-divrey torah.* We are commanded not to believe, not to accept, but to ***engage*** *with words of Torah.* Our statement of faith is that we find this engagement worthwhile. Torah's statement of ***faith in us*** is that we will succeed to finding ever-new meaning in it to nourish our generations.

Yes, there are days when the well feels empty, like a spring has gone dry. But our sages' comment "If it's empty, it's because of you," has taught me to say "I guess I'm having a bad day" rather than that Torah has failed. If this writing of *divrey torah* has taught me anything, it that new insight may come tomorrow. That too is a statement of faith.

וזאת הברכה
VE-ZOT HA-BERAKHAH
(Deuteronomy 33:1-34:12)

1 ה׳ מסיני בא...תורה צווה לנו משה

"Y-H-W-H comes from Sinai…Moses commanded us the Teaching" (33:2-4).

Our faith in Y-H-W-H comes to us because of the experience of Sinai, that of standing in that overwhelming presence, a moment that has never waned. Rabbi Barukh of Miedzybosh interpreted the verse, "The daily ascent-offering that was first made at Mount Sinai" (Num. 28:6) to mean: "Why do Jews constantly want to reach upward? Because they were already there at Mount Sinai!" Our verse can be read the same way: Y-H-W-H is always "coming from Sinai." In that moment of limitless love and awe, drawn together as one, we heard from the mouth of that powerful encounter: **"I am the One who liberates you from all your Egypts, from all your narrow straits! Worship nothing less as God!"**

These two *dibrot*, "speech acts," exist beyond all limits. They echo in our ears and hearts for all eternity. They are said to contain the entire teaching.

Moses follows up with *torah*, numerically 611. These are the spelling out of how to make the two commandments real in our daily lives. The Zohar calls them "611 counsels" by which to fulfill Torah's essential message.

2 תומיך ואוריך לאיש חסידך...האומר לאביו ולאמו לא ראיתיו ואת אחיו
לא הכיר ואת בניו לא ידע...יורו משפטיך ליעקב ותורתך לישראל ישימו
קטורה באפך וכליל על מזבחך

"Your oracle is with the one who is devoted to you (*<u>h</u>asidekha*)… Who says of father and mother 'I don't notice them,' who does not recognize his brothers or know his sons. Such shall offer Your

judgments to Jacob and Your teachings to Israel, placing incense in Your nostrils and offering wholeness on Your altar" (33:8-10).

The blessing of Levi contains the only use of the word *hasid* in the Torah. His devotion to Y-H-W-H and to equal justice demands that he set aside any favoritism in the hour of judgment, even to the members of his closest family.

It is this love of justice that permits him to "place incense in" God's nostrils, mitigating the wrath that blows forth from them when injustice rules the world. Human justice has to be able to pass a divine "smell test." When it does not, those nostrils get clogged up and nothing good comes forth from them. Our practice of justice keeps God from catching "a cold in the nose," when the divine forces of retribution might get released.

This is the most ancient theology of Israel. Even after all we've been through over those many centuries, it's still worth our attention.

3 אשריך ישראל מי כמוך עם נושע בה׳ מגן עזרך, ואשר חרב גאוותך

"Happy are you, Israel! Who is like you, a people who is saved in Y-H-W-H, the shield of your help. But pride is a sword that will destroy you" (33:29).

This translation offers a radical re-reading of Moses' final message to the people Israel, but I believe it is the one we need to hear today. It prepares the way for Zechariah's "Not by strength, not by power, but by My spirit" and for our sages' wisdom that "The power of Israel lies in their mouths," in their teachings, in what they have to say.

The return of the Jewish people to the arena of history, thanks to the Zionist movement, was redemptive on many levels. The Holocaust indeed proved to us how urgently it was needed. But the cost of this return has been tremendous; let us not be afraid to confront it. The choice of the name "Israel" for the state, and the almost universal support for the State of Israel among Jews, have transformed the meaning of our people's ancient name in the ears of our generation. "Israel" no longer sounds like "**a people saved in Y-H-W-H**" or like one that advocates a life of "But by My spirit." Israel is thought of as a major military power, as an exporter of deadly arms all over the world, and as a strong nation dominating and oppressing a much weaker one, sometimes brutally, over three quarters of a century. Its great successes and victories cause it to face the grave danger of "**Pride is a sword that will destroy you.**"

How do we restore the "wrestler with Y-H-W-H" who also lives inside this name Israel? How do we recover the notion that Israel – meaning the entire Jewish people, wherever we live – are a people dedicated to the teachings of Y-H-W-H and to doing good in the world, not only for ourselves? Is there a way for us to reclaim the mantle of "a kingdom of priests" that we dedicated ourselves to being at Mount Sinai? How do we again come to see ourselves as "**a people saved in Y-H-W-H?**"

4 ולא קם נביא עוד בישראל כמשה אשר ידעו ה׳ פנים אל פנים

"**And there arose no other prophet in Israel like Moses, whom Y-H-W-H knew face to face**" (34:10). Note that the verse does not say that Moses knew Y-H-W-H face to face, but that **Y-H-W-H knew Moses** that way. The inviolability of the divine face remains; no person may see God and live. Moses remains a human being. His greatness as a prophet stemmed from the fact that he was able ***to reveal himself*** fully before Y-H-W-H.

Our faith is in a God who seeks to ***know*** each individual human being. But we spend our lives hiding from God, from the possibility of letting ourselves be seen as we truly are. This has been true of humans since our first ancestors were exiled from – or fled – Eden. It is also the way Moses began his own relationship with the One who spoke to him from the burning bush. He "hid his face" (Ex. 3:6).

The forty-year journey from that moment to here was one in which Moses overcame both reasons we have for hiding from God: excessive ***fear*** and ***shame***. He let God see him fully, with all his faults. Because of that undefended state, he was able to hear the divine word, to translate it into human speech, and to respond to it without the hesitation caused by either of these. To say that there has been no one like him since is no surprise. But, say the Hasidic masters, each of us has "***an aspect of Moses***" within us.

5 לעיני כל ישראל

"For all the great signs and miracles that Moses wrought *le-'eyney kol yisra'el*, "for the eyes of all Israel" (34:12).

Wow! What he did for their eyes – and for ours! But that's what a religious leader does. He helps open their eyes, helps them to see – to see themselves, the world, and the teaching – in a new way. Moses may be called the original ***visionary leader***. It was through his eyes that this ragged bunch of slaves were able to see themselves as a free people. It was he who reminded them that they were the descendants of Abraham, the Children of Israel.

But, in the largest sense, what is it that Moses has helped all Israel to see? ***Bereshit bara' Elohim***! Through his Torah we have come to see that the whole world, all of Creation, is filled with the ever-creating presence of Y-H-W-H.

Torah has come into the world to remind us that we live in a created universe and to serve as a guidebook for responding to that truth.

חזק חזק ונתחזק !

Onward, from strength to strength!

תם ונשלם. שבח לאל בורא עולם

Complete are our readings,
Former and later.
All we have left
Is to praise our Creator!

Arthur Green, PhD, is recognized as one of the world's preeminent authorities on Jewish thought and spirituality. He is the retired Irving Brudnick professor of philosophy and religion at Hebrew College and rector of the Rabbinical School, which he founded in 2004, and professor emeritus at Brandeis University. He also taught at the University of Pennsylvania and the Reconstructionist Rabbinical College, where he served as dean and president. Green is author of several books including *Judaism's Ten Best Ideas: A Brief Guide for Seekers*; *Ehyeh: A Kabbalah for Tomorrow*; *Seek My Face: A Jewish Mystical Theology*; and *Radical Judaism*. He is long associated with the Havurah movement and a neo-Hasidic approach to Judaism.

We are

Monkfish Book Publishing

...an independent press publishing spiritual and literary books from a diverse range of perspectives. Genres include memoirs, wisdom literature, fiction, and scholarly works of thought. Monkfish books appeal to the seasoned or novice seeker as well as to the general public looking for reliable sources on spirituality. The readers we had in mind when we began Monkfish in 2002 were devoted spiritual seekers, the type whose passion for the spiritual quest would lead them to read across a dazzling array of traditions: Buddhist, Hindu, Jewish, Christian, Muslim, Native American and more. It has always been our intent to publish works of spiritual authenticity for the general public as well as the specialist and scholar.

Our books are available from booksellers everywhere.

Use this QR code to see recently published books:

Use this one to sign-up for our monthly newsletter:

www.ingramcontent.com/pod-product-compliance
Lightning Source LLC
Jackson TN
JSHW070602160226
97893JS00001B/1

9781966608219